Making Sense of Free

Dana Kay Nelkin presents a simple and natural account of freedom and moral responsibility which responds to the great variety of challenges to the idea that we are free and responsible, before ultimately reaffirming our conception of ourselves as agents. *Making Sense of Freedom and Responsibility* begins with a defense of the rational abilities view, according to which one is responsible for an action if and only if one acts with the ability to recognize and act for good reasons. The view is compatibilist—that is, on the view defended, responsibility is compatible with determinism—and one of its striking features is a certain asymmetry: it requires the ability to do otherwise for responsibility when actions are blameworthy, but not when they are praiseworthy. In defending and elaborating the view, Nelkin questions long-held assumptions such as those concerning the relation between fairness and blame and the nature of so-called reactive attitudes such as resentment and forgiveness. Her argument not only fits with a metaphysical picture of causation—agent-causation—often assumed to be available only to incompatibilist accounts, but receives positive support from the intuitively appealing Ought Implies Can Principle, and establishes a new interpretation of freedom and moral responsibility that dovetails with a compelling account of our inescapable commitments as rational agents.

Dana Kay Nelkin is Professor of Philosophy at the University of California, San Diego.

Making Sense of Freedom and Responsibility

Dana Kay Nelkin

OXFORD
UNIVERSITY PRESS

OXFORD

UNIVERSITY PRESS

Great Clarendon Street, Oxford OX2 6DP

Oxford University Press is a department of the University of Oxford.
It furthers the University's objective of excellence in research, scholarship,
and education by publishing worldwide. Oxford is a registered trade mark
of Oxford University Press in the UK and in certain other countries

Published in the United States of America by Oxford University Press
198 Madison Avenue, New York, NY 10016, United States of America

ISBN 978-0-19-960856-0 (Hbk)
ISBN 978-0-19-968476-2 (Pbk)

For Sam

Contents

Acknowledgments

My father first introduced me to the very serious problem at the heart of this book, a problem that has occupied me to varying extents since childhood, by describing in very simple, but powerful terms, the great threat to the conception of ourselves as free agents. He did such a beautiful job that I couldn't believe that not everyone was worried about this all the time. At the same time, he had such a broad smile and a twinkle in his eye at seeing me understand it, that I also thought with some relief that it couldn't be the end of the world. I managed to move on for the time being, but came to find myself drawn again and again to the so-called "problem of free will". And in graduate school, even when I intended to work on seemingly unrelated issues, I found myself thinking about the problem, and finally decided to tackle it directly. This book is a continuation of my on-going search for a solution. For enlightening me about free will, for sharing with me from the start his passion for philosophy, and for his love and support, I am ever grateful to my father, Norton Nelkin.

My experience as a graduate student at UCLA provided me with the foundation for this book. It was then that I discovered that not only had philosophers been wrestling with the problem of free will itself, but also that they had been analyzing the nature and source of our self-conception as free and responsible agents. I also learned to appreciate the values of clarity and rigor in writing and thinking, and continue to take my teachers and fellow students as models. I owe great thanks to my advisor Tyler Burge, who not only fully supported my change of topic away from one of the areas he himself seemed to be working on at the time, but whose incisive comments and questions helped me take my work in directions I couldn't have anticipated. I am also very grateful to my teachers, Barbara Herman, Andrew Hsu, Keith Donnellan, and Michael Otsuka, as well, each of whom showed me a different and new way into the problem.

Although they were not officially my teachers, John Martin Fischer and Gary Watson provided instruction and inspiration through their work from the time I started to work on free will as a graduate student. Now that I have come to know them, they have both, in their own ways, become models for me not only for their ground-breaking work, but for their lived belief that philosophy is a collective enterprise and for their constructive and supportive attitudes.

Derk Pereboom has contributed to this book in many ways. He read the manuscript both in parts, as well as in its entirety, many times over and has given me wonderfully constructive comments over the several years I have been working on the project. Although Derk is a "hard incompatibilist", arriving at a quite different conclusion than I do in the end, I am repeatedly intrigued by how much common ground there is between our views, and am continuously challenged when thinking about the points of disagreement between us. I am immensely grateful for our on-going philosophical conversation and accompanying friendship.

I have been very fortunate to have had wonderful colleagues and friends at both Florida State University and at the University of California, San Diego, who have also provided constructive feedback and support, and I am especially grateful to Dick Arneson, David Brink, Russ Dancy, Pat Matthews, Don Rutherford, and Eric Watkins. I am very lucky, too, to have such a wonderful community of colleagues working in related areas, and I'm especially appreciative for exchanges with Randy Clarke, Joseph Keim Campbell, Matthew Hanser, Agnieszka Jaworska, Michael McKenna, Al Mele, Eddy Nahmias, Tim O'Connor, Dan Speak, Manuel Vargas, and Carol Voeller.

Working with graduate students has provided me with a wonderful opportunity to learn and try out ideas, and I am grateful to those in my seminars for challenging and illuminating discussions, and especially to Justin Barnard, Nina Brewer Davis, Lisa Damm, Brad Hadaway, Per Milam, Theron Pummer, Erick Ramirez, Sharon Skare, and Michael Tiboris.

Michael McKenna and an anonymous reviewer for Oxford University Press provided extraordinarily detailed and incisive comments on the entire manuscript, and I can only hope to have done partial justice to them in revising the book in light of their insights. I owe great thanks to Peter Momtchiloff for encouraging and seeing the project through, and to the rest of the wonderful team at Oxford, especially Jan Chamier, Eleanor Collins, and Elmandi Du Toit.

I have benefited from much feedback on papers and talks, and would like here to give special thanks to recent audiences at UCLA, Cornell University, the University of Southern California, and the University of Geneva for their feedback on the talk on which chapter 5 is based.

For their aesthetic contributions, and, more importantly, their great friendship, I am grateful to Jennifer Phelps and Laurie Pieper. Many thanks, too, to Drew Wyeth, who photographed Laurie's painting, and to Elissa Thomson and Niki Even of the inspiring Outside the Lens organization for arranging the photography. For introducing us, and for much more, many thanks to my adopted Explorer Elementary family.

For their unconditional support from the beginning, I give deepest thanks to my mother, Nancy Morais, and my sister, Karen Nelkin Brandao.

For the love and encouragement of family as well as their keen insights, I thank John Brandao, Lee Morais, Ben Nelkin, Sarah Nelkin, Sue Metzner, and Regina Rickless.

For the best sense of perspective I could ask for, for their ubiquitous love and sheer joy, I thank my daughters, Sophie and Alice.

In countless ways, Sam Rickless made it possible for me to write this book. He gave me the book that prompted the thesis of my dissertation, and he helped me proof-read for the umpteenth time. In between, he brought to our discussions his amazing philosophical talent and clarity of thought that I hold as ideals, and he gave me gifts every day of his time, humor and optimism. And for all the conversations in which we asked about the meaning of life, and for Sophie, Alice and the other answers, he has my eternal gratitude.

Introduction

We have an unshakeable sense of ourselves as free and responsible agents. And yet we can easily be made to question whether this sense of ourselves is accurate—by sophisticated philosophical arguments, apparently simple generalizations from cases in which we are clearly not free and responsible, disturbing experimental results in psychology and neuroscience, and more. In this book, I defend a simple and, I believe, natural theory that responds to the great variety of challenges to the idea that we are free and responsible, and I offer a mutually supporting account of our conception of ourselves as agents. In so doing, I present a picture of our "sense of freedom and responsibility" in two different senses: an account of freedom and responsibility, and also an account of our sense of ourselves as free and responsible.

There are at least two ways in which these two projects are linked. One is that a very popular approach to our sense of ourselves as free agents interprets that sense in a very particular way—namely, as a commitment to the idea that we can choose among multiple undetermined options. This interpretation in turn has been used to motivate a particular picture of freedom itself, one that requires that the world be indeterministic in order for agents to be free. So figuring out exactly what our sense of freedom is—that is, what our conception of ourselves is, and why we have it—can have significant implications for the debate about the nature of freedom, and, by extension, about the nature of responsibility, for which freedom has often been thought to be a necessary condition.

A second way that the two projects have been linked can be traced back to Immanuel Kant and Thomas Reid among others, and concerns the task of answering the skeptic about freedom. As Kant wrote, "Now I say that every being which cannot act in any way other than under the idea of freedom is for this very reason free from a practical point of view".[1] The suggestion is that the necessity of thinking of ourselves as free entails that we really are. Reid took a somewhat more cautious, but still bold approach, writing that "This natural conviction of our acting freely, which is acknowledged by many who hold the doctrine of necessity, ought to throw the whole burden of proof upon that side . . . ".[2] For both Kant and Reid, the discovery that we must think of ourselves as free is a step in answering the skeptic (for Reid, a complete shift of the burden of proof, and for Kant, a decisive refutation— at least if we confine ourselves to conclusions within the practical point of view). While I see the evidentiary relationship between our self-conception and the nature and existence of freedom (and responsibility) as somewhat less straightforwardly supportive than both Kant and Reid, I do agree that what we learn about our own sense of ourselves can be fruitfully employed in the long-running debates concerning the instantiation of freedom and responsibility. And this is one of the main tasks in this book.

At the same time, I believe that each project has independent importance. For example, determining whether we are in fact "stuck with" a certain view of ourselves, whether as rational agents or as human beings, is interesting in itself. And if the answer to either question is "yes", and yet our view of ourselves is false, it would be interesting, at the least, to learn that one of our central commitments is an illusion. The question of what freedom and responsibility are, and whether they can be and are ever instantiated has immediate implications for the ways that we treat and feel about others, as well as ourselves. So while I believe that my approach to each question helps to illuminate the other, I also believe it is possible for a reader to accept one without the other.

In the first part of the book, I focus mostly on responsibility, and then return to the connection between responsibility and freedom in the last three chapters. There is a variety of notions of responsibility, and the one that I focus on here is the concept of moral responsibility, specifically of the sort required for deserved praise and blame.[3] At this point, I leave open

---

[1]   Kant (1785/1981, 448, p. 50).
[2]   Reid (1788/1983, p. 344).
[3]   This is similar to what Derk Pereboom calls "basic desert" (see, for example, Pereboom in preparation, and forthcoming). However, it is crucial to note that what is essential to blame and praise remains open at this point.

the question of what is essential to blame and praise, including, for example, whether blame is an essentially retributive notion, and return to this question in chapter 2. But it will be helpful at this point to distinguish this notion from other notions of responsibility. It is distinct from notions of simple causal responsibility, which would apply in a case in which someone inadvertently bumps into another while racing to save a life, causing a stubbed toe, for example. It can also be distinguished from a notion of responsibility according to which judgments of moral fault are attributed to agents, and agents' actions are appraised as being either virtuous or vicious. For attributing a fault to an agent of this kind does not appear to entail, by itself, that the one with the moral fault is deserving of blame for it.[4] For now, it is essential to note that the notion of responsibility at issue has been at the heart of debates over whether we have free will, where it is very often (although not always) presupposed that free will is essential to responsibility in the sense required for deserved praise and blame.

I begin in chapter 1 by setting out and motivating a view of responsibility that I call the "rational abilities view". Stated most simply, the view is that one is responsible for an action if and only if one acts with the ability to recognize and act for good reasons. I motivate the view, using examples, and then compare it to rivals of various kinds. While not obvious at the start, I show that the view is a compatibilist one, but one that shares some features with popular incompatibilist views. As stated simply thus far, the view might seem to ignore an essential connection between emotions and responsibility, but I also elaborate the view to show that emotional capacities have an important role to play.

One of the striking features of the rational abilities view is a certain asymmetry: it requires the ability to do otherwise when actions are *not* performed for good reasons or are not good, while not requiring the ability to do otherwise in the case of good actions performed for good reasons.[5] This makes the view vulnerable to criticism from almost everyone who has entered the debate, which includes both those who argue

---

[4] The notion of responsibility involved in the attribution of moral fault falls under what Watson calls "responsibility as attributability". I discuss the distinction between this notion and the one central to my investigation here in more detail in chapter 2.

[5] Susan Wolf adopts a view that is asymmetrical in this way, and first defended it in her rightly influential and aptly titled "Asymmetrical Freedom" (1980).

that the ability to do otherwise is always required for responsibility[6] and those who argue that it never is. Thus, the rational abilities view must be defended from two diametrically opposed directions, and I set out to do this in chapters 2 and 3, respectively. In chapter 2, I begin by addressing arguments primarily from incompatibilists who see the ability to do otherwise as required for responsibility when it comes to both praiseworthy and blameworthy actions. The ability to do otherwise has been thought essential for several reasons, including its connection to fairness of blame, its connection to one's being the ultimate source of one's own action, and because it has simply seemed true. I address variants of each of these lines of reasoning in chapter 2, and conclude that the rational abilities view has the resources to answer each. The discussion of fairness of blame in particular leads naturally into questions concerning the fairness of the so-called "reactive attitudes", such as resentment and indignation, as well as the fairness of inflicting harm or punishment. I suggest that the connections between blame and punishment are less direct than is often assumed, while retaining a robust notion of blame as something that can be deserved.

In chapter 3, I turn to challenges from the opposite direction. Here, it has been argued that so-called Frankfurt-style cases can be constructed for both praiseworthy and blameworthy actions, and so show that the ability to do otherwise is required for neither. By appealing to a particular understanding of "abilities", I argue that these cases do not show what is claimed of them. But the rational abilities view still faces a special difficulty when it comes to determinism. Does the rational abilities view in fact imply that we can be responsible for determined actions only as long as they are good and done for good reasons? If so, then that seems problematic. I argue that here, too, the rational abilities view has some flexibility and can address this most challenging objection. Finally, it might be asked why the ability to do otherwise in responding to *moral* reasons in particular should be required for responsibility, and I address this question, as well.

The discussion of abilities and determinism requires consideration of a powerful alternative to the rational abilities view, a view that has come to be known as the "agent causation" account of responsibility. The view has

---

[6] Or, more accurately, those who believe that the ability to do otherwise is always required either at the time an action is performed, or at an earlier time when a choice is made that results in the action. Such a view acknowledges the possibility of "tracing" the responsibility for the later choice to the earlier one. See Vargas (2005b) for a discussion of this sort of view.

a long and influential history, and has generally been assumed to be an incompatibilist theory.[7] In chapter 4, I consider this view in some depth, and show that there is a coherent compatibilist version of an agent-causal account of human action. I then question whether the incompatibilist version (which is incompatible with the rational abilities view) has any advantages over a compatibilist version (which is compatible with the rational abilities view). In the end, I argue that it does not, and that the rational abilities view is unthreatened by the true virtues of agent-causal accounts.

Chapters 2, 3 and 4 together reveal the extensive resources of the rational abilities view to answer a variety of challenges from both traditional camps in the debate—challenges to treat all responsible action as requiring the ability to do otherwise, and challenges to treat all responsible action as *not* requiring the ability to do otherwise. However, the question remains: what positive reason *is* there for an asymmetry? Aside from the fact that it is a consequence of an intuitively plausible view, can anything be said to explain it? In chapter 5, I explain how what has often been taken to be an axiomatic moral principle, namely, the Ought-Implies-Can principle, can do this work. The Ought-Implies-Can principle states that if an agent ought to perform an action, then she can perform it. This principle, as I argue, underwrites the claim that blameworthy actions require an ability to do otherwise, while it fails to underwrite a similar claim about praiseworthy action. Together with the arguments of chapter 2 against a blanket principle of alternate possibilities for all kinds of actions, this chapter constitutes a powerful explanation and rationale for the asymmetry of the rational abilities view.

In chapters 6 and 7 I turn to the question of whether the view developed thus far fits with, or is in tension with, our commitments as rational agents. I address a conclusion that can be found in the work of thinkers as different from each other as Aristotle, Kant, and Peter van Inwagen. It is the thesis that, as rational deliberators, we manifest a commitment to our own freedom. Two questions immediately arise: (i) Is the thesis true? And (ii) If so, what exactly are we committed to, in being committed to being free? In chapters 6 and 7, I provide a positive answer to the first question, and an elaboration of what our commitments come to. In particular, in chapter 6, I argue that insofar as we deliberate about multiple courses of action, we are

---

[7] One notable exception is Markosian (1999).

committed to our own deliberation having the potential to explain why we perform one rather than the other. And yet this does not thereby commit us to thinking of the world as undetermined. In chapter 7, I argue that we do presuppose that we are free agents in deliberating in the sense that our actions are up to us in such a way that we are responsible for them. The very nature of rational deliberation—of seeking reasons with a view to adopting and acting on the best (or at least good) ones—is such as to manifest a commitment to our freedom in this sense.

In Concluding Thoughts, I show how our commitments as rational agents fit with the rational abilities view developed earlier in the book. On the one hand, in showing that we are not committed to our being undetermined causes of our actions, a central motivation for a libertarian position is removed. On the other hand, in showing that we are committed to our being free agents in a sense related to responsibility, we have a challenge to the skeptic. Even if Reid was wrong to think that this insight thrust the entire burden of proof on the skeptic, it is a phenomenon the skeptic must account for. Further, the particular nature of the commitment provides strong mutual support for the rational abilities view itself.

I then go on to show how the various arguments of the entire book come together to provide a coherent compatibilist answer to the skeptic that incorporates a welcome flexibility on central questions such as those regarding both deep metaphysical issues involving the nature of causation and those regarding the precise emotional abilities humans must have to be responsible agents.

While each part of the book adds to and mutually supports the larger theory of responsibility and our conception of ourselves as free and responsible agents, a number of parts can also be seen as free-standing arguments. A compatibilist who adopts a symmetrical view of responsibility could, for example, embrace the reasoning about agent causation, while an incompatibilist who also adopts a symmetrical view of responsibility could accept arguments defending the necessity of having alternative possibilities in blameworthy cases. Thus, although the rational abilities view is a natural rival of influential compatibilist and incompatibilist views because it shares aspects with views of both sorts, the flip side of the existence of so much rivalry is that it can have something to offer all of those rival views, as well. At the same time, because the parts of the argument are mutually supporting, the whole has the potential to be genuinely greater than the sum of its parts.

1

A Rational Abilities View of Responsibility

1: The Theory Introduced and Motivated

When are people morally responsible for their actions, in the sense that they deserve praise and blame when they act well or badly? A natural answer, and the one I will defend, is that people are responsible when they act with the ability to do the right thing for the right reasons, or a good thing for good reasons.[1] The ability in question in turn has two components: the ability to recognize good reasons for acting and the ability to translate those reasons into decisions and actions. The appeal of the view is manifested across a wide range of our practices and judgments. For example, we believe that human beings gradually acquire responsibility as they gradually acquire rational abilities, and that those who are severely mentally impaired are exempt from responsibility for their actions.

The idea that what bestows responsibility is the possession of certain rational abilities is manifest in the judgments of responsibility codified in a variety of legal systems, as well. To see how, consider the insanity defense. There has been a great deal of controversy among legal scholars about just how to understand it, and I will focus briefly on an attempt to capture the basic idea in the Model Penal Code, an ideal system of laws proposed by the American Law Institute in 1962. According to the Model Penal Code, insanity is defined as a lack of substantial capacity to control one's behavior. In turn, substantial capacity is defined as: "the mental capacity needed to understand the wrongfulness of [an] act, or to conform . . . behavior to

---

[1] It may be that there is not a single right thing to do in a given situation, in which case one is responsible so long as one can do one of the good things available for good reasons.

the . . . law". The idea is that people are not responsible for their actions when they lack either the capacity to grasp reasons for acting (or not acting, as the case may be), or the capacity to translate those reasons into action (or omission). (One can see the history of the legal debate as an attempt to capture both cognitive and volitional abilities to respond to reasons.[2]) In general, when we find out that someone lacks a capacity for recognizing reasons or cannot control her behavior in light of them, we are tempted to excuse that person for her actions. Otherwise, in both legal and non-legal contexts, we tend to hold people responsible for their actions.

The case of children also illustrates this point. While there is a great deal of controversy over at exactly what ages children become responsible for various actions and at what ages they should be legally responsible, there is rough consensus that very young children are not responsible for their actions, and this, like the case of insanity, is well explained by the rational abilities view of responsibility. These cases suggest that in our ordinary practices, we presuppose that rational abilities at least tell part of the story about responsibility; that is, our treatment of these sorts of cases suggests that having certain sorts of rational abilities is required for responsibility. The theory coheres well with our ordinary ways of thinking in these cases.[3]

A number of philosophers have recognized the importance of rational capacities to responsibility. For example, some defend the idea that general rational capacities are required for responsible action (but not necessarily the ability to exercise them on each particular occasion one is responsible). R. Jay Wallace, for one, writes that "what matters is not our ability to exercise our general powers of reflective self-control, but simply the possession of such powers . . . ".[4] And according to John Martin Fischer and Mark Ravizza's influential view, one must act on a mechanism that is

---

[2] See Reider (1998); Fischette (2004).

[3] See Brink (2004) and Tiboris (in preparation) for a discussion of reasons to resist a recent trend to decrease the differences in legal treatment between adults and children. See also Morse (2002) who, writing from the legal perspective, takes lack of rationality to offer a unifying explanation of "the diverse conditions that undermine responsibility, including, among others, infancy, mental disorder, dementia, and extreme stress or fatigue" (p. 1064).

[4] (1994, p. 183). It must be noted that Wallace also provides a second condition for moral blameworthiness, namely, that the action in question must be wrong. Further, and equally importantly, Wallace does not take these conditions to define responsibility on their own. An agent is responsible in the first instance when her actions are the appropriate object of the

responsive to reasons.[5] But few defend what I see as the more literal reading of the claim that one must be able to do the (or a) right thing for the right (or some good) reasons. Susan Wolf is a notable exception, articulating what I believe is a view implicit in many of our practices, including legal ones. According to Wolf, one must "have the ability to do otherwise", that is, to exercise one's general rational powers in cases in which one does not do so.[6]

Seeing how the theory explains our judgments in cases like that of mental impairment and children is helpful. It will be helpful, too, to turn to some cases in which people genuinely struggle with the question of whether someone is responsible, as this can offer further insight into what helps us decide. Recently there has been much discussion about U.S. soldiers who inflicted severe physical and psychological pain on Iraqi prisoners. The question of whether the soldiers were responsible for their actions has been much debated. Private Lynddie England, whose smiling face in photographs showing her and her fellow soldiers forcing prisoners at Abu Ghraib into humiliating positions, has come to symbolize the worst of the U.S. presence in Iraq. While there were those who argued that she was fully responsible for her actions and should receive the maximum sentence, there were also many voices arguing that she bore little, if any, responsibility for her actions, given the circumstances. These voices were diverse, and appealed to a number of factors, including England's own cognitive impairments, which included information processing deficits, an unusual sensitivity to peer pressure, and a possible inability to distinguish right from wrong.[7] Many pointed to the military culture and pressures she was under at the time.[8] Some voices also included

---

reactive attitudes. In turn, the reactive attitudes are appropriate (and fair) when these two conditions are met. I will return to Wallace's challenging account later in the book.

[5] See, for example, Fischer and Ravizza (1998, pp. 81–2).

[6] Wolf (1990, p. 69).

[7] See Blumenthal (2005).

[8] "Someone familiar with Arab psychology, an Army intelligence officer or a CIA officer, must have known this and ordered what happened. What are the odds some low-ranking reservists came up with the idea out of the clear blue sky? . . . Yet so far only enlisted personnel are facing courts martial in the prisoner-abuse fiasco, and this is outrageous. Officers are responsible for what happens under their command. It is the officers, not the enlisted men and women, who should be held to account . . . Twenty-one-year-old reservists can't be expected to know when the genuine lines of the Convention are being crossed. Officers are expected to know this" (Easterbrook 2004). Moreover, a former high school psychologist who

appeals to a large body of psychological research suggesting that her obedience was *not* something to be predicted only because of her special personality traits, but rather because of the fact that the vast majority of people would act in a similar way.[9] The relevance of her own cognitive impairments is certainly to be expected, on the rational abilities view of responsibility. Yet the relevance of seemingly insufficiently important situational factors also fits well with this view.

To see why, it is worth considering some of the experiments that have led to the conclusion that situational factors, as opposed to anything like traditional personality traits, have a usually unrecognized influence on behavior. For example, in the 1960s, Stanley Milgram performed a series of studies in which subjects were told that they were part of a study on learning and memory.[10] Each subject was paired with an accomplice posing as a fellow subject, and each subject was told that, upon the request of the experimenter, the subject would provide electric shocks to his partner each time he missed an item on a learning test. With each missed answer, subjects were told, the electric shock would increase in voltage. The accomplices were trained to cry out in pain, exhibiting increasing discomfort, pain, and fear as each "shock" was administered by the subjects. Although a group of students told in advance of the experiments predicted that only 3 percent would continue to participate until the highest level of shock was given, subjects dramatically defied expectations. Although many exhibited signs of serious distress, twenty-five out of forty subjects in the original experiment continued to "shock" the person they believed to be a fellow subject until the cries of pain had completely ceased, until they reached a voltage level annotated with "Danger: Extreme Shock". Similar results were reached in subsequent trials.

Other classic "situationist" experiments include those that show that being in a group as small as two can dramatically decrease the likelihood that a person will help another in need, that being in the minority in one's belief about the relative lengths of two lines can dramatically increase the likelihood one will switch one's answer, and that all sorts of seemingly

---

worked with England said that because of her physical disabilities, he wasn't sure she could in all cases distinguish right from wrong or refrain from peer pressure (Bowers 2005).

[9] See Zimbardo (2004).
[10] See Milgram (1969).

irrelevant situational factors play a surprisingly large role in people's behavior. While there is great debate over how exactly to interpret the experimental results, it remains a live question *why* people are bothered by them, and why they have sometimes assumed that the results undermine our ordinary attributions of responsibility. At least part of why the alleged huge, but often unrecognized, influence of such factors seems undermining of responsibility is that it raises the question of whether people really can see and act on the right reasons in the particular circumstances they face.[11] It is natural to wonder whether many of the subjects of Milgram's experiments, for example, are somehow systematically prevented from seeing that the pain of their fellow "subject" is an overriding reason to stop shocking him. Perhaps they simply cannot see, because of the extraordinary power of the perception of authority, that an experimenter's directives provide a weak *reason* to continue. I believe that much of the worry that the results of the experiments undermine responsibility stems from the thought that the subjects are somehow lacking in the ability to do the right thing for the right reasons. Thus, the fact that situational factors are thought to operate in significantly similar ways in the case of soldiers like England raises similar questions about her responsibility.

Now I think the Abu Ghraib case is a particularly difficult one for people to come to a firm judgment about, let alone achieve consensus on, and this is so precisely because it is not at all obvious how much the soldiers' rational abilities really were impaired. For other cases of war crimes, it seems more obvious that soldiers' capacities are impaired beyond the extent to which they are responsible. In "From My Lai to Abu Ghraib", John Doris and Dominic Murphy nicely document the many situational factors that seem to simply rob one of the ability to exercise one's rational capacities.[12] The most obvious sorts of cases are on the battlefield, where the noise, confusion, smells, and pain are simply overwhelming. Doris and Murphy extend this conclusion to cases like Abu Ghraib, while acknowledging that the pressures at work there are more subtle. I am not as confident as they about extending their argument in this way, but I agree with the fundamental point that it is crucial to determine the extent to which soldiers have the ability to recognize and act on good reasons at the moment in question. In these sorts of cases, then, it seems that the

---

[11] I develop this line of reasoning in more detail in Nelkin (2005).
[12] Doris and Murphy (2007, pp. 35–8).

rational abilities view can explain not only our judgments, but also our uncertainty.

A second sort of case in which people struggle in assigning responsibility takes us back to the legal sphere. Death penalty cases provide an especially vivid window into how people think about a host of interrelated questions concerning responsibility, punishment, and personal history. Because there are usually two distinct phases in such cases—one to decide guilt or innocence and one to decide the penalty—individual defendants and jurors have an incredible freedom to decide what is relevant in considering whether to choose life or death. Now as we will see later, the relationship between responsibility and punishment is far from clear, and these sorts of cases raise a number of different questions, only one of which concerns the nature of responsibility directly. (For example, lingering doubts about the strength of the evidence that the defendant committed the relevant action can affect people's judgments about the appropriate penalty.) At the same time, considerations of responsibility are clearly one of the relevant factors, and appear, along with the lingering doubt mentioned above, to be among the most important. Thus, determining what jurors focus on in this regard is instructive. And while the fact that the real-life situation in which judgments are made is a complex one involving a number of interrelated factors in one way provides a reason to avoid it when trying to learn more about the nature of responsibility, it also provides a reason *not* to avoid it. On the one hand, it is true that it is hard for the individuals involved—let alone third parties—to isolate their judgments of responsibility from their judgments about appropriate punishment or their religious beliefs. On the other, the richness of the cases makes it possible to begin to see how people's various judgments might be connected.

For now, I would like to turn to some of the mitigating factors that are well recognized by courts and juries. Data collected by the Capital Jury Project suggest that,

Jurors tend to focus most on factors that diminish the defendant's individual responsibility for his actions. They attach significant mitigating potential to facts and circumstances that show diminished mental capacity, such as mental retardation or extreme emotional or mental disturbance at the time of the offense, but they have little patience for defendants who attribute their wrongdoing to drugs or alcohol. They express some concern for defendants who have been seriously abused as children, and still more for defendants who tried but could not get help for their problems. Nonetheless, the mitigation effect they give these factors remains limited. (Garvey 1998, p. 1539)

One way of interpreting the data gathered from polling capital jurors is that systemic mental impairment such as retardation has the most mitigating effect (next to lingering doubt as to whether the defendant committed the crime in question), and circumstances at the time, out of the defendant's control, such as extreme emotional disturbance, are also highly mitigating. Less powerful but still real mitigating factors in jurors' judgments include circumstances earlier in time over which the defendant lacked control and which helped form his (bad) character. These data nicely dovetail with the use of the insanity defense. Even where defendants don't qualify for that particular defense, the degree to which they possess rational abilities can affect jurors' judgments of their *degree* of responsibility (sometimes manifested in the severity of punishment deemed appropriate).

In a fascinating piece, "In The Face of Death", Alex Kotlowitz documented the experience of one jury that had been found to be "death-certified", that is, willing to impose the death sentence.[13] After finding the defendant, Jeremy Gross, guilty of brutally murdering a fellow convenience store worker, in what was by all accounts a cut-and-dried case, they went on to struggle with the question of whether to impose a death sentence and eventually agreed on a sentence of life in prison.[14] Surprisingly, given that all juries considering these questions are "death-certified", this decision is becoming more the norm than the exception, and one major reason for it is the increased use of mitigating evidence in the penalty phase of trials.[15]

There were a number of factors that appear to have influenced the jurors Kotlowitz interviewed. During the presentation of mitigating

---

[13] Kotlowitz (2003).

[14] At 2:40 am, Christopher Beers was the only employee in a convenience store on the west side of Indianapolis. He was 24 years old, had completed one year at Purdue University, and then run out of money for tuition. He had been working to earn money to return to school, and welcomed the night shift as a time to read. Jeremy Gross entered the store with a friend, holding a gun out of sight. Beers buzzed the two in, and then "Gross took long, hurried strides into the store, raised his right arm and started shooting". When Beers pleaded for Gross to stop after a bullet hit his chest, Gross followed him and shot him in the face. When Beers asked "Why, Jeremy, why?", Gross told him to shut up. All of this was captured on a surveillance tape which was eventually recovered (Kotlowitz 2003).

[15] Kotlowitz (2003).

evidence, it became clear that Gross had suffered a horrible childhood. His father was abusive, and his mother left only after trying to set his passed-out father on fire. Eventually taken from his mother, Gross had lived in twenty-seven places by the time he was sixteen. Despite being death-certified, after hearing the story of Gross's life, the jury voted not to impose the death penalty. While there were clearly a number of factors influencing the jury, at least some seemed to center on his diminished responsibility, for which his life story was evidence. For example, one wavering juror felt that though Gross had a "moral compass" it had been shattered by the abuse he suffered as a child. He said, "I began to think not that there's an excuse for what happened, but I had an understanding of his torment . . . Sympathetic is too strong a word, but I can't think of a better way to describe how I felt. I struggled with whether he knew the difference between right and wrong" (p. 49). This juror's report fits well with the idea that lacking robust rational abilities—including the ability to distinguish right from wrong—diminishes responsibility. The defendant's past was relevant to this juror at least in part because it explained how someone could now have such diminished capacities.

Not all cases are decided in the way this one was. But it is not unrepresentative, and, for that reason, reveals a great deal about what people think is relevant to making decisions about responsibility and punishment.[16] It is, of course, impossible to separate out all of the factors that go into jurors' actual judgments, and also any potential intermediate reasoning (for example, do they first make an explicit—or implicit—judgment concerning responsibility?). And yet, the situation is unique in our legal system in allowing jurors to decide on their own just what is relevant.

These cases should not replace hypothetical ones in which we are able to isolate factors in a way that we cannot always do with real ones. And we will have occasion to explore several of those in what follows. However, real cases and the real ways people respond to them are also important in determining the initial plausibility of the rational abilities view. Thus far, the rational abilities view seems to fit well with our very general approach in everyday life to judgments of responsibility, and even with cases in which we sometimes struggle to make such judgments.

[16] See Garvey (1998) and Sundby (2007).

So far, the cases we have considered have been cases of bad actions of kinds generally thought to be wrong. Thus, the questions we face in assessing them tend to be questions about whether someone is responsible and blameworthy, or instead excused or exempt from responsibility. What does the account say about good actions? Notably, the account only requires that, to be responsible, the agent have the ability to do the (or a) right thing for the right reasons, and does not require that the agent also have the ability to do something wrong, or act for bad reasons. Thus, in order to discern whether someone is responsible for a good action, we need to see whether she acts for good reasons in doing so, but not whether she also could have acted badly or for bad reasons. Here, too, I believe that the account accords with widespread practices. We tend not to withhold praise if we do not know whether agents could have acted badly. At the same time, we sometimes offer praise, even believing that the agent could not have done otherwise. For example, someone who does something heroic might say, "I couldn't help it. I had to do it". Many firefighters who risked their lives by entering the World Trade Center towers on September 11, 2001, speak matter-of-factly of rushing into the buildings. We do not pause to ask whether they could help it in order to praise them.

In its broad outlines, the rational abilities account seems to fit well with significant general aspects of our practices, both legal and social, concerning both good and bad actions. Of course, the fit might be illusory or seriously incomplete, or our practices might be explained in ways that don't require the truth of the account. It also may be that our practices are flawed, and that they ought to change in certain ways. But it is important to note that the account derives as least some of its initial plausibility from its fit with the general contours of our practices.

2: Situating the Theory among its Rivals

In fact, the rational abilities view seems so natural that it is somewhat surprising that it is not more widely accepted among philosophers who put forward conditions for responsibility. I suspect that one reason for this phenomenon is that when we delve under the surface, we very quickly come up against worries concerning an asymmetrical feature of the view and its implications in a deterministic world.

To highlight that asymmetrical feature, it will help to begin with an example. Suppose that you have promised to help a friend during a difficult time, and that following through is the right thing to do, despite the fact that doing so requires a serious sacrifice on your part. Now suppose that you have failed to keep your promise, and you are responsible for having failed. Must you have been able to do otherwise? That is, must you have been able to keep your promise? It seems that the answer is "yes", and it is an easy step from here to the idea that in general one must be able to have done otherwise in order to be responsible for one's actions. In fact, this claim, which Harry Frankfurt famously called the Principle of Alternate Possibilities, has seemed obvious to many. And it has been the first step for some in concluding that responsibility requires the falsity of determinism, as well. For if the world is determined, so argues the incompatibilist, then no one can do otherwise, in which case no one is responsible.[17]

Yet there is great debate about whether the ability to do otherwise is required for responsibility, and most parties seem to fall into one of two camps: (i) the ability is always required, and (ii) the ability is never required.[18] One of the distinctive things about the rational abilities view is that the ability to do otherwise is required for moral responsibility when one does a bad action or an action for bad reasons, but not when one does a good action for good reasons. Hence the asymmetry. And as a result of the asymmetry, the rational abilities view would seem to be vulnerable to challenging objections from both of the main camps in the debate. For example, when it comes to praiseworthy actions, some will argue that the view gets things wrong. One must be able to do otherwise in order to be responsible for a good action. Otherwise, one's actions are simply the inevitable consequence of past events over which one has had no control. And in that case, one cannot be responsible. This sort of challenge typically—although not always—comes from a certain group

---

[17] There are a number of ways of understanding determinism. For now, following van Inwagen, I take it to be the thesis that there is at any instant exactly one physically possible future (that is, one future is possible, given the actual past and the laws of nature). (See van Inwagen 1983, p. 3.)

[18] Again, things may be more complicated in that some views allow for "tracing"; according to such views, one can be responsible for an action at time t2 even though one cannot do otherwise at t2, as long as one's action is the result of an earlier action or decision when one could have done otherwise. See Introduction, note 6.

of incompatibilists, those who believe responsibility is incompatible with determinism.

On the other hand, many compatibilists would object that the rational abilities view gets things wrong when it comes to *blameworthy* actions. Even here, the reasoning goes, one need not have the ability to do otherwise in order to be responsible. Frankfurt introduced an example meant to show just this. Suppose that Smith is thinking about whether to kill his rival. Jones, wishing Smith to do just that, happens to be a talented neuroscientist who is able to manipulate electrodes implanted in Smith's brain to ensure that he decides to kill. But Jones is disinclined to interfere unless it is necessary to do so. So he decides to interfere only if Smith shows signs of wavering in his commitment. Fortunately (for Jones), Smith deliberates and decides to kill, never wavering. As a result, Jones does nothing. Is Smith responsible for his decision and consequent killing? It would seem so. Could he have decided differently? No, for Jones would have stepped in and caused him to decide to kill if he had shown any sign of wavering. Thus, it seems that we have a case of a bad action for which an agent is responsible, despite lacking the ability to do otherwise. Therefore the asymmetrical view, which requires the ability to do otherwise for blameworthy actions, must be mistaken. As we will see, this example is but one of a larger class designed to support the same conclusion, and collectively, they pose a serious challenge for the rational abilities view.

Yet, as I will argue in the next three chapters, the rational abilities view has the resources to answer objections from both camps. Before seeing how, it is worth noting that the rational abilities view is not alone in being asymmetrical, a point that is often overlooked. Any view that posits a specific ability will have this kind of character, too. For example, according to one version of a "real self view", one is responsible for one's actions just in case one has the ability to conform one's actions to one's true values (where those values represent one's "real self").[19] On this view, if one

---

[19] Watson (1975/2004) offers a view of this type, when he writes "The free agent has the capacity to translate his values into action" (p. 26). Here the evaluational system might be said to represent the "real self", and having the capacity to act on that system is what is necessary for free action. But it is important to note that Watson also suggests a different sort of view in the second part of the same sentence: "his actions flow from his evaluational system". Although this second claim seems to be a gloss on the first, I think they are actually quite different in meaning. I call the model described in the first claim a "capacity" model and the second model, according to which one must actually act on one's evaluations (and not simply have the capacity to do so), the "flow" model. Frankfurt (1971) also provides a classic locus of

actually conforms one's actions to one's true values, there is no need to be able to do otherwise to meet the condition sufficient for responsibility; but if one fails to conform one's actions to one's true values, then one must have the ability to do otherwise in order to be responsible. Thus, this view too is asymmetrical. This illustrates that asymmetry comes naturally with any condition that requires a substantive ability, and the rational abilities view is thus not unique in incorporating asymmetry.

Nevertheless, the asymmetry of the rational abilities view offers one explanation of why it has not been embraced by more philosophers. The problem is magnified further when determinism is introduced. For if determinism precludes the ability to do otherwise, then the rational abilities view entails that no one can be responsible for bad actions in a deterministic world, while leaving open the possibility that agents are responsible for good actions in such a world. This might seem a welcome result to some, but it also seems very odd indeed.

So far, we have seen that the rational abilities view is a very natural one, with many virtues. At the same time, its asymmetry makes it vulnerable to challenges from the two main camps in the debate concerning the nature of responsibility, and the asymmetry by itself appears to lead to an odd consequence when it comes to determinism. Before exploring the resources of the rational abilities view to respond to those objections, then, it will be helpful to compare the rational abilities view to others that, because of their symmetry, may appear to face fewer challenges.

One is a set of views that are compatibilist and, like the rational abilities view, place emphasis on the rational capacities of responsible agents. This set includes those classified as "reasons-responsiveness" views, following Fischer and Ravizza.[20] Like the rational abilities view itself, these views also

---

a real-self view. In summing up the view, Frankfurt writes: "Suppose that a person has done what he wanted to do, that he did it because he wanted to do it, and that the will by which he was moved when he did it was his will because it was the will he wanted. Then he did it freely and of his own free will" (p. 94). This passage is consistent with both a capacity model and a flow model, since the claim is that if one's actions (causally) flow from one's reflective desires, that is sufficient for acting freely. But is it necessary, as well? If so, then we would be forced to say that in typical "weakness of will" sorts of cases, in which one acts against one's reflective desires, one never acts freely. In order to accommodate these cases as free actions, a natural move would be to adopt a capacity model, according to which what is necessary is only the capacity to act on one's reflective desires.

[20] See, for example, Fischer and Ravizza (1998, pp. 62-91), and essays in Fischer (2006a), to trace the subtle development of Fischer's view.

acknowledge that responsiveness to reasons is central to responsibility, but they do so in a different way in order to accommodate the worries that arise for an asymmetrical view. For example, according to Fischer and Ravizza, one is responsible for an action only if one acts on a mechanism that would, in a set of different circumstances, respond to reasons.[21] Notice that this view is not asymmetrical in the same way as the rational abilities view: the ability to do otherwise is not required for any sort of action, good or bad. For both good and bad actions, the agent must simply act on a mechanism that would respond differently in at least some different circumstances. In addition, on Fischer and Ravizza's view, a mechanism's being such as to respond to different reasons in different circumstances shows that it "can react differently to the *actual* reason to do otherwise" (1998, p. 73). This sounds at first as though they are suggesting that responsibility requires an ability to do otherwise after all; but they go on to qualify the remark in a way that suggests that what is meant by "can do otherwise" is simply a general capacity rather than a particular ability to exercise it on a particular occasion: "This general capacity of the agent's actual-sequence mechanism—and *not* the agent's power to do otherwise—is what helps to ground moral responsibility" (p. 73).

While this view avoids certain objections facing the rational abilities view, I believe it has other difficulties that the rational abilities view can overcome.[22] One is that it replaces the idea that it is the agent herself who must have a reasons-responsive capacity with the idea that it is a mechanism of the agent that (at least primarily) has such a capacity, a change that on the face of it would seem less intuitive. To see why, consider some ordinary excuses for our actions, like "she couldn't help it, don't blame her". Here the incapacity that is supposed to excuse is attributed to the agent, not to a mechanism. We do not normally say or even mean things like "she acted on a mechanism that couldn't respond to the reasons there were". Of course, the reasons-responsive theory might

---

[21] "Responsiveness" in turn divides into two capacities that mirror those described by the rational abilities view: recognition and reactivity. See Fischer and Ravizza (1998), chapters 2 and 3 for a full elaboration of the moderate reasons-responsiveness view. Fischer and Ravizza also require that one meet a historical condition in order to be responsible for an action, namely, that one's action is one's own. See (1998), chapter 8, for an elaboration of this idea.

[22] For examples of other responses to Fischer and Ravizza, see McKenna (2000) and (2005), and Pereboom (2006).

still be correct without its being reflected directly in these kinds of exchanges. Nevertheless, it is an advantage of the rational abilities view that it reflects this widespread kind of excuse.

Also, the capacity central to the reasons-responsiveness view seems to have two parts or aspects: on the one hand, it is a capacity of the mechanism to act differently under different circumstances, and on the other, it is a general capacity to act differently given the actual reasons for acting.[23] One might worry that something is missing, namely, something more specific than a general capacity to act differently in the actual circumstances; for one might have the general capacity while being prevented in some important way from exercising it. This worry might be addressed by filling out what it means to have a general capacity, or by combining the account with additional conditions.[24] But it is a challenge for the view, and one that the rational abilities view has a way of overcoming. Or so I will argue.

Of course, in judging the relative strength of the views, we must look at a variety of factors, including surface plausibility, how the views accord with our intuitions about particular cases, and also how they can respond to those deeper worries we encounter when we delve below the surface.

There are also many other symmetrical compatibilist views, and we will have occasion to examine some of them in later chapters. For now, the reasons-responsiveness view of Fischer and Ravizza provides a good compatibilist foil to the asymmetrical rational abilities view. It will also be useful here to compare the rational abilities view to one other prominent set of competitors that require a symmetrical set of abilities for responsibility: namely, the ability to do otherwise, whether you actually do the right thing for the right reasons or not. There are many views according to which, in order to be responsible for any action, one must have had the ability to do otherwise when one acted, no matter what the nature of one's

[23] See also Wallace (1994, p. 183) and Scanlon (1998, p. 280). Each of these views has other quite distinctive features, but they both share with the reasons-responsiveness view under discussion the idea that what is required for responsibility is the general ability to recognize and act for reasons, rather than a specific ability to respond to the specific reasons at the moment.

[24] It is important to note that Fischer and Ravizza's account includes a second requirement for responsible action, namely, that one act on a mechanism which is in an important sense one's own. Fischer and Ravizza take this to be a "historical" condition, requiring the agent to have taken certain attitudes toward the mechanism in the past. The requirement of such a condition marks another difference between the rational abilities view and theirs. See Fischer and Ravizza (1998, chapters 7 and 8).

action. While a full comparative evaluation of the two kinds of views will have to wait, too, we can already see that they have different implications for at least some cases. For now, it is worth noting that the rational abilities view seems to have an easier time accommodating at least certain phenomena. For example, we are happy to praise people who act well, despite the fact that by their own reports, they simply couldn't help but do what they do. Martin Luther provides a dramatic example, reportedly saying of his refusal to recant his criticism of the Catholic Church: "Here I stand, I cannot do otherwise, so help me God". The fact that he cannot do otherwise does not seem to preclude praise. Similarly, to take an example of Wolf's, a woman who jumps into the sea to save a child drowning and who reports that she couldn't do anything else in the situation seems deserving of our praise. And in turn our praise seems to presuppose that she is fully responsible for her actions.

While I will return to these alternatives to the rational abilities view in later chapters, I hope to have made clear that the view is a very simple and natural one, and to have clarified some ways in which it stands in stark contrast to its competitors.[25] It is important to note at the outset that one reaction to surveying the views I have just sketched is to turn to skepticism. Perhaps *all* of the views have at least one devastating flaw, and this just shows that the concept of responsibility is an incoherent one, requiring conditions that cannot be jointly satisfied. This position deserves serious attention. One way of addressing it is to show that the apparently intractable challenges for one view can in fact be met. After attempting to do that in subsequent chapters for the rational abilities view, I will return to the skeptical position and compare their relative merits.

3: Kinds of Abilities

Let me now elaborate on what sorts of abilities are at stake in the rational abilities view.

The notion that being responsible requires only certain sorts of rational abilities might prompt one to ask whether the view is too "cold". The

---

[25] There are a wide variety of competing views worthy of discussion; I chose these two general categories for purposes of comparison because they illuminate key features of the rational abilities view, while providing a good idea of at least some of the main alternatives to it.

view might seem to ignore a huge literature connecting the reactive attitudes and other emotions to responsibility. For there is no explicit mention, for example, of any *emotional* capacities, such as those for empathy or guilt or remorse. And there is no explicit mention that responsible agents must themselves be able to see themselves as apt targets of reactive attitudes like resentment and gratitude. And yet, perhaps these capacities are central to responsibility. If so, then those often known as psychopaths—those commonly supposed to be lacking these capacities—should not qualify as responsible.[26] But since the rational abilities view does not require these capacities, the psychopaths appear to qualify as responsible on it. This is a challenge, but I believe the rational abilities view has the resources to address it, and doing so simply requires elaboration on the kinds of rational abilities in question, and what having them entails.

It is open to the advocate of the rational abilities view to acknowledge that emotional capacities are themselves required in order to have the rational capacities it mentions explicitly. The case of EVR described by Antonio and Hanna Damasio supports this sort of response.[27] After having a brain tumor removed from the ventromedial region of his frontal lobes, EVR seemed to recover fully. IQ tests taken after the surgery resulted in the same scores as tests taken before, and even certain tests eliciting the generation of options for social interactions were in the normal or superior range. His social knowledge appeared intact and accessible. However, his work and personal life soon began to unravel. At work, he now came in late, failed to finish tasks, and so on. He was soon divorced, remarried, and divorced again. The Damasios and their colleagues developed a hypothesis about what had happened: the surgery had resulted in a breaking of the link between his emotions and his judgment. This proved to be true. It turned out that EVR's emotional responses had become abnormal in various ways. For example, when shown horrifying pictures, his galvanic skin response was flat instead of showing a response. At the same time, he was able to recognize that before the surgery he would have felt something different in a similar circumstance. EVR seems to lack precisely the ability to recognize reasons and to translate that recognition into action required

---

[26] There is a great deal of controversy about exactly what psychopathology is. See Shoemaker (2007) and Watson (forthcoming) for recent discussions. For present purposes, what is important are the common assumptions mentioned in the text.

[27] Damasio (1995).

by the rational abilities view. Although he could generate copious options for acting, he also observed that "after all that, I still wouldn't know what to do!" (p. 49). Antonio Damasio and his colleague, Antoine Bechara, devised further experiments that led them to a more precise theory concerning the relationship between emotions and decision making, namely, that emotional responses can mark certain alternatives as simply unviable. As a result, one's available alternatives are narrowed, and it is possible to reason through them. Without emotional responses marking certain alternatives in this way, one simply lacks the cognitive resources to think through every possible option. According to this theory, which Antonio Damasio calls the Somatic Marker Hypothesis, the absence of emotional markers makes it harder to assign value and disvalue to various alternatives, and decision making suffers dramatically as a result. Whatever the exact story of the cognitive and emotional mechanisms turns out to be, a natural conclusion from cases like EVR's is that the rational capacities themselves require emotional ones. Thus, the rational abilities view is consistent with the claim that emotional capacities are indeed required for responsibility.

This sort of response does not address the suggestion that emotional capacities or the capacity to feel the reactive attitudes are required for responsibility *independently* of their contribution to requisite rational capacities.[28] But if these emotional capacities are necessary *in virtue of* their indispensability for having rational capacities, then the rational abilities view can accommodate this phenomenon.

What exactly is the relationship between these capacities and the ability to do the right thing for the right reasons? It would be nice for the rational abilities view to have an answer; it would certainly be more complete if it did. I will begin in this endeavor by sketching out a framework of options and exploring one recent proposal.

First, we need to confront the options of recognizing a necessary or a contingent relationship between emotional capacities and the requisite rational ones. Some argue that certain emotional capacities are necessary

---

[28] Fischer and Ravizza mention the reactive attitudes in a condition separate from their requirement of moderate reasons-responsiveness for responsibility. As noted, they include a separate historical condition, according to which one must view oneself as an apt target for the reactive attitudes (1998, chapter 7). (Arguably, one must have the capacities to feel certain emotions in order to view oneself in this way.)

for having the rational ones (it isn't just something about us as humans, while martians, say, could be responsible without these).[29] In other words, in order to recognize the reasons that are out there, you need to experience certain emotions, or at least be capable of doing so. Even if this is true for human beings, though, we might decide that it is so contingently, or even necessary in an important way for humans in particular.[30] Perhaps there could be a species of beings for whom emotional experience was not required in order to take other people's pain, say, as a reason not to harm them, and to act on such reasons. Ishtiyaque Haji imagines such a being, Data*—not too different from Mr. Spock in Star Trek, who is responsible.[31]

Second, one can pick and choose among the various emotional capacities. Do they all come as a package, or might some be required in order to act on good reasons, while others are unnecessary?

Third, one might think that the emotional capacities are required for the recognition of reasons, or for acting on the reasons one recognizes, or for both.

To see how to navigate among these choices, I will start with a line of reasoning offered by Paul Russell, who seems to opt for the necessary connection between the possession of emotional capacities and the possession of rational ones. He defends the following thesis:

MS: The responsible agent must be able to feel and understand moral sentiments or reactive attitudes.[32]

Russell accepts the further claim that for an agent to be responsible, she must be able to *hold* herself and others responsible, where this requires possessing the reactive attitudes. Russell argues that lacking the reactive attitudes prevents one from recognizing, as well as from being motivated by, moral reasons. In support of his claim, Russell has us imagine a parallel with fear. Suppose Jill is incapable of feeling fear. Still, she can recognize dangerous situations and ones that may harm her. She also understands that other human beings react differently than she does to these situations. "In this sense," writes Russell, "Jill has an entirely 'external' or 'superficial' understanding of fear...". Russell concludes that Jill is not a full

---

[29] See, for example, Ramirez (in preparation) for discussion of this view.
[30] See McKenna (forthcoming) for discussion of this point.
[31] Haji (2003, p. 72).   [32] Russell (2004, p. 293).

participant in normal human life so far as we "reason and engage with each other about dangerous and harmful situations and objects".

Now consider Jack, who lacks all capacity for "moral sense". Jack is intelligent, however, so he appears to respond to reasons. "That is to say, Jack can recognize and follow moral norms" and can anticipate sanctions for not doing so. Still, violating moral norms does not affect Jack in the normal way. "Jack is morally *cold*". He is not motivated to care about his moral qualities because of his own or others' reactive attitudes. Just as with Jill, Russell concludes, Jack is not a full participant in normal moral life.

According to Russell, Jack is able to motivate himself by means of "external" sanctions, but he lacks any "internal" system of sanctions or incentives, as associated with moral sentiments. Having an internal system, according to Russell, allows us to treat the sanctions in question as appropriate or fair, and in these cases, the agent accepts or endorses the moral considerations and norms that serve as the basis of the adverse reactive attitudes.

While I find the cases invoked very interesting, I think the argument is flawed, for two reasons. The first is that it does not distinguish among the great variety of reactive attitudes and aspects of moral sense. It might be possible to have some without others; for example, one might think that empathy is particularly well-suited for recognizing reasons for actions. But perhaps it is possible to feel empathy without guilt or resentment. There is some developmental evidence to suggest that children develop the capacity for empathy before that for guilt and resentment.[33] And some actual adults, perhaps Gandhi among them, have been able to feel tremendous empathy while trying to rid themselves of the capacity for feelings of resentment.[34] If successful in their endeavors, they lack the capacity to feel certain sorts of attitudes, while retaining others. Yet such a person could fail to be responsible on Russell's view, because that view is animated by the idea that the *reactive* attitudes are what allow you to hold people responsible. It is not clear that empathy by itself can do this work of allowing you to hold others responsible, and yet it is, in my view, a very natural candidate for *reason-recognition*. Resentment and guilt are, admittedly, better suited for the job of holding responsible, among the reactive

---

[33] See, for example, M. Lewis (1993), and Hoffman (2000).
[34] See chapter 3 for more discussion of Gandhi.

attitudes. Perhaps having any one of these means you have all the others, but that is far from obvious. A convincing case might be made that because of the way humans develop, they must have the reactive attitudes in particular. But it is somewhat less plausible at the outset that this is true for any responsible, and, indeed, moral agent.

A second, but related, problem with the reasoning can be brought out by means of the analogy with fear. Jill is abnormal, true enough. And she might get herself into big trouble, as people with relatively low fear responses do sometimes. But she can still recognize dangerous situations as providing reasons for action, even if it is more roundabout and intellectualized for her. Similarly, I grant that Jack is abnormal, but it requires more argument to show that lacking the capacity to feel guilt and resentment prevents him from recognizing moral demands as binding. Again, the charge of "coldness" in Jack's responses might be mitigated by recognition that absence of the reactive attitudes in particular does not entail a lack of *emotion*, including, notably, empathy. And it is simply a leap to suggest that only external rewards and sanctions can be what is motivating him.[35]

Where does this leave the rational abilities view? With a welcome flexibility, I believe.

While it is certainly consistent—as stated in its canonical form—with a strong requirement of a broad set of emotional capacities like that suggested by Russell, my inclination is to see whether it is possible to make do with less. So far, I have sketched some possible ways of filling out the rational abilities view that make room for emotional capacities to play a role in the determination of responsibility. I will return to this question in chapter 2, where I suggest that at least the reactive attitudes like resentment may play a lesser role than is often thought. But it is a virtue of the rational

---

[35] An interesting set of real-life cases are those with autism. See Damm (2010). This is an interesting group in part because there is at least some good evidence that those with autism have robust moral concepts (for example, they make the moral/conventional distinction) and attribute responsibility in similar ways to those without autism. At the same time, there is some evidence that they lack typical capacities for empathy. It is an interesting question what emotional deficits there are, and how they affect moral capacities. It is reasonable to conclude that they do possess deficits that result in diminished responsibility, but it is less clear why that is the case. It may be that their diminished responsibility is due to complex perceptual deficits that prevent the application of moral principles in particular situations rather than through a general lack of capacity to recognize and act on reasons.

abilities view that, in its most general form, it does not hinge on whether possession of the reactive attitudes is necessary for moral responsibility.

Thus far, I have been addressing the challenge that the rational abilities view might have consequences that are intuitively too *harsh*, since it might appear at first not to require emotional capacities of any sort. And I have argued that appearances might be misleading here, since the possession of some of the relevant rational abilities might—at least for human beings— require a range of perceptual and emotional capacities. But there is another challenge that comes from the other direction. Perhaps, one might argue, the view is too *forgiving*. If agents must be able to recognize *moral* reasons in order to satisfy the rational abilities view, then our psychopaths *would not* count as responsible, and yet they seem—at least to some—to be paradigms of responsible agents deserving of blame.[36] This challenge, like the first, forces us to elaborate on the nature of the rational abilities in question. Is recognition of moral reasons in particular required for responsibility or is it sufficient that an agent be able to recognize only other sorts of reasons for action? I believe one must be able to recognize moral reasons, and thus this is included in the rational abilities required to be responsible. This is a controversial issue, however, that I will address in chapters 3 and 5, where I explore in more detail worries about the nature of the ability to do otherwise.

In sum, the rational abilities view requires that morally responsible agents have a set of rational abilities that allows them to recognize and act on good reasons, where these include moral reasons. These abilities may in turn require a range of perceptual, cognitive *and* emotional capacities, at least for human beings. But the view as so far stated leaves it open that different perceptual, cognitive and emotional capacities could stand in for the ones we humans use in different kinds of agents.

4: Responsibility and the Reactive Attitudes

We have just seen that one way in which responsibility and the reactive attitudes might be related is that being a responsible agent might require the capacity to react with attitudes of indignation, guilt, and resentment,

---

[36] See Scanlon (1998, p. 284) and Talbert (2008, p. 517).

for example. Capacities for reactive attitudes toward oneself or others might be among the capacities any rational agent (or any human rational agent) needs in order to be responsible. But there is another way that the reactive attitudes have been thought to be related to responsibility: one's being responsible is to be understood directly in terms of either the *tendency* or the *appropriateness* of holding one responsible, where "holding responsible" is a matter of having reactive attitudes like resentment and guilt.

Now there are a number of different versions of this sort of view, and their differences are of great importance. For example, on one kind of view, inspired by Peter Strawson's "Freedom and Resentment", responsibility is to be understood entirely in terms of the tendency to be held responsible, where, in turn, this tendency is understood as the tendency to be met with the reactive attitudes. This account suffers from a well-known problem, however.[37] On this view, there appears to be no room for us to say that reactive attitudes, and corresponding judgments of responsibility, are unjustified. Whatever actions tend to produce the attitudes are simply ones for which people are responsible. And yet it seems clear that people make mistakes—even large numbers of people can be unjustified in their reactions and corresponding judgments of responsibility. For example, some people are prone to blame infants for their behavior, for example, but they are making a mistake. On the kind of view that only appeals to the tendency or proneness toward the reactive attitudes in explicating responsibility, there is not room for mistakes based on the fact that their targets are not really responsible for their actions. But it seems an essential fixed point that people can make mistakes about these things. One natural move is to understand responsibility not as the tendency to be met with reactive attitudes, but with the appropriateness of so being met.

Indeed, this is also a kind of view inspired by Strawson. According to this view, responsibility is constituted by the appropriateness of "holding responsible"; there are no fixed conditions, independent of the appropriateness of others' reactions, in terms of which responsibility can be understood.[38] However, this move faces problems of its own. For there

---

[37] See, for example, Watson (1987/2004).

[38] See Ramirez (in preparation) and Zimmerman (in preparation) for a very helpful categorizing of views that includes views of this sort. Ramirez bases his account to some extent on a more general neo-sentimentalist view of evaluative concepts.

is the well-known difficulty of explaining how we are to discern the conditions for "appropriate" responses without appealing to independent features of the agent and situation in question, such as her rational capacities and opportunities.[39] And yet, once we have done this, it seems that we have pointed the way toward general independent conditions for responsibility that need not mention the *reactions* people have (or might have) to the actions in question.[40] Why then continue to maintain that responsibility can only be understood in terms of reactive attitudes, rather than thinking that the appropriateness of the attitudes depends on whether people really are responsible? Another way to put the question is in terms of explanatory priority. Which is more fundamental—responsibility or the appropriateness of the attitudes? Does one depend on the other or are they mutually dependent?

The view I have offered thus far provides independent conditions for responsible action, even if these conditions themselves include the possession of emotional capacities. Further, it seems that the appropriateness of reactive attitudes is—if anything—dependent on their targets' satisfying the requisite conditions. And this is the simplest way of making a connection between responsibility and the reactive attitudes, once we have independent conditions for being responsible.[41] Whether it is appropriate to feel guilt about one's own actions depends, among other things, on one's capacities at the time, and on one's not being interfered with in a way that prevents one from exercising them.

---

[39] See, for example, Watson (1987/2004, p. 228) and McKenna and Russell (2008, pp. 10–11).

[40] Wallace (1994) attempts both to offer a view that understands responsibility essentially in terms of the appropriateness of responding with reactive attitudes, but also offers very general conditions under which these attitudes are appropriate. Fischer and Ravizza also introduce the notion of responsibility as a "Strawsonian" one: "Someone is morally responsible insofar as he is an appropriate candidate for the reactive attitudes..." (p. 6). But they then go on to offer quite independent conditions on responsibility, as we have seen. Thus, it is not clear how we are to read the "insofar" in their statement. If we read it as entailment, the view is consistent with our having an independent way of understanding moral responsibility. Only if we read it as claiming that responsibility is entirely and exclusively constituted by the appropriateness of reactive attitudes would we see it as Strawsonian in a stronger sense. See McKenna (forthcoming) for subtle discussion of the relationship between responsibility and the reactive attitudes.

[41] See Zimmerman (in preparation) for a similar conclusion, and an illuminating analogy. Zimmerman compares the question of whether responsibility or the appropriateness of the reactive attitudes has priority, to the question in metaethics of whether "being good" or "the appropriateness of reactions of approval" has explanatory priority.

A view that takes correct attributions of responsibility to ground and justify the appropriateness of reactive attitudes, rather than the other way around, will be at least partly vindicated if the independent conditions so far developed can be shown to be both plausible and resistant to challenges. It is to this task that I now turn.

2

Deep Assessment and Good Action

In this chapter, I take up challenges primarily from incompatibilists who argue that when it comes to both praiseworthy and blameworthy actions, the ability to do otherwise is essential to responsibility.[1] I begin with a set of powerful arguments that appeal to the notion of fairness, including one posed by Gary Watson that targets asymmetrical views in particular. These arguments also raise a number of important questions about the relationship of responsibility to other notions such as sanctions and the reactive attitudes. I then turn to two other arguments that reach the same conclusion in different ways and that I believe have been very influential in driving incompatibilism about responsibility: one that reasons via the idea that the ability to do otherwise is related to one's being the source of one's own actions, and another that takes the ability to do otherwise to be partially constitutive of responsible action.

1: Fairness Arguments

A very powerful motivation for the claim that the ability to do otherwise is required for responsibility is that fairness requires it. In its standard form, it begins with the idea that it would surely be unfair to blame people if they

---

[1] It is important to note that not all incompatibilists believe that responsible action is grounded in the ability to do otherwise, and also that some compatibilists believe that the ability to do otherwise is required for responsible action. For example, as we will see in section 3, some incompatibilists believe that the ability to do otherwise is at most a byproduct of another condition—an agent's being the ultimate source of her actions—that requires indeterminism. And some compatibilists, as we will see in chapter 3, offer accounts of the ability to do otherwise that are consistent with determinism.

could not help but do what they do, and so people cannot be responsible for the bad actions they perform if they lack the ability to do otherwise. Here is the argument:

The Intrapersonal Fairness Argument Concerning Blameworthy Actions[2]

(1) X is responsible and blameworthy for an action @ only if it would be fair to impose sanctions on X for @.

(2) It would be unfair to impose sanctions on X for the performance of an action @ if X lacked the ability to do otherwise.

Therefore,

(3) X is responsible and blameworthy for the performance of an action @ only if X had the ability to do otherwise.

Interestingly, when stated in this way, the argument concludes—strictly speaking—that *bad* actions, or actions done for bad reasons, must require the ability to do otherwise in order to be blameworthy. So at least initially, the rational abilities view seems to sidestep the argument, since it *requires* an ability to do otherwise for blameworthy actions.

Still, it might seem at first as though an argument parallel to the traditional one concerning blameworthy actions would be just as compelling:

The Intrapersonal Fairness Argument Concerning Praiseworthy Actions

(4) X is responsible and praiseworthy for an action @ only if it would be fair to reward X for @.

(5) It would be unfair to reward X for the performance of an action @ if X lacked the ability to do otherwise.

Therefore,

(6) X is responsible and praiseworthy for the performance of an action @ only if X had the ability to do otherwise.

Yet despite the apparently perfect parallel, the second argument is not motivated in the way that the first seems to be. It seems only fair that one

---

[2] I call this an "intrapersonal" argument because it concerns only a single person, and does not require comparative judgments concerning more than one person. I explain the contrast more fully in what follows.

have an opportunity to avoid doing something wrong and blameworthy, and thus to avoid harm, if such harm is to be imposed; but it is notable that we don't speak of the unfairness of lacking an opportunity to avoid acting well and so missing out on a benefit. The parallel lacks the initial intuitive pull of the first.

Watson agrees, as we will see, and offers good reason to believe that this argument is not as compelling as the one concerning blameworthy actions, leaving room for a genuine asymmetry that can ground the asymmetrical rational abilities view. However, he then goes on to offer another argument in its place that nevertheless shares with it a fundamental appeal to fairness. Thus, as Watson argues, the asymmetrical view is vulnerable to an objection concerning fairness after all: an ability to do otherwise is required for both bad *and* good actions to be responsible ones.

In what follows, I consider Watson's argument and argue on behalf of the rational abilities view that it can be answered. If it can, and if the traditional argument regarding blameworthy action still stands, then it would appear that the rational abilities view is in a strong position—and receives support from an unexpected source. For if there is an asymmetry between good and bad actions when it comes to fairness, there would be a natural explanation (and possibly even justification) of its asymmetrical treatment of the ability to do otherwise. Perhaps this is right. However, I am moved by some reasons to reject the traditional argument, as well. Unfortunately for the rational abilities view, if all fairness arguments are rejected, then the view appears to be left without an explanation of its asymmetrical treatment of good and bad actions. So in the remainder of this chapter, I explain the reasons that support rejecting the traditional Intrapersonal Fairness Argument Concerning Blameworthy Actions, and then in chapter 5, I go on to offer an alternative explanation and justification of why there is an asymmetry between good and bad actions when it comes to the ability to do otherwise.

Although I will here attempt to defend the rational abilities view against the challenge at hand, I hope my response will have broader appeal, as well. For I believe that much of what I say here (although not all) can also be adopted by those who defend symmetrical compatibilist accounts of responsibility.

Watson's Interpersonal Fairness Argument Concerning Praiseworthy Actions

In "Two Faces of Responsibility", Watson distinguishes between two notions of responsibility—"responsibility as attributability" on the one hand, and "responsibility as accountability" on the other. Watson draws a number of conclusions after drawing this distinction, contributing to an extended objection to the rational abilities view.

To see how, we need an explication of this key distinction between two sorts of responsibility. Let us focus first on blameworthiness, as Watson does. There are two kinds of blame. An example of the first is the judgment that a person's stealing of books is "shoddy". Following van Inwagen, Watson notes that this is a judgment that even a philosopher who is sincerely skeptical about moral responsibility can make. Or to take another example, suppose that "someone betrays her ideals by choosing a dull but secure occupation in favor of a riskier but potentially more enriching one, or endangers something of deep importance to her life for trivial ends . . . then she has acted badly—cowardly, self-indulgently, at least unwisely".[3] These sorts of judgments attribute moral faults to agents, and to make these judgments just *is* to blame the agents in this sense. This is a kind of appraisal that concerns agents' virtues and vices and so Watson calls it an appraisal from the *aretaic* perspective. The blame in question is blame in the "attributability" sense. In contrast, when we blame someone in the "accountability" sense, we invoke moral norms to which we hold people, and we treat them as deserving of sanctions for their violation. Notable among those sanctions, according to Watson, are the reactive attitudes such as resentment. The examples Watson gives are meant to illustrate the possibility of being responsible, and even blameworthy in the attributability sense, while not in the accountability sense. In the case of the woman who betrays her ideals, we blame her, but do not necessarily think she is accountable to anyone for her actions. In the case of the book stealer, it seems at least coherent for the skeptic about responsibility in the accountability sense to blame someone who has stolen his books in the attributability sense.[4]

---

[3] Watson (1996/2004, p. 266).
[4] One might worry that the distinction is not yet sufficiently clear. Here is an example in which it may be easier to accept the existence of blame in the attributability sense and not in the accountability sense: a toddler who behaves in a way we could accurately describe as "mean", while not at the same time thinking that he has violated any obligation or standard

Now Watson has the resources to argue against the rational abilities view by providing a diagnosis of its superficial plausibility: the asymmetrical view is appealing only insofar as we are blurring this distinction between two notions of responsibility. Recall that on the view in question, one is responsible to the extent that one acts with the capacity to respond to good reasons. It turns out then that when you do so respond, you thereby display the relevant capacity, even if you couldn't have done otherwise. So, for example, a woman who jumps into the waves in order to save a drowning child, but couldn't have done otherwise, is responsible and praiseworthy. (Following Watson, call this woman Rosa.) On the other hand, if someone does not respond to relevant reasons (for example, by not jumping in to save the child) then whether she is responsible or not will depend on whether she could have done otherwise. If she could not have done otherwise, she lacks the relevant ability, and so is not responsible. In short, the ability to do otherwise functions in an asymmetric way— you need it if you act badly, but not if you act well. According to Watson, to the extent that this is plausible, it depends on a slide from one sort of responsibility to another. When we agree that Rosa, the woman who saves the child and can't do otherwise, should be praised, we are thinking in terms of the aretaic sense. But, in contrast, when we withhold blame in the case of, say, the victim of the deprived childhood who fails to act well, we have moved to the accountability sense of responsibility. Call this second woman Joan. Note that we can still find Joan to be selfish and mean-spirited, and, so, blameworthy in the attributability sense, while denying that she is responsible in the accountability sense.

This "diagnosis" of our intuitions provides an initial challenge for the rational abilities view. There are a variety of ways a defender of the rational abilities view might respond at this point, including an appeal to the intuitive plausibility of the view itself. Further, as Watson notices, his account actually *makes room* for a certain asymmetry when it comes to praise and blame, and it might seem tailor-made to support an asymmetrical view when it comes to avoidability. The reason for this is that responsibility in the sense of accountability is, on Watson's view, understood in terms of the fairness of one's openness to sanctions on the basis of one's

that applies to him. Another might be someone who has a serious mental disorder, but whom we would not unreasonably call "cruel".

potential for flouting moral requirements. But there is no obvious counterpart in the case of praise. No worries about fairness of sanctions, then,
arise in the case of praise, and so perhaps being praiseworthy in the
accountability sense does not require avoidability. As Watson writes,

> considerations of fairness might still support an asymmetry solely within the
> perspective of accountability. For if the requirement of avoidability derives from
> the idea that we should not be made to suffer from sanctions which we had no
> reasonable opportunity to avoid, then the requirement will have no relevance to
> the conditions of appropriate praise. The special objection to responding adversely
> to those who could not do otherwise simply does not apply to the case of favorable
> treatment.[5]

In other words, the Intrapersonal Fairness Argument Concerning Praiseworthy Actions is unmotivated in the way that the parallel one concerning
blameworthy actions is. All looks well for the rational abilities view. But,
alas, Watson identifies a different worry that remains unanswered.[6] Again,
the problem concerns fairness, but this time it is a matter of *interpersonal*
fairness. Suppose that Rosa is praised for her unavoidable action in saving
the child. Joan, who failed to act well, but couldn't help it, can complain
that a system that benefits Rosa but not Joan is unfair. After all, Rosa is no
more deserving of benefit than she is.

Here is one way of articulating the argument in more detail, where
"responsible" is understood in the accountability sense:

---

[5] (1996/2004, p. 284). One might argue that we should simply reject a fundamental
presupposition of this explanation, namely, that there is no "accountability" sense of praiseworthiness; accountability only applies to blameworthiness. (I thank a reviewer for this point.)
I think doing so would be hasty, however, as we seem to have a notion not only of deserved
blame, but also of deserved praise. Whether this entails desert of *sanctions* and *rewards*, however,
is a question I will take up shortly. While I will suppose in what follows that there is a univocal
notion of responsibility distinct from mere attributability that includes both praiseworthy and
blameworthy actions, it is an open question what the precise appropriateness conditions are for
each. To raise just one puzzle in this connection, there is, arguably, a species of supererogatory
actions, actions which in some sense go beyond what one is obligated to do, which seem on the
surface even better candidates for praise than actions which simply fulfil obligations. There is no
obvious counterpart when it comes to blameworthy actions. I return to this issue briefly in
chapter 5.

[6] It is important to note that Watson does not claim that the problem is intractable, only
that it must be addressed. As Watson puts it, "once we view praise and blame in terms of the
fairness of assigning rewards and sanctions, as it seems we must from the perspective of
accountability, we cannot dismiss this complaint out of hand" (p. 285).

The Interpersonal Fairness Argument Concerning Praiseworthy Actions

(1) X is praiseworthy and responsible only if it would be fair to reward X.

(2) Joan does not deserve a reward.

(3) Neither Joan nor Rosa could do otherwise.

(4) Because neither Joan nor Rosa could do otherwise, and because Joan does not deserve a reward, it would be unfair to give rewards to Rosa.

(5) If neither Joan nor Rosa could do otherwise, and if Joan does not deserve a reward, then it would be unfair to give rewards to Rosa. (from (4))

Therefore,

(6) It would be unfair to give rewards to Rosa. (from (2), (3), and (5))

Therefore,

(7) Rosa is not praiseworthy and responsible. (from (1) and (6))

Answering the Interpersonal Fairness Argument Concerning Praiseworthy Actions

A first question at this point is how far the argument generalizes. If Joan were not in the picture, perhaps there would be no unfairness in distributing a reward to Rosa, and thus, there would be no reason to doubt that she is responsible in the relevant sense. Is her being responsible in the accountability sense contingent on who else is around to make a complaint? I believe that the argument is meant to aim for generality; on such a reading, the mere possibility of a Joan would be enough to generate the conclusion of the argument.

However, these considerations do reveal that there is a different notion of fairness at work here than in the intrapersonal arguments, and, thus, they raise a challenge that the argument turns on an equivocation. This interpersonal argument invokes a new interpersonal, or distributive, notion of fairness.

To see that there are really at least two distinct notions of fairness at work, consider a legal context in which both interpersonal and intrapersonal considerations appear. For example, it is often claimed to be unfair to impose the death penalty on the grounds that it is unfair in its application. The death penalty debate provides an interesting context in which it is sometimes conceded that, considered in isolation, the punishment would be fair (or just), but given the existence of others (for example with different skin color) receiving differential treatment, it is not. Thus, the debate illustrates the very different kinds of considerations that are at stake in the two kinds of arguments, intrapersonal and interpersonal. In contrast to the intrapersonal arguments, the interpersonal arguments target *systems* as much as particular instances of treatment. And, indeed, Watson suggests that the entire accountability system is really the target of this argument. Considering these differences suggests that there might be an important equivocation in the Interpersonal Fairness Argument Concerning Praiseworthy Actions if (1) appeals to the same (intrapersonal) notion of fairness as in the Intrapersonal Fairness Arguments, while (4) appeals to an interpersonal or distributive notion of fairness.

One way of defending the argument from this charge would be to invoke a bridge principle of sorts, so that unfairness of the interpersonal kind entails unfairness of the intrapersonal kind. Yet the legal debate just described gives us reason to doubt that there is a very general principle of this sort since it seems to manifest the live possibility that a practice could be unjust in a distributive, interpersonal sense, while it remains fair or just in an intrapersonal sense to treat an individual in a certain way. However, there may be a narrower sort of bridge principle, according to which a practice that is *necessarily* unfair in the distributive sense is unfair in all senses. I am not sure if this is the best way for the defender of the argument to respond, but for present purposes, I will not pursue this question further. Instead I will press a challenge to a particular premise in the argument.[7]

---

[7] Note that there is a parallel Interpersonal Fairness Argument Concerning Blameworthy Actions, too. The parallel argument goes as follows:

(1) X is blameworthy and responsible only if it would be fair (in all senses) to sanction X.
(2) Joan does not deserve to be sanctioned.
(3) Neither Joan nor Rosa could do otherwise.
(4) Because neither Joan nor Rosa could do otherwise, and because Joan does not deserve to be sanctioned, it would be unfair to sanction Rosa.
(5) If neither Joan nor Rosa could do otherwise, and if Joan does not deserve to be sanctioned, then it would be unfair to sanction Rosa. (from (4))

Therefore,

(6) It would be unfair to sanction Rosa. (from (2), (3), and (5))

Therefore,

(7) Rosa is not praiseworthy and responsible. (from (1) and (6))

In particular, I want to focus on the claim that Rosa deserves her rewards no more than Joan, *the reason being* that neither one can do otherwise (i.e., (4)). For there is reason to doubt that the complaint of unfairness that arises in the reasoning about Rosa and Joan is one that targets asymmetrical views in particular. To see why, suppose that a third woman, call her Sylvia, acts well, and yet could have acted badly, too. She has all the capacities one could hope for, and more. Still, Joan is stuck with only the capacity to act badly. Could Joan not still make a charge of unfairness, just as she did in connection with Rosa? Joan is entirely left out; she cannot hope to reap any benefits associated with being responsible. If this complaint is legitimate, then the charge of unfairness made against Rosa does not hinge on the idea that she gets the benefit of praise despite lacking the ability to do otherwise; rather, the charge is that Joan happens to lack *whatever* capacities are required for reward (whether they include the ability to do otherwise or not). Yet now the problem that initially seemed to target accounts that allowed for praise without alternatives is now a problem for any account of responsibility that allows for praise.

One response to Joan's complaint would be to say that Joan's situation exemplifies the problem of moral luck. What Joan does is ultimately determined by a number of factors, including her genetic make-up, her childhood circumstances, her developmental history. And she has no control over these. Thus, it is a matter of luck that she acts in the way she does, and that she fails to possess the capacities Rosa does. And, further, given that it is a matter of luck in this way, it is unfair to deprive her of the rewards Rosa reaps. But then Joan's complaint, albeit quite serious, does not make essential appeal to the requirement of avoidability. Importantly, she has a complaint, but it is not unique to the rational abilities view.

Another response is to say that Joan's complaint of unfairness does not impugn our judgment of responsibility on either Rosa's or Sylvia's part. It is unfair that they get to be accountable agents (with all the benefits and sanctions that go along) and she doesn't, but there is no incoherence in saying this; there is no contradiction in attributing accountability while acknowledging unfairness in its distribution. Further, it shows that this interpersonal complaint of unfairness need not be especially problematic for asymmetrical views that allow accountability without avoidability, for it also applies to accounts of accountability that *do* require avoidability.

If a special sense of unfairness lingers when one thinks about Rosa benefiting when she could not have done otherwise, then it seems to come from an *antecedent* reluctance to see Rosa as accountable. One already judges that Rosa is not accountable, and then reasons to the unfairness of rewarding her and not Joan. But then the initial intuition that Rosa is not accountable is what is really doing the work. In that case, a defender of the asymmetrical view could say: "I have located a genuine asymmetry when it comes to fairness. And now we can discuss our conflicting intuitions about the particular case" Or she could say: "At the very least, this argument is not what is doing the work for you".

However, we cannot yet rest easy that all considerations about unfairness have been accounted for. For there is one more set of cases that raises a question of interpersonal fairness. So far, we considered a question of interpersonal fairness between Rosa and Joan, and I argued that the same charge could be made by Joan against Sylvia as well, so that any unfairness that arises for Joan does not arise in virtue of Rosa's *inability* to do otherwise. Now let us explore the relationship between Rosa and Sylvia directly. Suppose that Rosa, who cannot do otherwise, and Sylvia, who can, each save one of two simultaneously drowning children. Can Sylvia justifiably complain about having to share kudos, or a prize with Rosa? If so, it seems that there is a kind of interpersonal fairness associated with Rosa's rewards, given her inability to do otherwise.

This is an interesting and challenging case. But I believe that filling out the details of Rosa's inability can undermine any initial sense of unfairness one might feel. For, by hypothesis, Rosa acts precisely for the same clear reasons that Sylvia does: she sees a child drowning and realizes that the child's death is an easily preventable (though inconvenient) and terrible, terrible thing. Recognizing all of this, Rosa jumps in in order to prevent the child from dying. Do we still feel that we would begrudge her a share of the kudos or prize in this case? One reason why it could, for some, seem that there would be unfairness in this case is that we understand Rosa's not being able to help it as a kind of "automatic" response, or a psychological compulsion. But when we think about Rosa's reaction as arising from her recognition of the powerful reasons there are for her acting in the way that she does, I believe such an initial response loses at least some of its strength.

An additional aspect of the case that might generate a sense of unfairness is the appeal to a prize. Perhaps to an even greater extent than in the case of punishment, it is very difficult to find consensus on what counts as appropriate when it comes to rewarding good actions. Offering money, for example, which is indeed divisible, is sometimes thought to be an inappropriate response to a person's performing a good action like saving a drowning child. Offering praise does not raise the question of appropriateness in the same way, but, on the other hand, praise is not obviously divisible in the same way that money is.[8] Thus, it is not clear that Sylvia actually loses anything that is otherwise appropriately hers by virtue of Rosa's having (inevitably) saved a child and been rewarded with praise for it. It might be here, too, that the example generates an initial response of unfairness in part because we are thinking of the division of a prize as cutting into Sylvia's reward; but if we focus merely on praise and not prizes, the strength of the intuition is also somewhat undercut. It is true that Sylvia is deprived of the chance of being praised precisely for being *unique* in her having performed a particular action, but I find it tempting to resist giving this in itself much weight on reflection.

To the extent that a sense of unfairness remains, it might be because of another unstated background assumption, namely, that what Sylvia did was in some relevant sense *harder* than what Rosa did. One might think that the fact that Rosa could only do the one thing, while Sylvia had a genuinely causally open choice, suggests that what Sylvia did was harder. Sylvia, unlike Rosa, had to overcome the temptation to pursue, let us suppose, a less inconvenient opportunity. Here, I believe, we face two questions: (a) does difficulty matter to one's praiseworthiness? And (b) is Sylvia's task more difficult than Rosa's? While I do not believe that the answer to (a) is at all obvious, I want to focus here on (b). The reasoning for an affirmative answer given above, which I believe is very natural, is not in the end convincing. Why does the mere ability to do otherwise reveal difficulty, and, conversely, why does the lack of ability to do otherwise reveal ease? Answering these questions depends on getting clearer about what is meant by "degree of difficulty". One natural way of understanding it is this: amount of effort and/or sacrifice required. But on this understanding, it may very well be that Rosa's act calls for an equal degree of difficulty. Perhaps she had to work extremely hard (perhaps even harder than Sylvia if she were a less fluid swimmer) to reach the child she

---

[8] In some ways, the case might be analogous to the love parents feel for their children. It need not be "divisible" in the sense that there is a finite quantity that is divided into smaller and smaller quantities depending on the number of children one has.

saved. Now there might be other interpretations of difficulty that build in "resistance of a genuinely causally open alternative". But since so resisting an alternative might be quite easy in the first (effort) sense, we need some non-question begging reason for requiring this condition. Until we have such a reason, it seems that an initial sense of interpersonal unfairness between Rosa and Sylvia is left without support, and indeed, is undermined by a fuller description of the case.

The Intrapersonal Fairness Argument Concerning Blameworthy Actions

It would seem at this point that the asymmetrical rational abilities view is in an excellent position. For the Intrapersonal Fairness Argument Concerning Blameworthy Actions is compelling, while its counterpart concerning Praiseworthy Actions is not; further, even the Interpersonal Argument Concerning Praiseworthy Actions fails to hit its target. So we seem to have a genuine asymmetry concerning fairness that can explain (and even justify) the asymmetry of the rational abilities view when it comes to the ability to do otherwise.

However, I believe that there are good reasons to question the Intrapersonal Fairness Argument Concerning Blameworthy Actions. Insofar as we have a stipulative definition of responsibility in the accountability sense, (1) cannot be questioned. But I will argue that there is at least a notion that shares much with Watson's that is distinct from responsibility in the attributability sense, and that is very important to us. On that understanding of responsibility as accountability, (1) can be questioned, and that is what I propose to explore in this section.

Must accountability be understood in terms of the fairness of providing sanctions and rewards? There certainly seem to be important connections here, but I want to question whether they are as direct as is often supposed. To help focus here, consider the possibility of a Mahatma Gandhi-like figure who does not believe we ought to respond with the reactive attitudes or with punishment. Such people raise an important set of questions, posed by Watson himself in other work.[9] Gandhi, for example, led the movement for Indian independence from Britain, fought discrimination by caste, religion, and sex, and worked for the alleviation of poverty. He did all this while advocating a non-violent civil disobedience

---

[9] See (1987/2004, pp. 257–8); (2001/2004, p. 316). See also Darwall (2006, p. 83).

approach, providing a model for movements all over the world. He clearly felt that there were wrongs committed on a wide scale, but at the same time strongly advocated change without violence and punishment, and there is some evidence that he did not condone retributive sentiments.

Must such people abandon the notion of accountability altogether? It seems possible that they can continue to think of themselves and others as obligated to meet certain standards. Obligation here means simply that one ought to do certain things, all things considered. This notion of obligation seems to go beyond attributability, and yet, the possibility of Gandhi (or someone like him in this respect) suggests that it is not incoherent to say that one is obligated to meet certain standards without being automatically committed to the claim that it is fair to impose sanctions for failing to meet them. If the link between accountability and the fairness of sanctions *could* be broken in this way—so that accountability did not *by itself* entail fairness of sanctions—then the claim that avoidability is required for fairness of sanctions could simply fail to apply to its target.[10]

It has been argued, however, that Gandhi's case only appears to suggest a conceptual separation of sanctioning reactive attitudes and responsibility and these cannot really come apart. Wallace, for example, argues for a similar conclusion and explicitly considers Gandhi and Martin Luther King as potentially undermining of it. In the end, Wallace concludes that Gandhi's and King's apparent avoidance of "disapproval and the sanctioning behavior that expresses it" while continuing to "hold their opponents accountable for the moral wrongs they committed" is consistent with an essential link between holding people responsible and the reactive attitudes (1994, p. 72).

To understand Wallace's argument, a bit of background is necessary. For Wallace, being responsible is to be understood in terms of the fairness of holding people responsible. Holding responsible, in turn, is to be understood in terms of adopting and expressing reactive attitudes which are essentially connected to sanctioning activity (p. 93). Thus, his conclusion is that one is responsible only if it is fair to adopt and express reactive

---

[10] Also, and even more briefly, it is worth thinking about non-moral sorts of responsibility in this connection. If there are indeed other sorts (for example, responsibility for one's aesthetic choices or athletic performances), then we can ask here, too, whether sanctions and rewards play the same sort of role. (There doesn't seem to be a complement to the reactive attitudes, or at least such a complement would not seem to be required.)

attitudes such as resentment, which involves the disposition to sanctioning behavior. His view is quite subtle, and I leave out additional details here. What is important for our purposes here is that, like Watson and others, he sees an essential conceptual link between responsibility and sanctioning reactive attitudes.[11] Thus, he acknowledges that the cases of Gandhi and King "seem to tell against the claim that the stance of holding people responsible should be understood in terms of the susceptibility to such emotions as guilt, resentment and indignation" (p. 72).

But Wallace takes this to be mere appearance. He offers a response to the challenge that begins by seeing Gandhi's and King's attitudes as including forgiveness and love, and concludes that the conceptual connection to reactive attitudes is intact even for them. As Wallace writes,

> To forgive someone, in the spirit of love, is a complicated stance. It presupposes that one views the person to be forgiven as having done something that would make resentment or indignation a fitting response—one cannot rightly forgive a person for having done something that would not have rendered one of these reactive emotions appropriate in the first place. Rather, in forgiving people we express our acknowledgment that they have done something that would warrant resentment and blame, but we *renounce* the responses that we thus acknowledge to be appropriate. (1994, p. 72)

I believe that this argument rests on two assumptions that are worth bringing out.

(1) Gandhi's and King's attitudes are ones of forgiveness, and
(2) Forgiveness presupposes the "acknowledgment that someone has done something that warrants resentment and blame", where resentment and blame are essentially sanctioning (that is, harms imposed for the offense).

It follows that even Gandhi and King, when they recognize and forgive wrongdoing, must assume that the wrongdoers in question have acted in ways that warrant the sanctioning of attitudes of resentment and blame. If this is right, then I would be unsuccessful in my attempt to suggest that Gandhi (or someone like him) is a kind of counterexample to the claim that responsibility in an accountability sense must be thought of as entailing the idea that sanctions are appropriate.

---

[11] See also Watson, who takes the reactive attitudes to "involve a readiness to adverse treatment" (1996/2004, p. 279).

However, I believe each of the assumptions behind Wallace's argument can be questioned, and in seeing how, we can also discover some interesting features of both resentment and forgiveness.

First, it is not at all obvious that Gandhi was concerned with forgiveness. And there is some reason to believe that he was not.[12] One reason is conceptual. Forgiveness seems to be an attitude that one who has been wronged has toward the person who has wronged her. For example, it is natural to say that you forgive someone who spread a false and harmful rumor about you, but it is not clear that you even could forgive someone for spreading a false and harmful rumor about your friend. There is something right about the idea that it is not *your* place to forgive. If it is anyone's place, it is your friend's.

Now, as a citizen of India, Gandhi was wronged. But his main focus was on his fellow human beings, not himself. So at least when it came to his public projects, forgiveness would not seem to be defining of his approach. Still, one might reply at this point that Gandhi was engaged in a kind of *analogue* of forgiveness that we can have as third parties on behalf of others.[13] Yet even this would not be among the first descriptions of Gandhi to come to mind. Rather, Gandhi's attitudes could be described as a complex mixture of empathy, love, and acceptance. And, in fact, when asked to explain the success of the Indian independence movement, Gandhi's answer was "love and truth".[14] I do not mean to say that Gandhi never forgave or felt feelings associated with forgiveness. However, I believe it would be a mistake to *assume* that the reason behind his lack of expressed resentment and demand for sanctions was a prior act of forgiveness, or even some third-party analogue of it.[15]

Next consider premise (2), a claim that adopts a particular picture of forgiveness premised on the acknowledgment that someone has done something that warrants the sanctioning attitudes of resentment and

---

[12] See Gandhi (1957/1993).

[13] Note that Benn (1996) coins the term "quasi-forgiveness" as an attitude we can take as third parties. He understands it as an overcoming of one's feelings of indignation and so on (pp. 377–8).

[14] See Shirer (1979).

[15] One might object at this point that Gandhi's behavior is consistent with a number of different motivations and psychological explanations, including forgiveness and beliefs about the appropriateness of sanctions. I agree. I cannot say with any confidence what Gandhi was feeling or thinking (although it would be nice if I could). Instead, I can only claim that it is possible to imagine his situation in the way described in the text.

blame. I believe that this is a very popular way of understanding forgiveness among philosophers, and that the contemporary classic writings on forgiveness by Jeffrie Murphy, in which he describes forgiveness as an "overcoming of resentment", are largely responsible for its popularity (1982, p. 504). In turn, Murphy attributes this sort of view to Bishop Butler's sermons on resentment and forgiveness. While I see the appeal of the view, I believe that many contemporary philosophers have actually misread Butler on this point, and yet that they were nevertheless correct in their claims that he was on to something important.

First, notice that the key claim about the nature of forgiveness really divides into two separate claims:

(2a)   Forgiveness presupposes the claim that resentment and blame are warranted.

(2b)   Resentment and blame are essentially sanctioning.

Briefly consider (2b). Some, including Pamela Hieronymi, Tim Scanlon, and George Sher, have questioned this assumption.[16] I am somewhat sympathetic to their conclusions on this point, while disagreeing with some of their reasoning. But for now I would like to focus on question (2a). For even if resentment and blame itself are essentially sanctioning, we do not thereby have an answer to whether forgiveness entails commitment to sanctions. We need an argument for understanding forgiveness in the way Wallace does. For there are other, and arguably, equally plausible, ways to understand forgiveness, according to which forgiveness requires the acknowledgment of wrongdoing, but where the question of appropriate sanctions is left open. It may be that there are really a variety of phenomena that all go by the name "forgiveness", and it may be that there

---

[16] For example, Hieronymi (2004) argues that blame, in the first instance, is a judgment that someone has acted with ill will. It has a certain "force" or significance in virtue of its importance in interpersonal relationships. For these very reasons, Hieronymi concludes that it is never unfair to blame on account of the special force of blame; blame is only unfair in some sense if the judgments involved in blame are false or perhaps poorly arrived at (p. 129). I am sympathetic to the conclusion, but do not agree with all of the details in the reasoning. Sher (2006) offers an account of blame according to which it is not essentially sanctioning, as well. On his account, blame requires both a "blame-constituting" belief that a person has acted badly (or has a bad character) and a "blame-constituting" desire that the person not have done so (or not have the character traits in question) (p. 14). In Sher (2005), he considers and rejects another fairness argument against a principle that is similar to (2) in the Intrapersonal Fairness Argument Concerning Blameworthy Actions, but is instead focused on the fairness of blame rather than the fairness of sanctions.

is no neat set of necessary and sufficient conditions that map out a single notion. I will here offer a characterization of forgiveness that I believe captures at least one important phenomenon in interpersonal relationships that goes by that name, and according to which (2a) is false.

On the view I propose, forgiveness does entail certain beliefs, attitudes, and intentions, including the belief that a wrong has been committed against one. It also includes a personal release of obligation of a sort. How does this work? It is important to note that a personal release does not mean that the wrongdoer ceases to be obligated in various ways, including to provide compensation to the person wronged. One might find this puzzling at first; but there are different ways of understanding how the wrongdoer can still be obligated despite having received a personal release by the wronged who has forgiven. Garrard and McNaughton, for example, suggest that forgiving involves a lack of insistence on an apology and on penance, while remaining consistent with asking for repentance and reparation. It is thus crucial to forgiving that there is no request for a "humbling" of the wrongdoer before one.[17] When I forgive, on their account, I do not "hold it against the wrongdoer for wronging me". Another way of understanding how there can be a personal release of sorts without there also being a lifting of obligation *tout court* is by analogy with the distinction between the criminal and civil law. In civil law, a plaintiff brings a complaint directly against a defendant, whereas in the criminal law, the state brings the complaint. A person who forgives releases the wrongdoer from a personal obligation, but not from all obligation. *Qua* the particular individual wronged, a person gives up demands. But this is consistent with making demands *qua* citizen, for example. To draw on a different analogy, consider the release from a promise. A friend might release me from my promise to repay a debt to him, but I might still have an obligation to make the repayment nonetheless. Similarly, a friend might forgive me for not repaying a debt, but that does not mean that I should not compensate him. Even if he does not "hold me to it", it does not follow that I should not repay him.

It seems to me that this sketch captures key elements of forgiveness in the belief that one has been wronged and in the giving of a personal

---

[17] See Garrard and McNaughton (2003, p. 47). Presumably, this view would need to be filled out to account for the phenomenon of forgiving the dead—assuming that is something people can do.

release. Forgiveness can surely involve many other things, as well. For example, *typically* it may involve or lead to the overcoming of resentment. But it need not. As Garrard and McNaughton point out, someone in whom forgiveness as a quality is deeply embedded might never feel this sort of emotion in the first place and still be able to forgive. From the other direction, I can imagine forgiving someone while still having recurrent feelings of resentment. I may disapprove of these feelings or wish I did not have them, but the fact that I have them does not seem necessarily to undermine the fact that I have forgiven. I might have forgiven a grade school teacher for her harshness, even if I occasionally feel a momentary resentment at the memory of it.

(Here Butler's work is a model, as he argues that we are obligated to forgive others, but *not* obligated not to feel the natural emotions of resentment and indignation. This is a coherent view only if Butler does not conceive of forgiveness as the forswearing of resentment. And Butler's own words make it clear that he did not: for Butler, what we are obligated to do in forgiveness is to forswear an *abuse* of resentment.[18])

Similarly, forgiveness is often accompanied by a restoration of a relationship. But it need not always be. A wife may forgive an abusive husband without canceling her divorce filing. Thus, phenomena such as overcoming hostile emotions and restoring relations might accompany forgiveness in many cases without being necessary.

Does this picture leave out a crucial element of forgiveness, namely the belief that a sanctioning attitude was warranted in response to the action? I do not believe such an element is necessary, although like the restoration of relations and the overcoming of resentment it might often accompany forgiveness. At the least, no explicit consideration of the proposition would seem to be necessary. After all, those with forgiveness "deeply embedded" might not feel the emotions in the first place. And some who do might not see their attitudes as essentially sanctioning. To attribute this theoretical proposition (and one that might be false) to anyone who forgives would seem to require an over-intellectualized process. The question becomes, then, whether people are *implicitly* committed to such a proposition insofar as they forgive.

---

[18] See Butler (1726/1896, pp. 151–2). See also Newberry's (2001) excellent defense and elaboration of this reading of Butler.

And in the context of the argument at hand, we need more than just an assertion that they are.[19] While it is plausible that forgiveness is often accompanied by an attempt to rid oneself of resentment, it remains an open question whether forgiveness must be accompanied by *any* particular attitude about the warrant or lack of warrant for one's reactive attitudes.[20] What seems essential to at least one central notion of forgiveness is something more fundamental: the judgment that one has been wronged and a certain sort of personal release from a kind of obligation in the face of that fact.

Now one might argue against this, and in defense of premise (2a), that I have presented a pared-down notion of forgiveness, and that there is a notion of forgiveness that also requires a belief in the warrant of sanctioning attitudes. In response I would say that while there might be such a phenomenon, there is no reason to suppose that understanding forgiveness in this way will preserve a univocal reading of the whole argument. To the limited extent that (1) is plausible—and I have given reasons for doubting it—it is so on the characterization I have given. Wallace writes that if Gandhi or others really were to abandon the belief that the reactive attitudes were appropriate, we would have to say that "they are no longer in the game of holding people morally responsible at all" (1994, p 73). But in the face of people, both real and imagined, who seem to renounce sanctioning attitudes and actions, but who fight for the most fundamental rights of their fellow human beings against collective wrongs, demanding that people change their behavior in important ways, we need more of an argument for believing that they do not really hold people responsible or to obligations.

---

[19] Interestingly, while Murphy (2003) and others have seen the defining feature of forgiveness as an overcoming of justified resentment or related attitudes, others have described it in strikingly different terms. For example, Bennett (2003), drawing on some work of Jean Hampton's, sees what he calls "personal forgiveness" as overcoming understandable, but *inappropriate* attitudes such as resentment, while possibly continuing to blame. Bennett and Hampton see resentment as including a doubt about whether one is really worthy of the respect which one demands, and only in moving beyond resentment does one regain that healthy self-respect that was threatened by a wrongdoer. Once one is fully confident in oneself as worthy of respect, one does not feel resentment, on their view, even if one feels other things, like contempt (pp. 137–42).

[20] Another reason for questioning this entailment comes from theological treatments of forgiveness. For example, on one view, God cannot feel emotions such as resentment, but this does not preclude God from forgiving. At least in theological contexts, the connection between resentment and forgiveness seems somewhat tenuous.

In the end, Gandhi—or perhaps people like him in certain ways—are understandable. And it seems plausible that they hold others (and themselves) responsible in a strong sense that is distinct from attributability, while rejecting the appropriateness of sanctioning reactive attitudes. Arguments to the contrary appear to fall short. Views that claim an essential connection between responsibility in a deeper sense and the appropriateness of sanctions continue to face a challenge here, in the idea that such people at least seem to have a coherent grasp of a robust concept of responsibility without believing that it entails (let alone is defined by) something about the appropriateness of sanctions. In turn, this would suggest that if there is a conceptual link between the two, it is a more subtle one than is often supposed. And this suggests that the first assumption in the traditional argument should not be accepted without qualification.

Where We Are

We have seen first a set of intrapersonal arguments appealing to fairness that suggest a symmetrical treatment of praiseworthy and blameworthy actions such that both require that the agent acts with the ability to do otherwise. But further reflection suggests that these arguments should not be treated in the same way because of an asymmetry built into the notion of responsibility as accountability (at least as elaborated in terms of sanctions). Examination of an interpersonal fairness argument requiring the ability to do otherwise for praiseworthiness shows that it fails, as well. It seems, then, that not only can the rational abilities view answer the argument that fairness considerations dictate a symmetrical treatment of the ability to do otherwise in requiring it for all actions, it can even appeal to an asymmetry in intrapersonal fairness considerations to *support* its asymmetrical treatment of alternatives. However, I have not embraced that argument here. Instead, in chapter 5, I will suggest an alternative route to explaining its asymmetry when it comes to the ability to do otherwise.

But first, let us turn to other considerations—distinct from fairness—that can also motivate the worry that the rational abilities view has it wrong when it comes to good actions. One way of motivating such worries is to suggest that the inability to do otherwise precludes responsibility, but only because it points to something else in virtue of which responsibility is impossible: namely, one's being the source of one's actions. And yet a third way of defending the key claim is very direct:

the ability to do otherwise is itself necessary for responsibility, and this has direct intuitive appeal. I will take up the first suggestion in section 2 and the second in section 3.

2: Source Arguments

Some have argued for incompatibilism on grounds other than that responsibility requires the ability to do otherwise. Determinism, it has been argued, precludes responsibility not because it precludes the ability to do otherwise, but because it entails that an agent's decision to act is produced by a source over which she lacks control.[21] What really matters for responsibility is not the possession of options, but rather the kind of control over one's actions that one cannot have if they are determined by past events. If, for example, to take one of the cases described in chapter 1, Jeremy Gross lacked the ability to do otherwise, because any potential alternatives were somehow blocked, but he was himself the undetermined source of his decision to kill his co-worker at the convenience store, then he could be responsible. While the two ideas—(i) that an agent's ability to do otherwise is what is important to responsibility, and (ii) that an agent's being the true source of her actions is what is important to responsibility— have often been assimilated or at least not clearly distinguished, the two are distinct ideas and one can accept one without the other.[22] Pereboom himself accepts the second idea, which he calls "causal-history incompatibilism", but not the first, which he calls "leeway incompatibilism".

Nevertheless, Pereboom acknowledges that alternative possibilities "not necessarily of the robust sort" might be entailed by the indeterministic feature of the kind of causal history that is required for responsibility (2001, p. 37). In other words, although alternative possibilities are not what *makes* someone responsible, they are *entailed* by one of the features *in virtue of which* someone is responsible. To illustrate, consider Jeremy Gross's case again. Suppose that he were in fact the undetermined source of his decision to kill his co-worker. This does not entail, as Pereboom points out, that Gross could have refrained from killing. That option could have simply been blocked in any number of ways, including the fact that were

---

[21] See Pereboom (2001, pp. 1–2).

[22] See Pereboom (2001, pp. 1–6); Fischer (1982); O'Connor (2000, pp. 20–1). See Kane (1996) for arguments that we should accept both ideas.

he to have wavered, some brain event would have caused a lethal seizure. At the same time, perhaps the fact that his action was undetermined entails that there was more than one way things could have gone with Jeremy. He could have shot his victim in the head or the heart, for example. Neither of these options was blocked. Or he could simply have had these two short-term prospects: lethal seizure or killing. Pereboom points out that these options do not appear to provide a pair of robust alternatives, where having a robust alternative to one's actual action explains *why* one is responsible. Intuitively, if Jeremy's alternative were, rather than having a lethal seizure, an action on his part such as deciding not to kill, such an alternative would at least seem intuitively more promising in providing an explanation for Jeremy's responsibility. But the fact that he could have had a seizure or shot his victim in a slightly different place doesn't seem relevant—at least in itself—in explaining his responsibility. Yet, claims Pereboom, Jeremy can be responsible, in virtue of being an undetermined source of his actions, even if his alternatives are not robust ones. At the same time, being an undetermined source of his action might imply the existence of *some* alternatives, even if it is not in virtue of them that one is responsible.

Thus, it is important that the rational abilities view have the resources to face the challenge that having alternative possibilities is *always* required for responsible action, whether good or bad—not because having those options is itself what makes one responsible, but because having them is entailed by what really matters, namely, that one is the undetermined source of one's action. Pereboom has provided a very subtle version of such a line of reasoning in his "four-case argument" for incompatibilism. In what follows, I will set out the argument, and respond to it on behalf of the rational abilities view. Some of the responses are available to all compatibilists, but at least one is unique to the rational abilities view.

The argument centers around four cases, each of which is deterministic and in each of which an agent satisfies compatibilist conditions sufficient for responsibility. For example, the agent in question satisfies Fischer and Ravizza's reasons-responsiveness condition on responsibility and possesses Wallace's powers of reflective self-control. The agent also acts with the endorsement of his "second-order" reflective desires, or his desires that his first-order motivations be effective, thus satisfying a paradigm real self view.[23] Each scenario features Professor Plum who "kills Ms. White for the sake of some personal advantage" (p. 111).

In Case 1, "Professor Plum was created by neuroscientists, who can manipulate him directly through the use of radio-like technology, but he is as much an ordinary human being as is possible, given these unusual features. The neuroscientists manipulate him to undertake the process of reasoning by which his desires are brought about and modified. They do this by pushing a button just before he begins to reason about his situation, thereby causing his reasoning process to be rationally egoistic".[24] Filling out the case, we can imagine that "by way of neural intervention the manipulators enhance Plum's disposition to reason self-interestedly at the requisite time, so that they know that it is ensured, causally, that he will decide to kill Ms. White".

In Case 2, "Plum is like an ordinary human being, except that he was created by neuroscientists, who, although they cannot control him directly, have programmed him to weigh reasons for action so that he is often but exclusively rationally egoistic, with the result that in the circumstances in which he now finds himself, he is causally determined to undertake the moderately reasons-responsive process and to possess the set of first- and second-order desires that result in his killing Ms. White..." (2001, pp. 113–14).

Case 3 is even more like the ordinary situation than either Case 1 or Case 2. In that case, "Plum is an ordinary human being, except that he was determined by the rigorous training practices of his home and community so that he is often but not exclusively rationally egoistic (exactly as egoistic as in Cases 1 and 2). His training took place at too early an age for him to have had the ability to prevent or alter the practices that determined his character. In his current circumstances, Plum is thereby caused to undertake the moderately reasons-responsive process and to possess the first- and second-order desires that result in his killing White..." (p. 114).

And, finally, Case 4 is "the normal case"—at least if determinism is true: "Physicalist determinism is true, and Plum is an ordinary human being, generated and raised under normal circumstances, who is often but not

---

[23] See Frankfurt (1971).
[24] See Pereboom (forthcoming). Pereboom there responds to reactions to his original Case 1, set out in (2001), and alters and fills out Case 1. See Fischer (2004), Mele (2005) and Baker (2006) for some reactions to the original case.

exclusively rationally egoistic . . . Plum's killing of White comes about as a result of his undertaking the moderately reasons-responsive process of deliberation, he exhibits the specified organization of first- and second-order desires . . . ".

The argument has the following structure. In Case 1, we are invited to respond with the intuition that Plum is not morally responsible for his actions. And yet, we should also acknowledge that Plum meets the compatibilist conditions. Pereboom notes that if compatibilists resist this conclusion because of worries about moment-to-moment manipulation, the case could be modified to include a time-lag between the manipulators' activity and the relevant mental states that result. Thus, the case seems to serve as a counterexample to the compatibilist views.

Case 2 can also serve as a counterexample on its own, but it gets a boost in this department by comparison with Case 1. Since there seems no relevant difference, and in both cases the obstacle to responsibility seems to be Plum's lack of control over the source of his action, it seems that we begin to have a diagnosis of why Plum is not responsible in either case.

Case 3 is not relevantly different from Case 2, and so it seems impossible for the compatibilist to argue that Plum is responsible in Case 3. Again, in both cases, "causal determination by factors beyond Plum's control most plausibly explains his lack of moral responsibility". Similar reasoning applies for Case 4, and now we have what seems like a general refutation of compatibilism. If this is correct, then it would seem that the rational abilities view, even though not mentioned explicitly in the argument, falls along with each of the other compatibilist views.

But I do not think we need to accept the conclusion of the argument, for at least two reasons. A first response to the argument is to run it backward. That is, we can start by concluding that we should treat Case 4 differently from the way advocates of the argument want to, and by parity of reasoning, end up treating Case 1 and/or Case 2 differently, as well. I believe that there are at least three different ways to implement this general strategy. The first begins by appealing to a different intuition in Case 4.

In particular, if one has the intuition that people are responsible if they are in a situation like Plum's in Case 4, then, assuming Pereboom is right that there is no relevant difference between Cases 4 and 3, or between Cases 3 and 2, we ought to conclude that Plum is responsible in those cases, as well. Pereboom offers a response to this: we don't have intuitions of that sort;

rather, we have intuitions that real people are responsible, but not that they are at the same time determined. There is some evidence for this conjunctive claim, but I believe the jury is still out. It is true that subjects tend to reject the idea that we live in a determined world, at least when asked in certain ways.[25] And it is true that in some studies in which subjects are asked about the compatibility of determinism and responsibility in the abstract, results have suggested that subjects have incompatibilist intuitions.[26] On the other hand, in some studies, subjects are given scenarios in which protagonists are described as inhabiting a deterministic world, and perform a serious crime, described in detail.[27] A large number of subjects report that they would blame the protagonists in these situations. Collectively, these studies provide us with an interesting puzzle, but at least for now, it is not obvious what we should say about people's intuitions in general.[28] Arguably, if the crime is described in sufficient detail, we can generate intuitions about Case 4 that would allow for a kind of "work-backward" strategy as a response.

Michael McKenna has also suggested a "work-backward" strategy, but instead of starting from an *intuition* about Case 4, it begins with an agnostic position about Case 4.[29] Since the proponent of the four-case argument does not want to beg any questions at the outset, he argues, we should acknowledge that it is "not evident" that Plum is not responsible in Case 4. But given no relevant differences between Case 4 and Case 3, we should also withhold judgment about Case 3, and so on. Pereboom has responded by arguing for an initially open view of the case, which can change in light of relevant reasons such as comparisons to other cases. Although the difference in starting points is subtle, it is significant. Where McKenna argues for an agnostic position that does not change in light of our responses to additional cases, Pereboom argues for an open position that can (and in his view, should) change as we are faced with relevantly similar cases.

This seems to me a good response. At the same time, this does not by itself show that no work-backward strategy can succeed. The first kind of

[25] See Nichols and Knobe (2007, p. 669).
[26] See Doris and Knobe (forthcoming), and Nichols and Knobe (2007, p. 670).
[27] See, for example, Nahmias et al. (2005, pp. 568–9).
[28] I discuss this puzzle in more detail in Nelkin (2007a).
[29] See McKenna (2008, especially pp. 147–54).

implementation—that begins with an intuition about Case 4—is one option. Further, we are in a situation in which we have a number of intuitions about a number of cases—some realistic and some unlike our ordinary experiences (as far as we know), as well as different theories that fit more and less well with each one. For if intuitions about real cases, together with an independently plausible theory, *entail* responsibility in Case 4, then the strategy can still be used as a response to the argument in yet a third way. Notably, Case 3 may be a quite realistic case in which intuitions may very well be compatibilist for many. At the very least, it allows us to avoid the conclusion of the four-case argument. For no matter what, it seems we are going to end up with recalcitrant intuitions of one kind or another. The question is what theory does a better job overall of accommodating our intuitions. The four-case argument provides a strong challenge to compatibilist views, but it is one that they can meet by bringing to bear intuitions about other cases, as well as a plausible theory that explains (ideally) our intuitions even in recalcitrant cases. For example, the fact that manipulation is often associated with the implantation of rote or automatic responses might be clouding our reading of the cases so that we do not fully acknowledge that the protagonists have the relevant compatibilist capacities. This response is somewhat less satisfying than working backward from clear intuitions about Case 4 itself, but it is possible to use both in combination.

Thus, compatibilists have a variety of "work-backward" strategies from which to choose in responding to the four-case argument. A second and complementary response appeals to the specific features of the rational abilities view. One might argue that while Plum may satisfy a variety of compatibilist conditions, he does not clearly satisfy the conditions set out by the rational abilities view. In particular, on this view, one needs the ability to do otherwise only in the case in which someone does something bad or for bad reasons. So, *at most*, one needs indeterminism for those actions. For this reason, it would be instructive to vary the example so that Plum acts well. Suppose, for example, that we replace Case 2 with the following. The neuroscientists have created Plum so that he fully under-stands and recognizes good reasons for acting. He is moved by people in distress and desires to help them so as to relieve their suffering. Suppose that one day he finds himself in a situation in which he can help a child only at great risk to himself. He thinks about the relevant considerations and decides that all things considered, helping is the right thing to do and resolves to do it. The intuitive force of this example seems to me to swing the other way. At the very least, it is much less appealing to say that Plum is not responsible. If indeed there is an asymmetry in our reactions to the cases, it suggests an explanation other than that we find people not to be responsible when their choices are determined by causes beyond their control. What capacities one has when one acts is what is essential here. This line of response both questions whether Cases 1–3 serve as independent counterexamples to the rational abilities view, and also points to an alternative explanation for our intuitions that allows us to resist the general conclusion against compatibilism.

This response reveals that the rational abilities view is "ahistorical" in the sense that it does not require either an indeterministic history or a special compatibilist one. But that is not to say that history is irrelevant to responsibility. What history one's actions have can also make it the case that one lacks some crucial abilities one needs to be responsible. So, for example, Jeremy Gross's history is important precisely because it precludes his seeing the reasons there are at the time for acting differently than he does. In many cases in which people lack the relevant abilities (or capacities and talents more generally), we can find a genetic explanation for this in a particular kind of unfortunate history. But it is not the history itself that precludes responsibility; it is the result of that history. This consequence of the rational abilities view is an attractive one because it gives a place for the importance of history in agents' actions, but it also does not require a history with particular features—either incompatibilist or compatibilist. Even though there are compatibilist positions that are "historical" in requiring certain kinds of histories that are consistent with determinism, in sharing worries about manipulation and other histories with incompatibilist positions, it is harder for them to say why one should be a compatibilist. For example, a compatibilist view that required that, say, one's motivations not be the result of manipulation, will have a hard time with just the sort of argument we have been examining. For what is the relevant difference between manipulation and a natural process, where both have the same determined results? This is a challenge a non-historical view like the rational abilities view simply does not face, since it does not object in the first place to manipulation per se.

Fischer and Ravizza offer a more sophisticated historical condition, namely, that an agent have "taken responsibility for the mechanism on which she acts". Taking responsibility in turn requires that an agent see her own motivations as causes, that she accept that she is a fair target of the reactive attitudes as a result of her exercise of agency, and that she have these views of herself on the basis of appropriate evidence (1998, pp. 210–13). Further, the condition requires that she take responsibility for acting on the mechanism she acts on, and, as has been noted, it is not clear exactly how this is supposed to work.[30]

It is not ruled out, then, that a compatibilist historical condition can work; but it faces difficulties that a non-historical view simply avoids. And there is a way in which the rational abilities view is able to get the best of both worlds: it does not require a certain kind of history, but it can at the same time acknowledge the importance of history in generating the abilities relevant to responsibility. Again, one reason why manipulation seems so worrisome is that in real life it is often associated with the implantation of motivations that are not sensitive to reasons, or with the raising of children in a way that prevents them from being able to recognize good reasons for acting. For this reason, manipulation can play an important role in how we come to judge someone as responsible or not; but manipulation is not by itself the culprit, it is the result that matters, a result made probable by certain kinds of manipulation.

Although this general point is available to other non-historical views, such as real self views, I believe the rational abilities view is particularly well suited to support it. To see why, consider that a real self view can also suggest that history has a genetic role to play, in, say, one's not being able to act on one's value judgments. But it is one's lack of ability at the present time rather than the process that matters. Still, this will not explain why manipulation bothers us when it is the mistaken value judgments themselves that are instilled as a result. It is still tempting to think that even though the conditions of this real self view are met in such a case—one's motivations and value judgments are perfectly aligned—the fact of manipulation precludes responsibility. In contrast, the rational abilities view can provide a different judgment in this case, depending on the details of the case. If the manipulation is direct in such a way as to bypass the agent's recognitional or motivational capacities, then the agent is not responsible, even if her implanted values and motivations line up in the right way. If manipulation results in an agent's being able to recognize and act on good

---

[30] See, for example, Bratman (2000, pp. 457–8).

reasons, then it is much less tempting to worry that the manipulation raises difficulties in attributing responsibility.

In sum, the rational abilities view has distinct advantages over both historical compatibilist views and other non-historical compatibilist ones in being able to address manipulation arguments against compatibilism. At the same time, it can take advantage of responses to such arguments that are in principle available to all compatibilist views. To see these points in action, let us turn to a final and even simpler manipulation argument, due to Al Mele (2006).[31]

Suppose that Diana creates a zygote, Z, which develops into Ernie, and assembles it in such a way as to ensure that Ernie will bring about E by A'ing thirty years later. "Diana ensures a lot more than that. A complete description of the state of the universe just after Diana creates Z—including Z's constitution, of course—together with a complete statement of the laws of nature entails a true statement of everything Ernie will ever do" (p. 188). Ernie is a "mentally healthy, ideally self-controlled person who regularly exercises his powers of self-control and has no relevant compelled or coercively produced attitudes...his beliefs are conducive to informed deliberation and he is a reliable deliberator". With this in mind, consider this reasoning:

(1) Because of the way his zygote was produced in his deterministic universe, Ernie is not a free agent and is not morally responsible for anything.

(2) Concerning free action and moral responsibility of the beings into whom the zygotes develop, there is no significant difference between the way Ernie's zygote comes to exist and the way any normal human zygote comes to exist in a deterministic universe.

(3) So determinism precludes free action and moral responsibility.

Like Mele, I believe that the real action is in premise (1).[32] What should we say about it? I believe that much depends on the details here, which are not fully spelled out in this argument. If we suppose that Ernie has the relevant abilities to detect, adopt, and act on good reasons, then it is, at the very least, easier to deny premise (1) than if Ernie is stuck without, say, an

---

[31] Also see Mele (1995, pp. 144–76) and (2006, pp. 164–73) for extended discussions of a historical compatibilist account that explicitly requires a lack of manipulation of a certain kind.

[32] This discussion is based on an earlier one in Nelkin (2007a).

understanding of why other people's pain is a reason not to act in certain ways. Suppose that "E" is Ernie's helping a friend to leave the hospital after an emergency surgery. Ernie acts in the way he does because he sees his friend in need and realizes it will be easy to help. This scenario is very different from the following: imagine that Ernie has been designed to act only in his self-interest, not recognizing anyone else's interests as a reason for acting. At the time in question, Ernie E's, that is, he pushes a button to blow up a large building he owns, which is inhabited by hundreds of people, in order to collect on the insurance. In this case, given the lack of rational abilities he has been endowed with, it is much harder to think of Ernie as responsible. Thus, in this case, too, history can matter in so far as it results in an agent's having one set of abilities rather than another.

When it comes to this argument, all compatibilists would do well to run the argument backward—using one of the same strategies employed against the four-case argument. Here, too, all compatibilists can use the appeal of broad theories, as well as intuitions about normal cases, to weigh against the intuitive force of the argument. But I believe the intuitive force of the premises can also be blunted directly if we ask for an elaboration of the details that are relevant to determining whether the conditions required by the rational abilities view are satisfied. The view prompts the asking of further questions about the scenario, different answers to which can make a difference to the intuitive appeal of the premises. In this way, the rational abilities view has a special advantage when it comes to answering the causal-history incompatibilist.

Finally, it is worth returning to the connection between causal-history or source incompatibilism, and the ability to do otherwise. For even if it were true that indeterminism were necessary for responsibility in virtue of its being a requirement for an agent's being a source of her actions in the right way, it does not automatically follow that an agent must be able to do otherwise. Strictly speaking, according to at least some kinds of causal-history incompatibilism, there must be alternatives for the agent in the sense that things have to have been able to go otherwise. But it does not follow from this that the agent herself have to have been able to act otherwise. In that case, while causal-history incompatibilism would constitute a challenge to the compatibilism of the rational abilities view, it would not constitute a challenge to it on the grounds that it has the wrong implications for praiseworthy actions in failing to require an ability to do otherwise.

3: Leeway Arguments

So far, we have looked at two important kinds of reasons why the ability to do otherwise might be thought to be required for responsibility in all cases, including both praiseworthy and blameworthy ones. The first included an appeal to fairness and the second included an appeal to the idea that we must be undetermined sources of our actions. The rational abilities view offers unique answers to both challenges. It remains to examine one more set of reasons for thinking that the rational abilities view gets things wrong in not requiring the ability to do otherwise in cases of good actions.

In particular, one might adopt the position that the ability to do otherwise is essential for responsibility in a more direct way. It might be thought that there is some sort of conceptual link between responsibility and the ability to do otherwise that does not make use of the idea of fairness, nor of one's being the ultimate source of one's actions. How might this work?

The simplest argument for this conclusion consists of a direct appeal to the plausibility of the principle of alternate possibilities:

> (PAP)   A person is morally responsible for an action only if he could have done otherwise.

PAP does not distinguish between good and bad actions; for any action, alternatives are required. Thus, if PAP is correct, then the rational abilities view could not offer a complete account of moral responsibility.

Let us now evaluate the claim that PAP is intuitive. Harry Frankfurt and many others have offered what appear to be counterexamples to the claim, and I will discuss some of these in the following chapter. But even in the absence of clear counterexamples, it is worth noting that if the entire argument consists in the intuitive force of PAP, then it must be weighed against an intuitively plausible view inconsistent with it, together with other intuitions concerning examples. It is also possible to construct principles not unlike PAP with which it might be argued that PAP is naturally confused. Frankfurt, for example, provides this one:

> (PAP')   A person is not morally responsible for what he has done if he did it only because he could not have done otherwise.

The idea behind Frankfurt's alternative principle is that what really troubles us about cases described as ones in which agents cannot do otherwise is not the mere fact that they cannot do otherwise. It is that they do what they do precisely because of whatever it is that prevents them from doing otherwise. To take a familiar case, if one does not save a drowning child because one is tied up with a rope, then one is not responsible for not saving the child. But it isn't because one cannot do otherwise, it is because one didn't save the child precisely because one couldn't. Suppose, on the other hand, that there is an agent who simply does not value saving children at small cost to himself. He chooses not to save the child. Even if he could not have done otherwise, Frankfurt suggests, he is responsible, as long as what causes his choice and action is his own reflection and commitment. PAP seems attractive because it is easily confused with another true principle. I do not mean to endorse PAP', but I do think it illustrates very nicely the possibility of finding principles that explain the appeal of PAP without entailing it.

Thus, the appeal to the intuitiveness of PAP comes up against other intuitions, plausible and appealing theories, and diagnoses of why PAP might seem right even if it is not. Ideally, then, a defender of leeway incompatibilism should take the intuitive force of PAP to be a starting point, something to be combined with some sort of explanation of why it is true.

One explanation goes like this: (1) free will just is the ability to do otherwise,[33] and (2) responsibility entails free will. But both premises of this argument might be questioned. Or rather, one might ask whether the kind of freedom required for responsibility consists in the ability to do otherwise. Fischer and Ravizza, among others, concede that there is a notion of freedom that consists in the ability to do otherwise, and then, by arguing in favor of a particular conception of responsibility that does not require it, conclude that responsibility simply does not require the ability to do otherwise.

Similarly, one might argue that control requires the ability to do otherwise, and since responsibility requires control, it, too, requires the ability to do otherwise. However, since there are different notions of control, we can accept the idea that responsibility requires control while remaining open as to whether it requires the ability to do otherwise. Which is the right notion? I believe that the only way to answer this is

---

[33] See van Inwagen (1983, p. 8).

to continue to develop the competing views, part of which I undertake in this book. The plausibility of the views as a whole must ultimately be taken into account.

In sum, it would help the leeway incompatibilist to say more about why the ability to do otherwise is required for responsibility. But we have already set to the side two powerful suggestions: that the ability to do otherwise bears a special connection to responsibility via fairness, and that it bears a special connection to responsibility via one's being the true source of one's action. (And even if fairness turns out to be relevant after all, it is possible for the asymmetrical rational abilities view to accommodate this, by appealing to an asymmetry in fairness considerations themselves.) As for the proposal that either a notion of freedom or control is (partially) constituted by the ability to do otherwise, this, too, can only be a starting point. For what notion of freedom or control is at stake in responsibility is itself a contentious question, to be answered only by developing competing pictures.

4: Where We Are

At this point, the rational abilities view has shown itself to have resources to answer a number of arguments that the ability to do otherwise is required even for good actions done for good reasons. However, one might worry that by rejecting the three rationales for the ability to do otherwise, we are left without resources to explain why the ability to do otherwise is required for responsibility for *any* kinds of actions, good or bad. Showing that the ability to do otherwise is required precisely for blameworthy actions, but not praiseworthy ones, requires a special treatment. In this chapter, I have aimed only at disarming rationales for requiring the ability to do otherwise in *every* case of responsible action. In chapter 5, I offer a positive account of why the ability to do otherwise is required for blameworthy actions alone.

3

Abilities

In the last chapter, I examined challenges to the rational abilities view from those who argue that the rational abilities view has the wrong implications when it comes to praiseworthy actions. In this chapter, I turn to challenges from those who argue that the view has the wrong implications when it comes to blameworthy actions.

1: Heroes, Villains, and Abilities

One might agree with advocates of the rational abilities view that one can be responsible for acting well without the ability to do otherwise, but disagree with their claim that one cannot be responsible for acting badly without such an ability. Fischer and Ravizza take just this position, rejecting the asymmetry that is built into the rational abilities view. Their objection depends largely on appealing to "Frankfurt-style" cases, arguing that such cases work for both praiseworthy and blameworthy actions, showing that we can be responsible for *either* kind, despite lacking the ability to do otherwise.[1] Their first case is called "Hero", and in it a woman, Martha, is walking along a beach when she sees a child struggling in the water: "she quickly deliberates about the matter, jumps into the water, and rescues the child". Had she considered *not* saving the child, "she would have been overwhelmed by literally irresistible guilt feelings which would have caused her to jump into the water and save the child anyway" (p. 376). Intuitively, Martha is morally responsible, even though she could not have done otherwise. Her disposition to guilt feelings played no role in what she did, despite making it impossible for her to do otherwise.

---

[1] Fischer and Ravizza (1992, pp. 375–6). For Frankfurt's original case, see Frankfurt (1969). Frankfurt also credits Robert Nozick with independently constructing a similar case.

Now consider a second case, "Villain". Joe is an evil man who knows that a child watches the sunset at the end of a long pier every day. Joe has decided to push the child off the pier, causing her to drown. Max is just as evil.

> Max is pleased with Joe's plan . . . but Max is a rather anxious person. Because Max worries that Joe might waver, Max has secretly installed a device in Joe's brain which allows him to monitor all of Joe's brain activity and to intervene in it, if he so desires. This device can be employed by Max to ensure that Joe decides to drown the child and that he acts on this decision; the device works by electronic stimulation of the brain. Let us imagine further that Max is absolutely committed to activating the device to ensure that Joe pushes the child should Joe show any sign of not carrying out his original plan. Also we can imagine that there is nothing Joe could do to prevent the device from being fully effective if it is employed by Max in order to cause Joe to push the child into the treacherous surf.
>
> In fact, Joe does push the child off the pier on his own, as a result of his original intention. He does not waver in any way. Max thus plays absolutely no role in Joe's decision and action . . . (Fischer and Ravizza 1992, p. 377)

Joe seems to be morally responsible for his actions, just as Martha is for hers. In neither case does what prevents them from doing otherwise actually play any role in causing an action. Thus, Fischer and Ravizza conclude about Wolf's asymmetric view that the "asymmetry thesis is false, rather, good and bad actions are symmetric with regard to the requirement of alternative possibilities for moral responsibility" (p. 377).

Interestingly, a proponent of the rational abilities view can accept Fischer and Ravizza's intuitions about the cases without rejecting the asymmetry in question. The reason is that we can say that while Joe in Villain and Martha in Hero both lack the ability to do otherwise in some sense, they both *have* such an ability *in the relevant sense*.

In the context of responding to the original kind of Frankfurt cases, such as Villain, in which the agents are blameworthy for their actions, this general strategy has been adopted in a number of different ways. To take just two examples, it has been argued that in the original Frankfurt cases the protagonist can either do X "on his own" or as a result of intervention and that the protagonist can do something other than what he does for which he would be entirely blameless.[2] In the time since these analyses of the examples were proposed, more sophisticated Frankfurt-style examples

---

[2] See Naylor (1984) and Otsuka (1998) respectively.

have been constructed (as we will soon see) that purport to avoid vulnera-
bility to this kind of response, and yet more responses have been offered in
turn.[3] I will here explore the prospects of a particular version of this general
strategy of identifying an ability to do otherwise in Frankfurt-style cases.

As Wolf herself understands the possession of an ability, an agent has an
ability to X if (i) the agent possesses the capacities, skills, talents, knowledge
and so on which are necessary for X'ing, and (ii) nothing interferes with or
prevents the exercise of the relevant capacities, skills, talents and so on
(1990, p. 110). Since in Villain, Max's presence actually plays no role in
Joe's action, and, we can presume, Joe has the talents and skills to refrain
from pushing the child off the pier, Joe's ability to so refrain is intact,
despite Max's presence. Similarly for Martha in Hero. Now of course,
there is *a* sense of "ability to do otherwise" in which both Martha and Joe
lack such an ability. Joe will push the child off the pier, even if he wavers,
and Martha will save the child even if she considers not saving the child. In
this sense, having an ability to do X is precluded when it is inevitable that
the agent will not do X (call this the "inevitability-undermining" sense).
But in another sense, both have their abilities to do something different
from what they do intact.

Fischer and Ravizza recognize that the success of their argument hinges
on what notion of "ability" is at stake. Yet, they argue, even on Wolf's
understanding of "ability", Joe lacks the ability to do otherwise "for were
he to try to [do the right thing for the right reason], Max's device would
prevent his exercising the relevant capacities, skills, etc., required to refrain
from pushing the child into the water" (1992, p. 378, note 9). I believe
that this is a misreading of Wolf's characterization. What is needed to
remove one's ability to do something in the relevant sense (call it the
"interference-free capacity") is either the removal of the capacities, talents,
skills, and so on (the presence of which is not in dispute), or the actual
interference with or prevention of the exercise of those capacities. The fact
that Max's device *would* interfere with or prevent such an exercise in
counterfactual circumstances does not entail *actual* interference or prevention. For this reason, Fischer and Ravizza's Frankfurt-style case does not
constitute a decisive objection to the asymmetry of the rational abilities

---

[3] For example, see Mele and Robb (1998) and (2003), and McKenna (2003), and
Pereboom (2001) for additional Frankfurt-style examples, each of which is meant to address
these (and other) responses to the original Frankfurt cases.

view. It does raise the important question of how we should understand "ability" in this context.

The interference-free conception of an ability described earlier is ambiguous in an important way. One might understand it to require only a general capacity, so that if I am on a desert island with no keyboard, I can still be said to have the ability to type. I need not be in circumstances at all friendly to my typing—that is, I need not have a typewriter or computer within a thousand miles or have the use of uninjured fingers in order to retain this general capacity. The general capacity in this sense seems insufficient for the kind of ability that is needed in order to be responsible. Even in the Frankfurt-style cases, it seems that the protagonists have more than this; they have the skills, talents, and knowledge, but they also have unimpeded use of their bodies and uncluttered piers in their sights. The circumstances provide all that they might need to act, but for a *counterfactual* intervener. That is, the circumstances are conducive for their acting, except that something *would* intervene in some way, on some sign or other. The idea of being interference-free that I prefer, then, is that nothing is actually preventing you from acting otherwise (though it *would* under different circumstances). It is true that this notion is distinct from what Austin called an "all-in" ability, in which one has the opportunity to exercise one's general capacity in the circumstances, or from what I earlier called an "inevitability-undermining" sense.[4] But it is noteworthy that it goes beyond the notion of mere general capacity, and at the same time appears to be all that is needed in the way of ability for responsibility, if we share Frankfurt's intuitions about his cases.

The account sketched so far provides a way to resist the claim that the ability to do otherwise is not needed for either blameworthy or praiseworthy actions; at the same time, it faces important challenges. First, it might be argued that there are still more sophisticated Frankfurt-style cases that serve as counterexamples to the claim that responsibility requires the ability to do otherwise, even in this interference-free sense. Second, it might be argued that this notion of ability is not one we work with in our daily lives, or see as centrally connected to freedom and responsibility.

Let us start with the first challenge. Even if Hero and Villain do not undermine the rational abilities view built on the interference-free

---

[4] See Clarke (2009) for a very useful framework of different notions of ability. Also, see Austin (1956).

conception of an ability, other cases might. A case proposed by Derk Pereboom might seem to be just such a case. The first part of the case proceeds as follows: Joe is considering whether to claim a certain tax deduction, all the while knowing that it would be illegal, but that he would probably not be caught and convicted. Joe has a

> very powerful but not always overriding desire to advance his self-interest no matter what the cost to others, and no matter whether advancing his self-interest involves illegal activity. Furthermore, he is a libertarian free-agent. Crucially, his psychology is such that the only way that in this situation he could fail to choose to evade taxes is for moral reasons ... In fact, it is causally necessary for his failing to choose to evade taxes in this situation that a moral reason occur to him with a certain force. A moral reason can occur to him with that force either involuntarily or as a result of his voluntary activity ... However, a moral reason occurring to him with such force is not causally sufficient for his failing to choose to evade taxes. If a moral reason were to occur to him with that force, Joe could, with his libertarian free will, either choose to act on it or refrain from doing so (without the intervener's device in place) ... But to ensure that he chooses to evade taxes, a neuroscientist now implants a device which, were it to sense a moral reason occurring with the specified force, would electronically stimulate his brain so that he would choose to evade taxes. In actual fact, no moral reason occurs to him with such force, and he chooses to evade taxes while the device remains idle. (2001, p. 19)

It seems that Joe is responsible, despite lacking the ability to do otherwise. Does Joe lack that ability to do otherwise *in the interference-free capacity sense*? Not obviously. It is plausible to say that Joe has the relevant capacities to do the right thing, despite failing to do so. Is there interference? It seems not; the device in Joe's brain functions much like Max in the Villain case in that it never does anything. It is only "waiting" to act, so to speak, in the event that it is triggered.

At this point, however, Pereboom suggests a modification to the case that he claims shows that Joe does in fact lack the interference-free capacity to do the right thing:

> Suppose that a patient has a tumor that puts pressure on his brain so that he can no longer do cutting-edge mathematics. If the tumor were not putting pressure on the brain, he could do the mathematics. But imagine that it is causally impossible to remove the tumor, or for its existence to cease in any other way, without the patient dying. Then, it would seem, he does not have the capacity, free of interference, to do cutting-edge mathematics. Analogously, suppose that in Tax Evasion the intervener has implanted his device in Joe's brain, which is triggered by the requisite level of attentiveness to moral reasons, but she has also made it causally

impossible to remove or disable the device without killing him. As a result, he permanently cannot choose to refrain from evading taxes. Under these circumstances Joe would appear not to have the capacity, free of interference, to choose to refrain from evading taxes. But still, it seems he could be morally responsible.[5]

If this is right, then Joe is a counterexample to the rational abilities view; one can act badly without being able to act well, even in the interference-free capacity sense, and yet still be responsible. However, this example depends heavily on the use of an analogy to a tumor, and it is here that we can begin to resist the reasoning. In the tumor case, it is claimed, we think of the mathematician as lacking the ability to do high-level mathematics even in the interference-free capacity sense. If we think of the implanted device as relevantly similar to the tumor, we should draw the parallel conclusion in Joe's case.

We need more detail about the tumor case in order to see how the parallel is supposed to work. In general, I believe, we think of tumors as destroying brain tissue, and so destroying the capacities and skills needed to engage in certain mental activities. A less standard way of thinking of a tumor would be as more akin to the counterfactual intervener in the Villain case—as "waiting in the wings" so to speak. In this scenario, the mechanisms for doing mathematics would remain untouched; but some how if they were engaged, the tumor would ensure that they could not result in a correct mathematical judgment. Now it matters very much which of these two different scenarios we have in mind when we draw the parallel to Joe's case. On the first scenario, the parallel is one in which Joe lacks the capacities and skills necessary for doing the right thing. But in that case, it isn't obvious or intuitive that Joe is responsible for not doing the right thing. On the second scenario, the parallel is one in which the device still functions as a counterfactual intervener, albeit one that is there to stay. And in that case, it might be argued that Joe still has the ability to do the right thing for the right reasons in the interference-free capacity sense. Thus, even this purported counterexample can be resisted.

It is essential at this point to address the second potential challenge to the view set out. One might worry that in the interference-free sense of ability, one can have the ability to do otherwise while lacking any genuine

---

[5] In correspondence. This suggestion is based on a similar one that appears in Pereboom (2001, pp. 27–8), in response to a proposal of McKenna's, namely, that one requires a power to be the author of one's actions.

alternatives; thus, the intuitively appealing idea that alternatives are necessary for blameworthiness would fail to be captured if the interference-free sense of ability is used.[6] There would be no point, then, to speaking in terms of an ability to do otherwise.

One way to reply to this challenge is to suggest a corresponding sense of "alternative" such that if one has an interference-free capacity, one does have an alternative. But even if that is not the sense people often invoke in discussions of responsibility, one might argue that there is a natural confusion between the two senses. It might be that typically when one has the interference-free ability to do otherwise, one does have alternatives in the sense that is precluded by Frankfurt-style cases. Frankfurt-style cases are, after all, arguably not the norm. So we might mistakenly assume that if we have the ability to do otherwise in the interference-free sense, then we have alternatives in the inevitability-undermining sense.[7]

Finally, and most radically, a defender of the rational abilities view that invokes the interference-free sense of ability might opt for a limited sort of revisionism.[8] If there really is a tension between the interference-free sense of ability and our ordinary notion of alternatives, we ought to retain the former and jettison the latter when it comes to attributions of responsibility. In support of jettisoning this latter notion of alternatives, it is worth noting that we are not committed to it as rational deliberators; when we deliberate, we consider alternatives, but the notion of alternatives we employ does not commit us to a notion of alternatives that is precluded by Frankfurt-style cases. One strong motivation for incompatibilism in general, and, more specifically, for understanding alternatives required for responsibility in a way that in turn requires indeterminism, is based on the assumption that we are stuck with such a conception of alternatives in virtue of being deliberators. As deliberators, the reasoning goes, we

---

[6] This is a kind of objection also lodged against both traditional compatibilist conceptions of the ability to do otherwise and newer versions that appeal to recent work on the nature of dispositions. For some recent examples, see McKenna's (1998) reply to Campbell's (1997) defense of a traditional compatibilist account, as well as Campbell (2005); Clarke's (2009) response to a series of "new dispositionalists" including Smith, M. (2003), Vihvelin (2004), and Fara (2008); and Fischer (2008).

[7] Actually, the situation is more complicated than this, since at least some who offer Frankfurt-style cases distinguish between robust and non-robust alternatives. See Fischer (1994, pp. 140–1) and Pereboom (2003, pp. 186–8).

[8] See Vargas (2005a) and (2007) for a very helpful discussion of different types of revisionism.

necessarily think of ourselves as having multiple undetermined alternatives. But, as we will see in chapters 6 and 7, this is simply false. We are not
committed to our having alternatives that are undetermined, although we
are committed to our having alternatives for which our deliberation makes
a difference. This means that a powerful motivation for retaining (or even
adopting) a notion of alternatives in the context of responsibility that
requires indeterminism is undermined. We are simply not stuck with
a notion of alternatives in our deliberative lives that would be in tension
with a notion that does not require indeterminism.

At this point, a defender of Fischer and Ravizza's view might claim that
if in fact revisionism of a sort is required here, then at least one advantage
noted at the outset—namely, the greater intuitive plausibility of having the
capacity in question attach to the agent instead of the mechanism—is
undermined. For if the rational abilities view succeeds only if revision to
an everyday concept is acknowledged, then defenders of views like Fischer
and Ravizza's might also avail themselves of a similar move. Neither
would then be said to be "more intuitive" than the other. I believe that
this raises a deep question about what standard we should use in any area
where we are considering a revision in concepts.[9] At the same time, it is
worth pointing out that the rational abilities view together with the
interference free capacity view of abilities allows us to preserve a great
deal of what both compatibilists and incompatibilists have been concerned
to preserve. On the rational abilities view, there is a sense in which not
only does a responsible agent need the general capacity to do otherwise in
certain cases, but she also needs not to be interfered with in such a way that
she cannot exercise it on a particular occasion. These seem to be important
and intuitive conditions that are retained by the rational abilities view,
even if the view were to be seen as a moderately revisionist one.[10]

---

[9] I return briefly to this point in Concluding Thoughts.

[10] It should be noted that the rational abilities view and the reasons-responsiveness view of
Fischer and Ravizza share key commitments, including to the compatibility of responsibility
and determinism and to the view that Frankfurt-style cases successfully show that one does
not need an ability to do otherwise in *an inevitability-undermining sense* to be responsible. At this
point, it might be asked whether the difference between the two views is truly a substantive
one. There are in fact several substantive differences, including these: (i) the rational abilities
view does not appeal to counterfactual properties of a mechanism; (ii) the rational abilities
view is ahistorical, as we saw in chapter 3, requiring no "ownership" condition; and (iii) the
rational abilities view is asymmetrical where the reasons-responsiveness view is not.

2: Determinism and Abilities

Suppose then that the interference-free notion of ability is well-motivated. In that case, Frankfurt-style cases do not cause a particular problem for the rational abilities view.[11] But determinism is another matter altogether, as we saw at the outset. For if determinism is true, then it appears that one could satisfy conditions of the rational abilities view on responsibility if one does the right thing for the right reasons, but not if one fails to do so. In this case, we would have an apparently unacceptable asymmetry of responsibility attributions as a result of the built-in asymmetry of the view itself, together with a certain kind of world.

There are a variety of responses to make to this serious challenge. First, one might simply accept the conclusion and the contingency of the existence of blameworthy actions on the truth of determinism. After all, many incompatibilists are willing to rest the contingency of responsibility in general on whether determinism is true; is the situation for the rational abilities view really so much worse? Second, it is worth noting that other compatibilist views that appeal to capacities will face parallel challenges.[12] But these responses are not sufficient, for they merely show that the view is not unique in facing problems of this kind; the problems remain.

A more direct response is this: the worry here rests on an assumption that can be questioned, namely, that determinism itself entails a kind of interference with or prevention of the exercise of one's capacities. In one sense, determinism would seem to entail that the exercise of a capacity to do otherwise than one does is "prevented". But we need to be careful here, since in that sense of "prevent" the existence of a counterfactual intervener also prevents the exercise of Joe's capacity to refrain from pushing the child to his death, and we have seen that this is not a sense

---

[11] This point does not detract from the importance of Frankfurt-style cases. They do suggest that freedom and responsibility are compatible with at least one important notion of the ability to do otherwise, and force us to look elsewhere to figure out why determinism is threatening to freedom and responsibility.

[12] Of course, there are alternatives for compatibilists. In addition to "flow models" (see chapter 1, note 19), there is the unique view of Fischer and Ravizza, according to which at least part of what is required for responsibility is a disposition to do otherwise in *different* circumstances. Objections can and have been raised to these views on other grounds, including precisely the fact that they do not incorporate an ability to do otherwise; ultimately, then, these alternatives are not obviously to be preferred just because they avoid this particular worry about determinism.

that is relevant to responsibility. In one more robust sense of "prevent", in which something actually inhibits Joe's choices or actions, there is no prevention in Joe's case. Does determinism actually inhibit someone from exercising his or her capacity in the way that someone's being tied up with a rope obviously does, or does it otherwise entail that someone's capacity is inhibited? I believe that the answer is not obvious, and it is worth exploring a line of reasoning that suggests otherwise.[13] In this section, I make a start, and will add ingredients from later chapters to make a fuller case.

Reflection on Frankfurt-style cases might at first suggest that determinism is unlike a counterfactual intervener in a way that makes the first, but not the second, entail a prevention or interference with one's exercise of a capacity to do otherwise. One difference comes to mind immediately (and it did to Frankfurt): in the case of determinism, it seems that what makes it the case that one lacks the ability to do otherwise actually plays an explanatory role in one's action, whereas in the counterfactual intervener case, what makes it the case that one lacks the ability to do otherwise plays no such role.[14] Clearly, the fact that the counterfactual intervener plays *no* role is sufficient to show that his presence does not undermine responsibility. But it remains an open question whether *playing a causal or explanatory role* is sufficient for a state of affairs to interfere with one's capacities in a sense that undermines responsibility. Let us consider this suggestion:

(a) If a state of affairs plays a causal role in one's A'ing, then it interferes with one's exercise of the capacity to B.

This is clearly false. Any paradigm free action would seem to serve as a counterexample, as long as one's actions have causal antecedents. Thus, while *not* playing a causal role means that a state of affairs is *not* responsibility-undermining, it is not the case that playing a causal role means that a state of affairs *is* responsibility-undermining. So consider a second suggestion:

---

[13] Wolf constructs a "Leibnizian" scenario in order to show that *physical* determinism in particular does not entail interference or prevention in the relevant sense (1990, pp. 103–16). Fischer and Ravizza raise several strong challenges for Wolf's argument along these lines. In the text, I take a somewhat different approach.

[14] See Frankfurt (1969).

(b) If a state of affairs plays a *deterministic* causal role in action A, then it interferes with one's exercise of the capacity to B.

Unlike (a), (b) poses a real challenge to the rational abilities view. But even (b) can be resisted. First, note something interesting about (b). It is neither the fact that something causes an action, nor the fact that something in some sense guarantees that the action will take place (as in the classic Frankfurt-style cases) that is claimed to prevent one from doing otherwise; it is the combination of both of these features in a single state of affairs that is claimed to prevent one from doing otherwise. Does the combination succeed in a special way that neither component does on its own?

Let us consider two cases. In the first, George Bush authorizes the U.S. army to begin war with Iraq, deterministically caused to do so by his prior mental states and other earlier states of the world. In the second, Bush authorizes the U.S. army to begin war with Iraq, caused probabilistically to do so by his prior mental states and other earlier states of the world. In the second case, we can suppose that there was a ninety-nine percent chance of his acting in the way he actually did. Now we can imagine that Bush might claim later that he didn't have a choice in either case. It could have happened differently in the second case in the sense that it was not determined by strict causal laws, but in fact the earlier events were efficacious and he was unable to do otherwise in the sense that he could "do" nothing to affect the course of events once the earlier events had occurred. In the sense of having the ability to do otherwise that is connected with control, he had no *more* of this ability in the second case than in the first.

Thus, we face a dilemma. In the sense that seems relevant for responsibility, the ability to do otherwise does not seem precluded by determinism in a special way. If anything, determinism appears to be a particular instance of something more general, namely, mechanism, or the thesis of universal event causation. Thus, we can either embrace the idea that determinism serves to preclude the ability to do otherwise in the relevant sense, in which case we should also embrace the idea that mechanism more generally does as well, or we can be open to the idea that neither determinism nor other sorts of mechanism by themselves do so.

This is to transpose a form of argument that is familiar from the free will debate where its particular target is less focused. It is a powerful argument, but one that is usually set in general terms at the level of "free will", rather than in terms of a particular component of it. In other words, the familiar (and powerful) argument goes like this: "You say that determinism implies that no one is free because it takes away a person's control over things. But mere indeterminism does not help. It doesn't add to one's control". The version I am offering here moves the argument down a level: "You say that determinism implies no one has the ability to do otherwise in the relevant sense because it takes away a person's control over things. But mere indeterminism does not help. It doesn't add to one's control. So either way, no one has the ability to do otherwise".[15] The idea is to say that determinism and indeterminism stand and fall together, not only for whether one has free will and moral responsibility, but also for whether one has at least one key component ability.[16]

All of this leaves us with three options. The first is to continue to fill out the notion of abilities in a compatibilist way. The second is to pursue another conception of control altogether, one that relies on a different metaphysical picture. This is to accept the reasoning given above, while noting that it relies only on an event-causal libertarian picture. According to this second option, turning to an agent-causal metaphysics can help achieve a genuine ability to do otherwise that constitutes control and that avoids the reasoning that the compatibilist and libertarian are in the same boat when it comes to the ability to do otherwise. A final option is to retreat to skepticism, and to agree that neither determinism nor indeterminism is consistent with the notion of "ability" that really captures control.

My strategy is to pursue the first option, while at the same time welcoming a change in metaphysical pictures. Executing this strategy means doing a number of things, and I will take on these tasks in subsequent chapters. First, I will explore the theory of agent-causation in chapter 4, and show that while the theory has great virtues, and while it is typically understood as essentially libertarian, it need not be. Thus, the appeal of this alternative to a compatibilist conception of abilities is defused. Second, I will argue that we can find guidance into a deeper understanding of abilities by turning to our own conception of our

---

[15] In Nelkin (2001) I argue for the more familiar version of this argument.

[16] It is a bit more complicated than this. The ability to do otherwise is not a component of moral responsibility on the rational abilities view; but it is entailed by a component of moral responsibility when it comes to bad actions, or actions done for bad reasons.

alternatives in deliberation (the subject of chapters 6 and 7). Third, I address the skeptic in the final chapter.

So far, then, we have seen that objections based on Frankfurt-style cases to the asymmetry of the rational abilities view can be resisted. The threat of determinism is not thereby dismissed, however. In this section, I have sketched a strategy for meeting it, and will return to it in the next chapters. Before turning to that task, one last issue regarding the asymmetry of the rational abilities view needs to be addressed.

3: The Ability to Do Otherwise in Recognizing a Moral Reason

In chapter 1, I mentioned a worry about the rational abilities view that concerned its implications for people known as psychopaths. Since it makes no explicit mention of emotional abilities, it might seem at first to be too harsh; in other words, it seems to hold people responsible who lack even the capacity to sympathize with others. In response, I argued that the rational abilities view has considerable flexibility when it comes to emotional abilities. It may be, for example, that in human beings, having certain rational abilities requires certain perceptual, cognitive, *and* emotional ones. It is a virtue of the account, I believe, that it is consistent with different sets of empirical facts. And our uncertainty about the nature of psychopaths, as well as our incomplete knowledge about how various capacities are related in human beings, reflects the uncertainty—or at least lack of consensus!—we have about how to treat psychopaths when it comes to responsibility.

So far, then, we have seen how the view responds to the charge that it is too harsh. But there is an objection that is sometimes launched from the opposite direction: the rational abilities view lets people off the responsibility hook when it shouldn't. This is because you can do terrible and evil things without having the ability to do otherwise required by the rational abilities view. Psychopaths are a good example. Surely these people are responsible for their actions in virtue of their horrible motives, the pleasure they take in others' suffering, and so on. Their very lack of conscience is itself a reason to blame them.

This sort of objection comes from different directions. One finds it, for example, in Scanlon (1998) and Talbert (2008). On this sort of view, only a very general rational capacity is required for responsibility. To be responsible, one need not be able to act on the reasons there actually are in a given situation—notably moral ones. As long as one has the general capacity to recognize reasons for acting (say, one does fine with prudential reasons despite being blind to moral ones), then one is responsible (and blameworthy) for one's bad actions. For as long as one understands what reasons are in general, if one acts badly, not showing proper respect for the moral status of others, then one is, in effect, acting with a kind of contempt. One is saying that considerations about other people are not reasons for action, and this is to act with a kind of contempt that is blameworthy.

Despite the temptation to blame in these situations, I do not believe this reasoning works. When we really try to imagine moral blindness, it isn't clear that anything that could properly be called "contempt" is really in play. If there is no real grasp of the idea that hurting someone is a reason not to perform an action, then it is not literally true that the agent in question fully understands the proposition he or she is claimed to deny. Of course, genuinely morally blind people may be very bad and to be avoided and even locked up in some circumstances. But the case has not yet been made that they are responsible for their actions in anything like the accountability sense. Perhaps they are responsible in something more like the attributability sense described earlier, for all that this line of reasoning shows. At times, Scanlon seems to endorse something like this view: "If he is unable to see the force of some reason that counts against this attitude, this does not alter the fact that the attitude and the judgment that is warranted are properly attributable to him. Any errors involved in these attitudes are also attributable to him, and he is therefore properly criticized for holding them" (1998, p. 289).

But at other times, Scanlon seems to want to include the idea that in blaming the morally blind we are making a demand of them, and this seems to point in the direction of accountability. Further, Scanlon makes a distinction between making demands and imposing sanctions, a distinction about which I expressed a cautious optimism in chapter 2. There I suggested that there is a notion of accountability that is associated with obligation, but is not defined directly in terms of sanctions. As Scanlon shows, making this move allows him to forestall the following "unfairness" argument for the claim that the morally blind are not responsible:

(1) If it is unfair to blame an agent for a harmful action, then the agent is not responsible.

(2) Blame is a sanction.

(3) If an agent had no opportunity to avoid performing an action, then it would be unfair to impose a sanction.

(4) The morally blind have no opportunity to avoid performing harmful actions.

(5) It is unfair to impose a sanction on the morally blind.

Therefore,

(6) The morally blind are not responsible.

Scanlon resists the argument by denying premise 2, a move that I have also questioned in a different way in the previous chapter when I proposed a way of understanding forgiveness that presupposes blame but not a belief that sanctions are appropriate. Should the rational abilities view drop the restrictive requirement that one must be able to grasp moral reasons in order to be responsible?

I do not believe so. For this move, even if successful, can at best rebut the argument at hand. It cannot support the *positive* claim that the morally blind are responsible. And I believe that the very idea of a demand requires an ability to fulfill it. It does not make sense to demand of people that they change their attitudes if they are incapable of doing so in a very strong way.

Scanlon disagrees because he sees two aspects to moral criticism: moral criticism is special because a person is asked to reassess or defend her attitudes, and it is special because of the significance that "this form of justifiability has for an agent's relations with others" (p. 287). But for this point to be relevant to showing that moral criticism is appropriate (beyond attributability) for the morally blind, Scanlon would have to see each of these aspects as being individually sufficient for the appropriateness of moral criticism. That is, we would have to accept that the significance of the act for our relationships alone can make moral criticism appropriate, even if we are not really in a position to ask an agent to change in some way. Only if we see each aspect as individually sufficient can we avoid requiring the capacity to respond to a demand. And yet if we are to see the second aspect of moral criticism as separable from the first, then it seems that we must let go of the idea of a demand altogether. We must let go of any real "asking" of someone to act in a certain way.[17]

In more recent work, Scanlon understands a blameworthy action as one that "shows something about the agent's attitudes towards others that impairs the relations that others can have with him or her".[18] Taken in isolation here, the idea of demand is absent, but then so is the idea of accountability, it seems.

In the end, then, if we see Scanlon's position as regarding attributability only, there is no reason to doubt it. However, if, in appealing to the notion of a demand, he means to ascribe accountability to the morally blind, then there is good reason to resist. Although I have not questioned Scanlon's distinction between the appropriateness of demands and attributions of obligations on the one hand, and the appropriateness of sanctions on the other, I have tried to show that this distinction cannot do all the work Scanlon desires. For the ideas of demand and obligation are powerful ones, and these do require the ability to do what is demanded and fulfill one's obligations. By removing considerations of sanction and fairness from the table, Scanlon is able to rebut certain arguments for excusing the morally blind, but insofar as he leaves considerations of demand and obligation on the table, he is unable to rebut others that refer only to these ideas.[19]

Thus, while it is a somewhat open question whether the rational abilities required for responsibility themselves require particular emotional capacities, they must include the ability to grasp moral reasons.

---

[17] There is a tension, though, between the idea that each "aspect" is sufficient, and his diagnosis of his disagreement with opponents: "One might conjecture that the strongly different intuitions that people have on this issue reflect the fact that some are focusing mainly on one of these aspects of moral criticism while others are thinking mainly about the other". If either is sufficient, there should be no disagreement.

[18] (2008, p. 128).

[19] I discuss this point in more detail in chapter 5, where I argue for a general "Ought-Implies-Can" principle.

4

A Compatibilist Account
of Agent Causation

In the last chapter, I argued in favor of employing in the rational abilities
account of responsibility a compatibilist understanding of abilities to act in
ways other than one does. But the argument was incomplete. There
I offered a dilemma, showing that indeterministic causation by prior events
does not give the agent any more in the way of the relevant kind of *ability*
than does deterministic causation by events. This is to transpose a very
powerful and influential line of reasoning concerning free action to
support a conclusion about the relevant kinds of abilities. The basic idea
is the same, and can be found in many places.[1] Insofar as there is a lack of
control, or what is sometimes called "luck" from the point of view of the
agent, in the deterministic world, there is an equal lack of control when we
simply add indeterminism. Our choices, then, are these: to embrace
skepticism; to accept that the abilities required for responsibility (and for
blameworthy actions in particular) are compatible with determinism; or to
identify a way to break out of the dilemma that starts with an apparently
exhaustive choice of deterministic and indeterministic causation by events.

Pereboom characterizes the dilemma in a way that seems initially to
favor skepticism. Libertarians deny that one can have the relevant sort of
control in a deterministic world to be morally responsible. But

---

[1] Van Inwagen pointed out that his "Consequence Argument" has an apparent parallel
in what he calls the "Mind Argument". It appears at least that whether our actions are
determined consequences of prior events over which we have no control, or undetermined
consequences of prior events over which we have no control can make no difference to
whether we act freely (see van Inwagen 1983, p. 148). Van Inwagen and others (for example,
Finch and Warfield 1998) have tried to show that these lines of reasoning do come apart after
all. I disagree, and explain why in Nelkin (2001).

it is no remedy simply to provide slack in the causal net by making the causal history of actions indeterministic. (In preparation, chapter 3, p. 4)

He calls this "the problem of the disappearing agent". Once we see the world as a web of events, tied together with causal relations in accordance with causal laws—whether deterministic or indeterministic—it seems that there is no room for the agent herself to exert control in the world.[2]

It would seem then that the only possible way to avoid skepticism is to shift to an entirely different picture of the world and the agent's place in it. Pereboom believes that there are good empirical reasons not to make this shift, but others have embraced it as a viable way to avoid the dilemma and show that the agent is there after all. This position has come to be known as "agent causation", and the basic idea is that the agent herself—and not (merely) judgments, decisions, or any other mental events involving her—is the cause of her actions. Now if in this way we can break out of the web of causation that otherwise seems to constitute the causal world, then we can break out of the dilemma I posed in the previous chapter. If we are agent causes, perhaps our ability to cause things indeterministically is precisely what it is to have the relevant ability to act that is needed for responsibility.

This is a powerful idea, and one that has a long history. It might seem that in order to maintain a compatibilist view about both praiseworthy and blameworthy action, one would need to argue against the very possibility of agent causation in ways in which it has long come under attack. For example, agent causation has been thought to be incoherent, and impossible to reconcile with causation in the rest of the world. But I will not take that approach. Instead, I will agree that the best versions of agent causation can meet these challenges. My disagreement will be with two rarely questioned assumptions about the nature of agent causation, namely, (i) that it must be undetermined in a certain sense; and (ii) that it is fundamentally different in kind from causation that does not involve agents, where the latter only takes events as causal *relata*.[3] I will argue that once we acknowledge that agent causation can be compatible with a kind of determinism, we do not have good reason to prefer indeterministic

---

[2] See also Chisholm (1964) for a similar kind of dilemma—and third way.
[3] A notable exception who questions the first is Markosian (1999); a notable exception who questions the second is Watkins (2010).

agent causation to deterministic agent causation as a requirement for responsible agency.

Thus, this point provides a key component in the argument for a compatibilist account of abilities. But equally importantly, it offers a positive and attractive *metaphysical* account of responsible agency to underlie the rational abilities view. This chapter has two main aims, then. One is to add to the argument for a compatibilist understanding of abilities by undermining an influential competing incompatibilist account; the other is to show that the compatibilist can make use of many appealing aspects of that incompatibilist account in answering the "disappearing agent" problem.

I will begin by describing some common features of influential contemporary accounts of agent causation, and set out some challenges that all such views face. Then I will explore the virtues of a Kantian account of agent causation that questions assumption (ii)—namely, that agent causation is a unique kind of causation in the world, explaining the advantages of this view. With the Kantian view in hand, I will be able to construct a compatibilist version of the theory, one that questions assumption (i) above—namely that agent causation must be indeterministic. I go on to assess the relative advantages of the two Kantian views, arguing in favor of the compatibilist version. Finally, I compare the view to one other compatibilist version of agent causation.[4]

1: Contemporary Agent-causal Accounts and Challenges They Face

Roderick Chisholm wrote that

... if we consider only inanimate natural objects, we may say that causation, if it occurs, is a relation between *events* or *states of affairs*. The dam's breaking was an event that was caused by a set of other events—the dam being weak, the flood being strong, and so on. But if a man is responsible for a particular deed, then, if what I have said is true, there is some event, or set of events, that is caused, *not* by other events or states of affairs, but by the agent, whatever he may be.[5]

---

[4] But see Pereboom (forthcoming) for an interpretation of Descartes and the Stoics as compatibilist agent causationists.

[5] (1964/2003, p. 130).

Using a pair of medieval terms, Chisholm calls causation of events by events "transeunt causation" and causation of events by agents "immanent causation". The existence of immanent causation solves the problem of the disappearing agent; it explains how a person herself could be responsible for her actions. Free and responsible action, on this view, is action caused by agents, and not simply by events involving agents, such as judgments or decisions.

Now this view faces a number of challenges and questions, and I will focus on five here. Chisholm addressed some of these, and more recently, they have been addressed by defenders of newer versions of agent causation.

(1) *The Disappearing Reasons Problem*

One question facing agent causation theorists is whether in their view there is a role for reasons in free and responsible actions. One of the advantages of the (rejected) picture in which free and responsible actions are caused by agents' judgments and desires (which are events or states of affairs involving agents) is that it is easy to see how reasons are involved in the production of action. If one's decision is caused *by* one's judgment that saving a child is the best thing to do, then it is clear that one's reasons play a direct causal role. Part of what makes the action a praiseworthy one is that it was done for reasons, and good ones at that. But if the sole cause of the decision on the agent-causal picture is the agent (and not events involving her), then what role is there for reasons to play?

(2) *The Contrastive Explanation Challenge*

Agent causationists appear to be unable to answer certain kinds of questions that have been thought essential for determining whether someone acts freely and responsibly. For example, if the action was not caused by a datable event in time, what explains why it happened when it did instead of five minutes before or five minutes later?[6] Relatedly, why did the agent choose to save the child rather than let him drown? Nothing in past events or states of affairs, nothing in the reasons available to the agent ahead of time, can explain these "contrastive" facts.

---

[6] See C.D. Broad (1952, p. 215) and O'Connor (2000, pp. 74–6) for a response.

(3) *Challenges of Incoherence*

The charge of incoherence is a familiar one. Some seem to arrive at incoherence by means of reasoning like that involved in not being able to explain why something happened when it did.[7] Some have also claimed that causation is only intelligible in the context of changes taking place that cause other changes. And questions have also been raised about how agent causation can be reconciled in a coherent way with event causation. If an event occurs that would normally cause another event, can an agent intervene to cause either that event or another?[8] This challenge might be thought to be a question of how to fit agent causation into a coherent theoretical picture with event causation. But it might also be thought to be an empirical question, and I will treat this question separately.

(4) *Is it Substantive?*

Some have raised the worry that agent causation simply reduces to event causation or becomes superfluous. As Pereboom writes: "It would be helpful to have a sense of exactly what we must conceive in order to form a positive conception of ourselves as substance-causes in a way that does not permit *reformulation* in terms of our being causes by virtue of involvement in events".[9] Relatedly, Clarke writes that

> the problem arises how, in virtue of standing in this relation to some other property (or properties), the agent-causal property can confer on the substance possessing it, rather than on the event that is the substance's possessing it, a power to cause an effect . . . (2003, p. 192)

And Clarke believes that this question is related to a general question about how agent causation is supposed to differ from event causation.

(5) *Empirical Challenges*

Data and past experience suggest that the world is governed by general causal laws relating events involving both animate and inanimate objects, and that there is just no evidence for (while there is evidence against) any kind of "extra" causal relations at work.[10]

---

[7] See O'Connor (2000, p. 74) who reads the objection about timing as an objection to coherence.

[8] Watkins (2010).

[9] Pereboom (in preparation, chapter 3, p. 23, emphasis mine).

[10] See Pereboom (2001), for example.

Where do these challenges leave the libertarian agent causationist? Very creative answers to these challenges have been given. While I will not give a full exposition or evaluation here, I will sketch some of the main lines of response. When it comes to the role of reasons, contemporary agent causationists have tried to meet this objection in a variety of ways. One approach is to allow reasons to retain their causal role, albeit as causes separate from the agent herself.[11] Another option is to deny that reasons play a causal role at all, but to show that they have some other role, such as being the intentional objects of an agent-caused intention.[12]

---

[11] See Clarke (2003, pp. 133 ff.) who offers such an "integrated" account of causation of responsible action, according to which both the agent's having of reasons and the agent cause free and responsible action.

Pereboom (in preparation) offers a kind of dilemma that applies to this sort of account. On the one hand, if there is no connection between the statistical laws governing events and propensities for agent causation, then it seems that such a view has an unacceptable consequence in the form of "wild coincidences". It would be a wild coincidence if what is chosen freely over a large number of instances approximated precisely the expected outcomes of statistical laws that appear to govern event causation. On the other hand, if there is a connection between statistical laws governing events and propensities for agent causation for example, by the agent's having been "shaped by" antecedent events—then there is not the independence of the agent-causal power that was essential to provide what appeared to be enhanced control.

[12] O'Connor (2000) builds reasons into the intentional content of decisions so that reasons play a non-causal, but content-related, role in the production of action. According to his view, the agent acts for reasons when she acts to satisfy an antecedent desire, and she does that when she acts to cause an intention *to act so as to satisfy that desire*. More specifically: "The agent acted then in order to satisfy his antecedent desire that Φ if

1. prior to this action, the agent had a desire that Φ and believed that by so acting he would satisfy (or contribute to satisfying) that desire;
2. the agent's action was initiated (in part) by his own self-determining causal activity, the event component of which is the-coming-to-be-of-an-action-triggering-intention-to-so-act-here-and-now-to-satisfy-Φ;
3. concurrent with this action, he continued to desire that Φ and intended of this action that it satisfy (or contribute to satisfying) that desire; and
4. the concurrent intention was a direct causal consequence (intuitively, a continuation) of the action-triggering intention brought about by the agent, and it causally sustained the completion of the action" (2000, p. 86).

Various questions can be raised for this solution, including whether our intentions really have the form described—or at least whether they often do in cases of paradigmatically free and responsible actions. In more recent work, O'Connor has proposed that "reasons causally structure" an agent-causal capacity by "conferring probabilities" on it (2009, p. 198).

It is also worth noting that Chisholm himself tried to answer by citing Leibniz: "And we may also say . . . that . . . our desires may 'incline without necessitating'".

The question of contrastive explanation requires a different kind of approach. It seems that it can have no answer on this kind of agent-causal view, but that is not because it is an agent-causal view; it is because it is a libertarian view.[13] The best approach for the libertarian to take, in my view, is to acknowledge a lack of such an explanation, while pointing to other kinds of explanations that can in fact be given for the action. The action can still be caused by the agent (and possibly for certain reasons, depending on how the previous challenge is answered), for example.

Is the view coherent? A strong case has been made that the idea of causation is no less coherent when applied to agents than when applied to events. O'Connor, for example, takes the general concept of causation to have as its "core, primitive element" the "producing" or "bringing about" of an effect (2001, p. 68). Attempts to analyze causation conceptually in terms of counterfactual dependence or regularity miss this key aspect of causation. However, as we will see, the defense of coherence gains in plausibility as the nature of agent causation is spelled out. On the question of timing in particular, one response is to accept that there is no explanation to be given about why an action happened exactly when it did rather than at another time; but one can explain why it happened within a range of times, because it is only in that range that certain reasons are available.

Is the view substantive? Does it collapse into event causation? Pereboom appeals to the Stoic picture of responsibility, and suggests that a conception of ourselves as independent of any of our motivational states, in the sense of being able to act in accordance with them or not, is the key to having a positive conception of agent causation that it isn't possible to reformulate in terms of event causation.

---

[13] This worry about there being no contrastive explanation is sometimes referred to as the "luck objection". (See, for example, Mele 2006, p. 55.) Unfortunately, other worries have also gone by the same name, and I believe that confusion on this matter is responsible for many instances of people talking past each other. (See Nelkin 2007a, pp. 174–5, for an attempt to clarify this.) For example, sometimes "luck" just means "lack of control" or "outside the control of the agent". Understood this way, it is essential that any account of responsibility answer objections that luck is undermining of the view. If "luck" simply means "no contrastive explanation is available", then it is open to the advocate of an account to accept the premise and show why it is not undermining of responsibility. Thus, once the objection is phrased in terms of a lack of contrastive explanation, then I believe that it is clearer that the libertarian can agree that there is none available and then go on to explain why it is not necessary to offer one.

Perhaps, then, the Stoic view provides us with a positive conception of an agent, who, as a substance, has the executive independence from its states to make it the case that it is the substance possessing properties, rather than events that are the substance's possessing of properties at certain times, that is the first *relatum* in a causal relation. (In preparation, p. 26)

It is worth noting that there is a move from "independence from motivational states" to "independence from states", and it is relevant in this way. The former seems important for a notion of control, but the latter seems important for avoiding any kind of "reformulation". It isn't clear that one can avoid independence from *all* states, for one's possessing a causal power is always a candidate for a cause. But perhaps the real worry about "reformulation" is that the relevant agent-causal relations can be explained even in part with reference to laws relating particular states such as motivational ones. This worry is avoided as long as the agent does not act in accordance with natural laws relating the possession of certain properties to outcomes. And such a worry seems to be avoided in the Stoic picture adopted by Pereboom.

Libertarian agent-causation theorists, along with all other libertarians, face a special kind of challenge when it comes to reconciling free and responsible action with empirical data and theories of the world. Unlike compatibilist accounts, which do not generally require that the world be either deterministic or indeterministic, libertarians are committed to the natural laws being of a particular kind. There must be room for agents to act in ways that are not determined, given the actual past and natural laws. Agent-causal theorists have a variety of options here: one is to reject the idea that we are free, while maintaining that the only way we could be free is if a libertarian agent-causal theory were true (for example, Pereboom); another is to try to reconcile the claim that we are indeterministic agent-causes with the apparent regularity of the natural laws that seem to govern everything, including human action. Clarke's integrated account is an attempt to do this, although it raises questions about why we ought to believe that there are agent-causes operating *in addition to* event-causes.[14]

But there is a way of modifying the agent-causal libertarian view in order to make at least some of these challenges easier to address. Let us turn to that account now.

---

[14] See Pereboom's criticism (In preparation, ms. note 109).

2: The Kantian Libertarian Agent-causal Account

A sometimes unnoticed fact is that contemporary views broke from at least some of their historical antecedents by distinguishing between two radically different kinds of causes in the world—events and agents.[15] There is good reason to believe that Kant, among others, thought *all* of causation to be of a single general type, namely, substance causation. (In this, I follow Watkins' helpful interpretation.[16]) So not just human agents, but also billiard balls and coffee tables, are causes. A billiard ball has certain causal powers, and, when in certain circumstances, will cause certain effects in virtue of having those powers in those circumstances. Humans are distinguished in having special causal powers, of course, but they are not causes of a different fundamental type from causes involving inanimate objects. Thus, Kant's picture of human freedom takes place against a backdrop of a unified account of causation generally. What is it to be free on this picture?

On the Kantian picture, human actions can be free in part because they are undetermined. Unlike billiard balls, their natures and causal powers are not such as to determine a particular outcome. Human beings are also special in being rational agents. Their fundamentally free acts are their undetermined choices of maxims, where a choice of a maxim is a choice to perform a particular action for particular reasons in particular circumstances.

Now Kant's own picture was complicated further by a distinction between phenomena and noumena.[17] On this picture, "a human being acts morally if the soul, as a thing in itself, whose nature includes rationality, freely adopts a maxim ... that subordinates happiness to the moral law in accordance with its character ... " (Watkins 2010, p. 525). In turn, this ultimate noumenal choice determines the phenomenal character of human actions. I am going to set aside this aspect of the Kantian picture, and simply focus on a picture according to which human agents, among other substances, cause states and changes in virtue of exercising causal powers in various circumstances.

---

[15] See, however, Clarke (2003, p. 208) for references to Suarez (1597/1994) and also to Byerly (1979), Lowe (2001), and Swinburne (2000).

[16] See Watkins (2010) and (2005).

[17] It is also complicated by the fact that Kant was concerned to account for morally worthy actions in particular.

This picture is clearly different in a key respect from contemporary accounts that mix agent and event causation.[18] Importantly, at least some challenges are easier to meet if one adopts a more unified picture. The challenges that concern the fitting together of two radically different kinds of causation, or at least of radically different kinds of causal *relata*, do not apply at all to the Kantian account. For example, consider the challenge of incoherence that asks how agents can intervene in situations in which events typically cause other events. The question simply does not arise if all causal *relata* are substances. The view also has a clear answer to the question about how reasons play a causal role in action. Reasons can play a role, both in the circumstances in which an agent exists (with certain beliefs and desires), and also in the particular causal powers she exercises on a particular occasion (her power to act for a certain reason).

In facing other challenges, the view will be in a position similar to other libertarian agent-causal views. When it comes to the challenge that it cannot provide a contrastive explanation for responsible actions, the Kantian libertarian account can simply adopt the position that a certain kind of contrastive explanation cannot be given in the case of free and responsible action. Further, unless one adopts the two-worlds aspect of Kant's account, this account, too, will have to directly confront the empirical data that point to regularities of a kind that appear inconsistent with indeterministic agent-causes.

3: A Compatibilist Kantian Version

Once we have a uniform account of substance causation, it is easier to see how there can be a plausible compatibilist version. Billiard balls, for example, exert certain causal powers in their circumstances when struck by a pool cue, and it can be inevitable what their effects are. Given their own natures and causal powers, and the natures of and causal laws governing everything else in the vicinity, their effects are determined. Agents,

---

[18] Chisholm and Clarke, for example, are clearly working with a picture of the world in which there are two kinds of causes, events and agents. Interestingly, O'Connor's view is not as clear (2000). Although he contrasts agent and event causation (and claims both exist in our world), the account of "event causation" he ends up with looks quite a lot like substance causation. Citing Harré and Madden (1975), he writes that "When placed in the appropriate circumstances, an object manifests its causal powers in observable effects . . . " (p. 71). I do not find mention of the word "event" in the description at this point.

while having unique natures and causal powers, such as being able to act on certain sorts of reasons, can, at least in principle, exercise those causal powers even when, given their natures and circumstances, it is determined how they will act. The explanation of why they acted as they did will appeal to the fact that, in virtue of having a certain nature and causal powers, they acted for certain reasons.

This account distinguishes between (a) the metaphysical point that an agent—together with other substances—can be a cause and (b) the requirement that such a cause act indeterministically (in the sense that given all the facts about the past and laws of nature, more than one future is open). An agent's nature and causal powers may be such as to determine that she will act in particular way, given her circumstances. It may be that given her nature and causal powers, she must save a drowning child when she finds herself in the circumstances. Or it may be instead that given her nature and powers, although she is likely to save the child, she may refrain. Her nature may be such that she has a mixture of different kinds of causal powers, some that determine how she will act, and some that do not. Such a view allows for agent causation (understood as causation by a rational agent for reasons) in a deterministic world.

Now some have raised the worry that—*particularly if agent causation is understood in this way*—it simply reduces to event causation or becomes superfluous. Even if a positive conception of agent causation that is not reducible to event causation can be provided (such as the suggestion of Pereboom's discussed earlier), it might be thought that in a deterministic world in particular, there would be no room for agent causation that is not in some way superfluous.

Zimmerman expresses this worry: "Suppose that determinism is true. On such a supposition it would seem that any special type of causation that might be effected by agents would be wholly superfluous and hence it would seem that there is no reason to believe that such causation ever takes place".[19]

It is noteworthy that Zimmerman's worry depends on the assumption that event causation is the norm, and that if agents are causes, they are causes *in addition* to events. Because the view at hand is embedded in a unified account of causation, it rejects this assumption. At the same time, it

[19] (1984, p. 211).

is possible that part of what explains contemporary agent causationists' rejection of substance causation as having universal scope owes something to the idea that deterministic causation makes substance causation "superfluous" or reformulable in terms of causation by events involving agents.

It is important here, as before, to get clear on what "reformulation" means, and whether it is in fact problematic. If "reformulation" means that if we knew the agent's nature and causal powers, we could know how she would act in given circumstances, then this view of agents as causes (compatible with determinism) could be reformulated in terms of events and states and facts about the agent. But there is arguably a significant *metaphysical* difference between an event's, or state's, being a cause and the agent being a cause *in virtue of* her nature and causal powers. However, even if there is no metaphysical difference, but simply two equally good ways of describing the world, the fact that agents can legitimately be said to be causes, brings back the agent into the picture of action and so undermines worries about the "disappearing agent".[20]

At this point, it is important to note that if reformulation—of any of these types—is possible in a deterministic context, then it seems that *merely* adding indeterminism will not allow us to avoid it. To see this, it will be helpful to consider that some libertarian agent-causal views are "propensity-based" in that the agent has certain propensities, based on the agent's states, to cause what she causes.[21] For example, there might be a certain propensity, say, .9, that an agent will jump into the waves and save the drowning child. On this sort of view, for example, if agents cause in accordance with the same propensities that would be given by their being in the mental states that they are in, then it would seem that we could also reformulate in a parallel way to the deterministic case. This is not (yet) to say that indeterminism is not required for *free and responsible action*; it is only to point out that insofar as one is worried about

---

[20] In fact, allowing for a kind of equivalence has the potential to assuage a number of worries about how to account for the timing of actions on contemporary libertarian views. As mentioned earlier, one of the challenges facing libertarian agent-causal accounts is to explain why the agent acted when she did (rather than five minutes or six years earlier, given that she existed, then, too).

[21] For example, on Clarke's integrated account, "the propensity of an agent to cause a certain action is due (at least in part) to her having certain reasons, and her having those reasons will cause that action only if she causes it" (2003, p. 176). Further, it is a matter of natural law that the propensities of agents and the propensities of reasons to cause actions are the same. See Pereboom (in preparation) for detailed discussion of this view.

reformulation, one's worries should apply to both deterministic and inde-terministic, *propensity-based* views.

This leaves the possibility of indeterministic and *non*-propensity-based views. So before turning to whether a compatibilist account of agent causation can compete with incompatibilist ones when it comes to the question of *free and responsible* action, it will be important to explore whether there is an account of indeterministic agent causation that avoids any kind of reformulation. And here Pereboom's account, as well as the libertarian Kantian account, must be considered. As we saw earlier, Per-eboom offers a view according to which the agent acts independently of her motivational states. If an agent causes in the way his account provides for, then there is no alternative explanation that appeals to causal laws, deterministic or statistical. In this sense, there is no reformulation.

Such an account faces other difficulties, however. One—noted by Pereboom—is that it is hard to reconcile with the empirical facts. (In fact, it is for this reason that Pereboom adopts the position of Hard Incompatibilism, which is a kind of skepticism.) But another problem is that it remains difficult to see how this view of an agent's complete independence from her states and reasons captures *control* better than one that allows for dependence. We seem now to have an account that remains in key respects negative: the agent causes, but *not* in accordance with any propensities that parallel the propensities of her reasons.

Pereboom argues persuasively that there is a sense in which we have a positive and substantive conception of agent causation that does not reduce to event causation. That is the idea discussed earlier—namely, that the agent can assent to, dissent from, or suspend judgment about her motivational states. I agree that this is a positive conception of a kind of causal power. The question is whether it offers a positive conception of *enhanced control* over a picture in which an agent, in virtue of her rational powers and other aspects of her nature, will either act in accordance with certain propensities given by precisely those properties, or will certainly act in a certain way.

This is not to foreclose the possibility that the truth lies here. But in the absence of elaboration, it is not clear how we find enhanced control by the agent that is independent of her reasons and nature when these are understood as properties that ground her causal powers. It is notable that while Pereboom accepts that the agent-causal picture he describes is *prima facie* conceivable (to use terminology introduced by Chalmers[22]), it may not

---

[22]   (2002, p. 147).

be ideally conceivable in the sense that reflection could show it to be conceptually impossible. I think that an agent having a causal power is conceivable, even ideally; rather, what is in doubt is the possibility of having a causal power that provides *a unique kind of control* distinct from an agent-causal power that can be exercised by an agent determined by her own nature to act for certain reasons rather than others.

For this reason, it is not clear that merely avoiding reformulation of all kinds considered thus far is sufficient to achieve enhanced control. And in that case, it is not clear why we should be worried about reformulation per se, as long as the reformulation allows for true causation by an agent, with particular rational abilities, for reasons, and in virtue of her nature and the causal powers it supports.[23]

The Kantian view elaborated by Watkins might also seem to provide an alternative to a compatibilist or propensity-related indeterminist account of agent causation. On this view, the truly free choice happens at the level of the noumenal self, and that choice grounds the character of the empirical self, from which actions then flow deterministically. Here, too, however, we might wonder why the existence of what seems to be a completely inexplicable choice adds to the control we are seeking. (This question arises even when we set aside questions concerning the "grounding" relation between the noumenal and empirical selves.)

The question at hand is whether either the propensity-based incompatibilist view or a non-propensity-based incompatibilist view like those just described has advantages over the compatibilist account of agent causation. And it simply does not seem that either does—at least not without further elaboration. Neither incompatibilist view offers an account of enhanced control. In fact, the compatibilist one even offers certain potential advantages. For if our natures do make it the case that we are determined to cause what we do, then we can offer a contrastive explanation of our

---

[23] Pereboom suggests, in correspondence, that elaboration comes in the form of arguments for incompatibilism, notably the manipulation or four-case argument. If the argument shows that there must be an enhanced and indeterministic control for responsibility, then the requisite control is ruled out in a deterministic world. I agree with the conditional, but I reject the antecedent. (See chapter 2 for an argument to this effect.) Further, it is important that more seems needed to show that the manipulation argument, even if successful, would constitute an elaboration of the indeterministic agent-causal view; for skepticism of a conceptual (or "impossibilist") sort, rather than merely an empirical sort, would seem still to be a live option without a clear view of *how* the indeterministic agent-causal view accounts for enhanced control.

actions that appeals to our very natures. And, further, the compatibilist avoids the difficult challenge of reconciling responsible actions with the empirical facts, since it does not entail that responsibility requires that the world be indeterministic (and in a particular way). Thus, the compatibilist account has distinct advantages over the incompatibilist one.

Before concluding, it will be helpful to compare the Kantian compatibilist account just developed with another compatibilist account.

4: The Kantian Compatibilist Acount Contrasted with a Hybrid Compatibilist Account

The only other contemporary compatibilist agent-causal account of which I am aware is Ned Markosian's. In an elegant treatment, Markosian shows that there can be a compatibilist version of agent causation. I am sympathetic to a great deal in his discussion. I have only two significant disagreements with his approach, one of which is its concession to contemporary accounts of agent causation of a kind of hybrid picture of two very different kinds of causation.

Markosian offers the following version of agent causation, where "morally free" means "free in the sense required for moral responsibility" and A is an action:

(M) A is *morally free* iff A is caused by A's agent.

(M) appears consistent with the Kantian compatibilist account presented earlier. However, it is presented as sharing a key thesis with contemporary libertarian accounts, namely, the claim that agent causation is a special kind of causation reserved for (free) agents, while events involving non-agents are caused by other *events* involving non-agents. Because of this assumption, the compatibilism of this view does not come initially from the possibility of deterministic agent causation; rather it comes from the possibility that your agent-caused actions are *also* caused by events in a deterministic way. Markosian makes this explicit when he considers the objection that the intuition driving agent-causal theories really is incompatibilist in requiring an additional condition that an agent's actions not be caused by anything outside of the agent. To this, Markosian replies,

The reason it seems true that you cannot be morally responsible for an action that is caused by events outside of you, I would suggest, is that we tend to forget about the possibility of double causation. We forget that an action caused by some event outside of you could also be caused by you. (1999, pp. 269–70)

Once we realize the possibility of double causation, we are no longer drawn to the requirement that an action can have no causes outside of the agent. In illustration, Markosian offers a case in which one agent, Imran, passes the salt. He is caused to do so by the event of Yasmine's asking him to do so, as well as by himself. The fact that it has two causes, one of which operates deterministically, makes it the case that Imran's action can be morally free despite being determined. Understood as an overdetermination account, this is quite different from the one developed earlier which allows for deterministic *agent* causation. On the latter view, it is because of the natures of the agent and the substances around him that the agent will cause the things he does. Markosian's view, as described so far, allows for determination of actions in virtue of events being causes at the same time that the agent is causing the action in question. The picture thus far is a picture of overdetermination, and it raises questions both conceptual and empirical. For example, we might ask whether we could have any justification for believing in the existence of agent causation if all actual instantiations of causal relations were explained in terms of events. And we return to Pereboom's worry that it is too much of a coincidence to believe that events and agents would always cause in the same predictable ways.

Yet at the end of his paper, it becomes clear that Markosian's view is compatibilist in an additional way; he also accepts the possibility of deterministic agent causation that does not rely entirely on double causation. In considering a final kind of potential counterexample to the view, Markosian describes an agent who has been "forced" to be the way he is (by an abused childhood or by martians) and ends up a serial killer. As long as he causes himself to kill, he satisfies Markosian's sufficient condition for responsibility. And yet, intuitively, some might conclude that the agent is not responsible (and instead that the martians or abusive guardians are).

Now an initial supporter of a libertarian agent-causal view might accept a "double causation" view without accepting that agent causation itself can be deterministic and still constitute morally free action. So the objection is that the "agent causation" itself that is provided for in the account must be understood as indeterministic, even if it is granted that an additional causal process involving only events may be deterministic.

Interestingly, however, Markosian responds by accepting that an agent who is determined to cause his own actions can also be morally free, and explaining why we ought to accept it, despite an initial intuitive reaction to the contrary. The reason he gives is that the agent's action (killing) is morally wrong, and "if his actions are morally wrong, then they are morally free" (p. 272). This is a controversial assumption. To make this assumption, one must reject the idea of excused wrong-doing; that is, one must reject the idea that one can do wrong for which one is not responsible.[24] Now libertarians—even those who would countenance the idea of double causation when it includes an indeterministic agent-causal process—could simply refuse to allow such a case of *deterministic* agent causation to count as a responsible action. And they could do so while acknowledging that the agent's actions were, in some sense, morally wrong (albeit excused).

I would approach this case differently by conceding that additional (compatibilist) conditions might be required for responsibility. In particular, one must have certain general capacities for grasping moral reasons, and even the ability—understood as characterized in chapter 3—to act for good reasons. Only by filling out the case more fully could we tell if these further conditions were met. And only then could we have an intuition to legitimately test against them. So although I am very sympathetic to Markosian's approach here, I believe that there are additional resources available for answering these sorts of challenges. The best compatibilist version of agent causation can accommodate additional conditions on responsibility, so long as they are themselves compatibilist ones.

In sum, there are two main points of disagreement between the view I developed earlier and Markosian's, and one point of differing emphasis. The first point of disagreement concerns the adoption, on Markosian's account, of a hybrid view of causation, shared by contemporary accounts of agent causation. This aspect of the view leads to an initial emphasis on double causation as a model for a compatibilist theory of agent causation, although, as we have seen, Markosian has room in his picture for deterministic agent causation itself. However, in defending the compatibility of precisely such a determined agent-causal process with responsibility, Markosian appeals to a controversial assumption in undermining the intuitions

---

[24] I discuss this further in chapter 5.

generated by attempted counterexamples. In contrast, I believe that it is preferable to withhold intuitions before getting clearer about the details of the alleged cases; and to add to the compatibilist account additional conditions on responsibility that enable the account to be entirely consistent with the intuitions behind the alleged counterexamples. Once we do that, we can side-step the need to explain away at least some recalcitrant intuitions, can avoid appealing to the controversial assumption that rejects the possibility of excused wrong-doing, and can do so while employing plausible conditions on responsibility that are also compatibilist ones.

5: Conclusion

In conclusion, then, I have argued against libertarian versions of agent causation not because they are incoherent or even, primarily, because there is empirical evidence against them. Instead, I have tried to show that the best libertarian versions of agent causation are no better at securing enhanced control than the best compatibilist version. And the compatibilist version I developed here allows compatibilists to share in much that is appealing about the libertarian versions, including the reappearance, or, rather, the presence of the agent in the web of causality.

5

A Rationale for the Rational Abilities View: Praise, Blame, and the Ought-Implies-Can Principle

1: A Derivation from Ought-Implies-Can

In the last three chapters, we have seen that the rational abilities view has the resources to resist the pressure to treat all responsible actions in either of two uniform ways, namely, as requiring the ability to do otherwise (according to the traditional Principle of Alternate Possibilities), or as not requiring that ability at all (as Harry Frankfurt and others have argued). But one might naturally ask why there *should* be the difference suggested by the rational abilities view. In this chapter, I offer one explanation that, together with the intuitive power of the view itself, answers the challenge.

To begin, it will be helpful to distinguish between three particular principles, each with a narrower scope than the original Principle of Alternate Possibilities:

PAP-Blame: A person is morally *blameworthy* for what he has done only if he could have done otherwise.

PAP-Praise: A person is morally *praiseworthy* for what he has done only if he could have done otherwise.

PAP-Neutral: A person is morally responsible but *neither morally blameworthy nor morally praiseworthy* for what he has done only if he could have done otherwise.

Is there a reason for accepting PAP-Blame, but not the others? Interestingly, Frankfurt, whose name is virtually synonymous with the rejection of alternate possibilities in general, points the way. In a lesser-known paper, "What We Are Responsible For", Frankfurt notices that "the appeal of PAP may owe something to a presumption that it is a corollary of the Kantian thesis that "ought" implies "can".[1] Although Frankfurt immediately goes on to reject this presumption, I believe it contains a large kernel of truth.

Why would one make this presumption? To see why, focus for a moment on blameworthy actions—as most philosophers do when writing about responsibility. (Almost all the cases are ones where someone does some horrible deed like pushing innocent children to their deaths.) When people perform blameworthy actions, they do what they ought not to do and, instead, they ought to have done otherwise. Then, according to the Kantian thesis, it must be that they can do otherwise. Therefore, blameworthy actions require that their agents have been able to do otherwise.

Notice at this point that the reasoning seems to work nicely for blameworthy actions. As Frankfurt himself noted, though, it doesn't work for praiseworthy actions.[2] In fact, Frankfurt rejects the idea that the Kantian thesis really supports PAP for two reasons, one of which has to do precisely with this point:

> With respect to any action, Kant's doctrine has to do with the agent's ability to perform *that* action. PAP, on the other hand, concerns his ability to do *something else*. Moreover, the Kantian view leaves open the possibility that a person for whom only one course of action is available fulfills an obligation when he pursues that course of action and is morally praiseworthy for doing so.[3]

Although the reasoning is very condensed here, it is essential that the intuitive reasoning we used for blameworthy actions does not work for praiseworthy ones. Where we supposed earlier that blameworthy actions are ones whose performance violated an obligation (and so pointed to an

---

[1] Frankfurt (1983/1988, p. 95). As Kant wrote: "Now this 'ought' expresses a possible action, the ground of which is nothing other than a mere concept, whereas the ground of a merely natural action must always be an appearance. Now of course the action must be possible under natural conditions if the ought is directed to it ...". (Kant 1781/1997, A547/B575, p. 540).

[2] See also Widerker (1991) and Moya (2006), pp. 81–2.

[3] (1983/1988, p. 96). I will here follow Frankfurt in his use of "obligation". Although he does not elaborate, in the context of discussion of the Ought-Implies-Can principle, I understand him to mean "what one ought to do". As we will see, this is the sense of "obligation" adopted by other writers on the subject, as well. See Hart (1961), however, for interesting discussion of a variety of senses of the term in a variety of contexts.

ability unexercised, given the so-called Kantian thesis), praiseworthy actions involve no violation of an obligation, and so the Kantian thesis does not indicate any unexercised ability.

Now, let's spell out the Kantian thesis—or the Ought-Implies-Can principle—in more detail, as well. On the simplest version,

(OIC-first pass) If S ought to a, then S can a.

Now I'll need to elaborate on this in two ways for our purposes. The first is to say what sorts of things a stands for. We can substitute particular actions, of course, such as: keep one's promise to one's child to pick her up from school, or save a child from drowning. But I think it in the spirit of the principle that we can also substitute "refrainings" or "omissions", such as: refrain from pushing a child off a pier or refrain from insulting someone gratuitously. The principle seems targeted at our obligations generally—both our obligations to act and our obligations not to act in certain ways. The idea seems to be that we ought to be able to effect what we are obligated to do. We must be able to meet our obligations.

Second, if the Ought-Implies-Can principle is true, then we can also apply it to the past. So we can say that: if S ought to have done a, then she could have done a. Putting these points together, and making them explicit, we have the principle I'll refer to from here on simply as the Ought-Implies-Can principle, or OIC:

(OIC) (i) If S ought to have performed action a, then S could have performed action a, and (ii) if S ought not to have performed action a, then S could have refrained from performing action a.

Focusing once more on blameworthy actions, it seems plausible that

(1) If S is blameworthy for having performed action a, then S ought not to have performed action a.

But putting that together with OIC—or, strictly, the second part of it:

(2) If S ought not to have performed an action a, then S could have refrained from performing action a

yields PAP-Blame:

PAP-Blame: A person is morally blameworthy for what he has done only if he could have done otherwise.

For if S is blameworthy for having performed action *a*, then S could have refrained from doing what she in fact did; or, in other words, she could have done otherwise. (I will call this piece of reasoning from (1) and (2) to PAP-Blame "the Derivation".)

However, when it comes to praiseworthy action, it isn't clear how OIC could have any application. For, as Frankfurt pointed out, OIC is about what actions one ought to perform. But if one does what one ought, OIC says nothing about one's being able to do anything else. What we have, then, is a rationale for the asymmetry of the view, suggested by just the asymmetry Frankfurt noticed. I believe that he was right to see both that the Kantian Ought-Implies-Can principle seems to underwrite PAP-Blame, and also that it doesn't underwrite PAP-Praise (or even PAP-Neutral). But I will argue that he was wrong to dismiss so quickly its relation to PAP-Blame as merely apparent.

In fact, I will argue that, together with other plausible claims, the guiding idea of OIC supports PAP-Blame, while remaining silent on the idea that alternatives must be required for praiseworthy actions. In the remainder of the chapter, I will first spell out in more detail why there is no plausible counterpart reasoning for PAP-Praise in section 1, and then I will turn to evaluating the two premises in the Derivation of PAP-Blame from OIC in sections 2 and 3.

Of course, it does not follow that even if I could successfully defend all of these claims, the asymmetrical view is correct. Perhaps there is some other rationale or principle that entails alternate possibilities for every case of responsible action. But it is an important part of the case for the rational abilities view that there is a natural and plausible rationale (and one that has often been supposed to be axiomatic) that supports alternatives in the blameworthy case, and yet does not in the praiseworthy (or even neutral) case. Building on the arguments in chapter 2 against three prominent rationales for a *general* Principle of Alternate Possibilities, we have a strong case that insofar as alternatives are ever required for responsibility, they are relevant in just the cases predicted by the rational abilities view.

2: Praiseworthy Actions and Obligation

We have already seen that the conclusion of the Derivation applies only to blameworthy actions. And we cannot simply substitute "praiseworthy" for "blameworthy" in premise (1).

Doing so would yield:

> (1*)   If S is praiseworthy for having performed action *a*, then S ought not to have performed action *a*.

(1*) is clearly false, and so a non-starter. But we might modify it so it reads:

> (1**)   If S is praiseworthy for having performed action *a*, then S ought to have performed action *a*.

Now (1**) is not obviously false. It does not pair with OIC, however, in a valid argument for a parallel conclusion concerning praiseworthy actions. However, it could be paired with a *partner* principle to OIC to yield the conclusion that praiseworthy actions, too, require alternatives. I call the partner principle the "Ought-Implies-Can-Do-Wrong" principle:

> (OICDW) (i) If S ought to have performed action *a*, then S could have refrained from performing action *a*, and (ii) If S ought not to have performed action *a*, then S could have performed action *a*.

(Where OIC says that if I ought to save the drowning child, I can save her, OICDW says that if I ought to save the drowning child, I can refrain from doing so.)

Putting (1**) and OICDW together does yield the parallel conclusion regarding praiseworthy actions. (Call this piece of reasoning "the Counterpart Derivation".) But should we accept it? I do not believe so.

Unlike OIC, OICDW is not generally taken to be axiomatic, and is not often discussed. Nevertheless, one might defend it on grounds of symmetry, as Haji does.[4] (He is the main defender of OICDW that I know of, and defends it in the context of a subtle discussion of the relation of deontic notions like "ought" and "wrong" and notions of responsibility, like "blameworthy" and "praiseworthy".) Haji takes OICDW to be just as plausible as OIC itself. But he also

---

[4] See Haji (2002, pp. 28–31).

argues for it on the basis of a kind of presumption of symmetry. If you do something wrong, you have to be able to do otherwise (per OIC), and if you do something obligatory, it must be the case that you should be able to do otherwise in such a case, too. Obligation and wrongness are members of the same deontic family, and actions falling into each category ought to meet this same requirement. As a supporting analogy, he points to praise and blame, which, he argues, should also be treated symmetrically when it comes to the ability to do otherwise.

I do not find this reasoning convincing, however. The rational abilities view is itself a view according to which praiseworthy and blameworthy actions do not *both* require the ability to do otherwise. The asymmetry between praiseworthy and blameworthy actions, while perhaps initially unexpected, *simply falls out of* a unified and natural account of responsible action. The initial presumption of symmetry seems overridden by this fact. And being members of the same deontic family, as wrongness and obligatoriness are, does not in itself seem to constitute good reason to believe they must *both* satisfy the particular condition of being able to do otherwise. Thus, I conclude that OICDW is insufficiently motivated.

It is also worth pointing out that the Counterpart Derivation faces an additional difficulty. While (1★★) is not obviously false in the way that (1★) is, it is very controversial. For if there are supererogatory acts that include acts that are praiseworthy even if agents are not obligated to perform them, then (1★★) is false. The very idea of "going beyond the call of duty" would need to be rejected if (1★★) is true. Thus, the Counterpart Derivation only works to secure a blanket requirement of alternate possibilities for praiseworthy actions if supererogation is impossible; without that assumption, it can at best secure a qualified requirement of alternatives for the subset of praiseworthy acts that are non-supererogatory. A close examination of the debate over supererogatory actions is beyond the scope of this chapter, but it should be clear that a parallel derivation, unlike the Derivation itself, has serious problems from the start.

If, then, no true thesis in the ballpark of OIC, such as OICDW, supports PAP-Praise, but we can show that OIC supports PAP-Blame, we would have an interesting and powerful explanation of the rational abilities view. Let us look more closely at the Derivation.

3: Blameworthy Entails Wrong

According to (1), if I'm blameworthy for performing an action, then I ought not to have done it. That seems plausible. How can I be blameworthy for some action, if I haven't done anything wrong? Despite its intuitive appeal, many have argued against it. I would like to focus here on two related lines of reasoning against it. The first, most recently put forward by Scanlon (2008), centers around cases in which we act permissibly, but for bad reasons. The second, put forward by Zimmerman (1997), argues in a different way for the same conclusion, based on the idea that sufficient conditions for blameworthiness, which include most notably agents' judgments that what they are doing is wrong, are yet insufficient for wrongness.[5]

Scanlon on Blameworthiness and Wrongness

When someone is blameworthy, it is generally for doing something that was wrong. But wrongness and blame can come apart. The blameworthiness of an action depends, in ways that wrongness generally does not, on the reasons for which a person acted and the conditions under which he or she did so. So it can be appropriate to say such things as, "Yes, what she did was certainly wrong, but you shouldn't blame her. She was under great stress . . . " It can also make sense to blame a person when what he did was not impermissible. For example, it can be appropriate to blame a person who has done what was in fact the right thing if he or she did it for an extremely bad reason. (2008, pp. 124–5)

An example here is the agent who rescues a drowning child, but only for the reward he anticipates receiving. It would certainly be odd to say the agent acts impermissibly in saving the child; yet the agent seems blameworthy at the same time.[6]

---

[5] I am here using "wrong" and "ought not" interchangeably. Not everyone would agree. For example, Pereboom (2001, p. 147) suggests that while determinism may threaten obligation alongside responsibility, it need not necessarily threaten right and wrong. I will set aside this interesting position for now; I could restate everything in terms of obligation.

[6] See McKenna (forthcoming) for a related claim. In correspondence, McKenna offers a different case. An agent is not obligated to perform some act, A, but A'ing would be so easy and would help someone in great need. Would this be a case in which, though the agent is not obligated, she would be blameworthy, at least to an extent? This is an interesting case, but after it is filled out in a more specific way, it seems harder to generate both the intuition that the agent fails to be obligated while remaining blameworthy. For example, if the situation is like certain drowning child cases, in which it is easy to save a child who is drowning, at very low cost and no risk to oneself, then it begins to seem a case in which one is obligated to act, as well as being blameworthy for failing to do so.

Now my simple answer to this sort of apparent counterexample is to point out that what the agent is blameworthy for needn't be an action at all; and, further, if he is blameworthy for an action, it needn't be for, say, the rescuing of the child. It may be for a deliberate cultivation of certain (wrong) reasons, or for an omitting to look out for the morally salient features of the situation. And if you look more closely at Scanlon's description, although he suggests at first that blameworthiness and wrongness come apart in both directions, it isn't clear that he is committed to their coming apart in precisely the way needed in order to generate a counterexample to (1). That is, though he says that *the person* could be appropriately blamed for an action (and elsewhere that the action reveals a fault in the person), it is not explicitly claimed that the person is blameworthy for performing the very action that seems not only permissible, but morally required.

There is much more to say about this sort of case. For example, on other views opposed to Scanlon's (such as Matt Hanser's), what one ought to do is just *to act for certain reasons rather than others*.[7] On some such views, Scanlon might be incorrect in viewing the agent as violating no obligation. This would be an alternative way of resisting the apparent counterexample. But I believe that it is not necessary to take an opposing view of this kind in order to resist it.

Zimmerman's Plea for Accuses

Zimmerman, among others,[8] makes explicit that he means to offer counterexamples to (1). That is, he argues that one can be blameworthy precisely for an action that is not impermissible.

I see Zimmerman as making two related arguments, a general one, and one by example. He first argues that it is sufficient for being blameworthy for performing an action that one performs the action freely and that one believes one is thereby doing something wrong. However, he argues, these conditions are not sufficient for actual (objective) wrongdoing. Thus, one can be blameworthy without doing wrong or violating an obligation.

---

[7] Hanser (2005, pp. 443–4).
[8] See Haji (2002, pp. 46–53) and Vranas (2007, pp. 193–6).

Zimmerman claims that the following case, among others, is illustrative of these points. In fact, it seems that examples are supposed to support what Zimmerman takes to be the plausibility of the general claim. This case is similar in structure to Scanlon's, but Zimmerman has much more to say about it. Here it is:

Suppose, then, that Dan, a small child, is in danger, but that Paul does not realize this. Nonetheless, Paul picks Dan up and runs off with him, thereby in effect rescuing Dan from danger. The reason why Paul did what he did was that he thought that he would thereby upset Dan, and this was what he wanted to do, despite recognizing the wrongness of doing it. As it happens, though, Paul has upset Dan not at all; on the contrary, Dan is profoundly relieved to have been rescued by Paul.[9]

According to Zimmerman, Paul is to be blamed for acting as he did. But surely it was not wrong. "After all, he rescued Dan from danger, and this was surely the right thing to do under the circumstances".

Zimmerman then considers a move similar to the one I made earlier in response to Scanlon's case; namely, to identify some other action for which Paul is blameworthy, other than the clearly not impermissible "rescuing of Dan". (Note: I believe it is misleading to even say that Paul rescued Dan. More carefully, Paul did something that brought about Dan's avoiding a threat. But I think the description of "rescuing" is one that normally suggests that one who rescues intentionally aims at bringing another to safety.) Zimmerman imagines his interlocutor offering as a candidate for a wrong action *Paul's attempt to upset Dan*.

Zimmerman rejects this suggestion. He does so by attributing to his interlocutor the following underlying justification: "it is always wrong to attempt to do wrong". He then argues against this rationale. A key part of his argument goes as follows. Consider Huck Finn, who saves his friend, Jim, a slave, despite believing it wrong to do so. If we accepted the general principle that it is always wrong to attempt to do wrong, then we would come to the counter-intuitive conclusion that Huck Finn does wrong to attempt to save Jim.

---

[9] Zimmerman (1997, p. 236). Similar reasoning can be found in Zimmerman (2009).

It is unclear that this reasoning goes through. For it might depend on a particular theory of action individuation that equates attempting to do wrong with attempting to save Jim. However, it seems to me that the best response to Zimmerman here is to deny that the suggestion of Paul's wrongdoing depends essentially on the rationale that it is always wrong to attempt to do wrong. One might have quite another rationale for thinking Paul's attempt wrong. For example: his attempt is wrong because it was aimed at producing harm that served no good purpose. Or (if we want to avoid talking about an agent's aims when it comes to permissibility *à la* Scanlon): Paul's attempt is wrong because he should have known that it was likely to produce harm for no further purpose. I am not claiming to have got the details exactly right here, but it seems to me that unless Zimmerman can offer reasons for rejecting these and others, he has not offered a convincing reason to see Dan as either an illustration of his sufficient condition on blameworthiness, or a direct counterexample to (1).

In fact, I think Zimmerman is incorrect in his supposition that it is sufficient for blameworthiness that one believes one does wrong and performs a free action. Huck Finn, for example, appears to be a counter-example. For it is not clear that Huck is blameworthy for anything in the ballpark of saving Jim. But more obvious counterexamples might just be people who are mentally ill or seriously misinformed through no fault of their own. A teenager who dates someone of the same sex might have been brought up to believe that it was wrong for people of the same sex to be romantically involved, but her belief, together with her free action, seems insufficient for her to be blameworthy for it. Or take the very real case of the kidnapping of eleven-year-old Jaycee Lee Dugard, by Phillip Garrido and his wife.[10] She was held for eighteen years in the Garridos' backyard, and has two children with Garrido. Given an opportunity to admit her identity to the authorities eighteen years later, she took it. At that point, she believed that what she was doing was wrong, and in other respects, acted freely, but the idea that she is thereby blameworthy is extremely implausible. I conclude that this line of reasoning does not give us good reason to reject the very plausible (1).

---

[10] Mckinley and Pogash (2009). I thank Andrew Chignell for this example.

4: The Ought-Implies-Can Principle

Now this "ought" expresses a possible action, the ground of which is nothing other than a mere concept, whereas the ground of a merely natural action must always be an appearance. Now of course the action must be possible under natural conditions if the ought is directed to it . . . (Kant 1781/1997, A547/B575, p. 540)

In this section, I consider possible arguments for the Ought-Implies-Can principle, as well as important objections to it.

Rationales and Explanatory Power

The Ought-Implies-Can principle has often been taken to have the status of an axiom, a fundamental principle that supports other principles, but not in need of further support itself. However, two kinds of attempts have been made to provide positive arguments for the principle: (i) offering rationales that explain and ground its truth, and (ii) showing its explanatory power by pointing to phenomena that are otherwise unexplained without the principle. I believe that the second kind of argument provides strong support for the principle. While I do not rule out the possibility of an explanatory rationale for the principle, the ones on offer are insufficient, and their failure is at least suggestive of the idea that the principle is indeed axiomatic, in the sense that it is fundamental.

Let us turn, then, to the two rationales most frequently found in the literature. The first begins with the claim that the role of ought judgments is action-guiding. David Copp offers a good example of such reasoning:

Moral requirements are action-guiding. That is, their point is to guide agents' decisions among their alternatives. All-in requirements partition an agent's alternatives at the point of action into those that are permissible and those that are not. Hence, knowledge of what one is all-in morally required to do enables one to select a permissible action from among one's alternatives. Given this, an adequate theory would imply that an agent is all-in morally required to do A only if she can do A. Otherwise, a permissible action would not be among her alternatives, since a person's alternatives at a time are things she can do at that time . . . [11]

There is something appealing about this reasoning. But there is an ambiguity in the claim that the point of moral requirements "is to guide agents' decisions among their alternatives". If moral requirements are understood simply as propositions stating truths or falsehoods, then it is not clear that

---

[11] See Copp (2008, p. 71).

they have a point at all, let alone a point related to guiding actions. However, *stating* or *considering* or *actively judging* those same propositions might very well have a point related to the production of action. Yet even if it is true that ought-judgments (in the sense of mental affirmations) have a point, its bearing on the truth of the proposition captured by the Ought-Implies-Can principle is far from obvious. As Pereboom points out, *making* ought-judgments might have practical value even if the judgments—that is, their propositional objects—are false.[12]

A second kind of rationale appeals to fairness. It is worth considering two versions of this general line of reasoning. Fischer (who ultimately rejects the principle) writes:

> I think the most natural justification for acceptance of the [Ought-Implies-Can] maxim is that, if it were not valid, then there could be cases in which an agent ought to do X but cannot do X (and never could do X). Thus, given that if an agent ought to do X, then he would be blameworthy for not doing X, there could be cases in which an agent is blameworthy for not Xing and yet he cannot X. And this is objectionable—even unfair.[13]

Interestingly, this line of reasoning makes a principle concerning blameworthiness more fundamental than the Ought-Implies-Can principle. That principle is the conclusion of the Intrapersonal Fairness Argument Concerning Blameworthy Actions, discussed in chapter 2, namely,

(*) X is responsible and blameworthy in the accountability sense for the performance of an action @ only if X had the ability to do otherwise.

In chapter 2, I offered some reason to resist fairness principles of this sort.[14] But it is also worth noting that the reasoning relies on another controversial premise, namely,

(**) If an agent fails to do something he ought to do, he is blameworthy for not doing so.

---

[12] Pereboom (2001, p. 148).

[13] Fischer (2003, p. 248).

[14] I argued primarily against the supporting premises connecting blameworthiness with the appropriateness of sanctions. Fischer himself rejects the principle on importantly different grounds, as we will see in the next sections, based on Frankfurt-style counterexamples to PAP.

While I believe the premise has some genuine appeal, it goes against the very commonly accepted view that recognizes excused wrong-doing.[15] For example, it is widely accepted that someone who commits a wrong, say, breaking a promise, while coerced, for example, may be excused, and so not be blameworthy. But (★★) implies that this appealing view is incorrect. Applying (★★) to our example of breaking one's promise, then one is blameworthy for this wrong action, even if one is coerced. For all of those who accept the standard view of excused wrong doing, then there is no straight forward link between wrong doing and blame as captured in (★★).

Is there a way to avoid appeal to a principle about the fairness of blame? Copp offers a different kind of fairness rationale for the Ought-Implies-Can principle that does not mention either blame or sanctions at all, at least explicitly. He writes:

> It would be unfair to expect a person to do something, or to require that she do it, if she cannot do it. Similarly, morality would be unfair if it allowed that a person might be all-in morally required to do something that she cannot do—unless perhaps she cannot do it because of something she herself did at an earlier time that itself violated an all-in requirement. But it is not intelligible that morality might be unfair...[16]

This reasoning explicitly appeals to a claimed similarity between persons making demands of others and morality itself. But this presents a problem not unlike that facing the "action-guiding" rationale. The fact that it might be unfair for a person to demand something of another does not entail that a related proposition containing an ought-statement is itself unfair.

Of course, this point immediately raises the question of the *sense* of unfairness at stake here. For the reasoning to go through as set out, we need a clear and univocal sense of "unfairness" in both the case in which it is unfair for a person to make a demand and the case in which the proposition itself is unfair. I believe that it will be helpful, as before, to distinguish between an interpersonal kind of unfairness (in which it is unfair to treat two or more people in relevantly similar circumstances differently) and an intrapersonal one (which does not rely on any

---

[15] See chapter 4 for discussion of this point; as we saw there, Markosian is willing to accept something like (★★).

[16] Copp (2008, p. 71).

interpersonal comparison). The first kind can apply in cases in which I make a demand of someone. It might be unfair of me to make a demand of you, when I do not make it of myself or of others. But the unfairness of my making a demand in this sense would seem not to have a bearing on whether it is *true* simply that you ought to perform the action in question. Suppose it is unfair of me to ask Alice to pick up her toys if I don't ask her sister (or myself). It could still be true that she ought to pick up her toys. So the interpersonal notion of fairness does not seem helpful here. What about an intrapersonal sense of unfairness? One such notion applies in the case in which a burden is in the offing. (It isn't fair to burden someone with a life sentence for a parking violation.) But that requires some connection with sanction, perhaps via blameworthiness, as seems presupposed by the version Fischer sets out. In that case, though, this version of the fairness rationale collapses into something like that other version, which I have already rejected.

Those are not the only notions of fairness. A notion of "fairness" meaning "fittingness" or "appropriateness" could still work in the reasoning. And indeed there is something plausible about the idea that it wouldn't be fitting for morality to include requirements of actions that cannot be performed. However, it is not clear that such a notion would be elucidating by itself, let alone grounding of the principle itself. The reason it seems inappropriate for morality to include requirements that cannot be performed is precisely because of the *nature* of obligation, which encapsulates a directive to agents to act (or not to act). Once again, this suggests that the principle is more basic than the claims being made in support of it.

Does this mean that there is nothing more to say in support of the principle than that it is intuitively plausible? Not at all, for the principle itself can gain support from recognizing what is supported and explained by *it*. And, in fact, the principle can offer mutual support to other principles and to conclusions about particular cases. The notions of obligation and ability at issue can also be elaborated in illuminating ways. So far, I have simply tried to show that the most popular rationales that appeal to fairness and the action-guidingness of moral statements do not ground OIC in a more fundamental principle.

Consider, for example, cases that Howard-Snyder calls "second best options" (2006, p. 236). You promise to help a friend move at 8 am on Saturday. Stuck in traffic, you realize that you will not be able to make it. It seems that you acquire new obligations at this point—for example, to call your friend letting her know you will be late, to get there at 9 am, to stay later than you expected. The existence of these new obligations suggests that you no longer have the original obligation—precisely because you cannot fulfill it. (It would be odd, to say the least, if you had an obligation to arrive at 8 am *and* an obligation to arrive at 9 am.) Or consider a more dramatic example. A boulder falls on your friend. You try to lift the boulder and cannot. You immediately acquire the obligation to run for help. You are not obligated to lift the boulder, precisely because you cannot. The explanation for your new obligations in both of these cases—and others like them—is that you cannot be obligated to do what you cannot do. The existence of new, or second-best obligations, points precisely to this fact (see also Brink 1994, p. 231; and Vranas 2007, pp. 181–2).

The principle also explains why if you ought to do a particular thing, for example, pay a bill, then you ought to take any necessary means to doing so, for example, not depleting your bank account for other purposes, and writing a check to your creditor. It is precisely because you cannot fulfill your obligation unless you take these steps that you ought to take them.[17] Together with the intuitive appeal that has suggested its axiomatic quality, the principle's explanatory power provides strong support for the principle itself. Despite its strong appeal, however, it has come under attack from a variety of directions. I will here consider two that raise especially interesting questions about the connection of the principle to issues surrounding blameworthiness. These will also allow for an elaboration of the meaning of the principle itself.

A Challenge: Ought-Implies-Can, Properly Specified, Does not Entail (2)

I will start here with a challenge to the idea that I have correctly captured the principle, and that, once correctly captured, it simply does not support (2). Further, the very reasons for rejecting my formulation of the principle are reasons to reject (2) in particular. This objection, put forward by Gideon Yaffe, raises interesting questions about how exactly we are to understand the Kantian thesis. Yaffe takes it that the Ought-Implies-Can principle is best captured by the following:

---

[17] See Howard-Snyder (2006, pp. 238–40); but see too Graham (forthcoming) for an interesting alternative explanation of certain phenomena like these, that appeals to a distinction between different kinds of moral obligations. OIC, in my view, explains a wider variety of intuitions and in a way that offers more insight into *why* we have the obligations we do, but a full discussion must wait for a future occasion.

(Maxim) A person ought to perform a certain action only if he can do so.

Yaffe argues that from Maxim and (1), you cannot derive PAP-Blame. Rather, you need a new principle that refers explicitly to obligations not to act. He suggests the following:

(New Maxim) If an agent ought not to A, then it is possible that the agent *fails to A*.

However, from New Maxim and (1), you can derive only what Yaffe calls "Weak PAP":

(Weak PAP-Blame) S is morally blameworthy for doing A only if it is possible that S fails to A.

This is weaker than PAP-Blame because PAP-Blame requires that you be able to *do* otherwise or *refrain* from what you in fact do, not merely that something else could have happened such that you did not do what you actually did. For example, on the weaker version, it isn't that Joe needed to have been able to *decide* to refrain from drowning the child and perhaps walk away in order to be blameworthy for the drowning; for all the weaker version says, he could be blameworthy if he could have been struck by lightning and paralyzed in the moment before he acted.

Why does Yaffe think that New Maxim must be formulated as he does, as opposed to OIC, second clause, or as is captured in (2)? He offers a variety of cases that, if understood as he does, appear to provide counter-examples to (2). For example, he writes, "we often quite adequately discharge our obligations not to act simply by passively *not acting*, and not by actively performing some alternative. The man struck unconscious right before the moment at which he must not do some terrible thing, doesn't do it at that moment, and so does nothing wrong, despite the fact he doesn't *do* anything else . . . " (2005, p. 308). (Importantly, doings include refrainings in this context.) Similarly, he offers an example of discharging our duty not to steal while asleep. If we can fulfill obligations not to act without being able to do or refrain from doing anything, then we must also *have* such obligations without being able to do or refrain from doing anything. Behind this seems to be an idea that while some obligations require acting (or refraining), others require only that we not "cross lines" of certain sorts. And the latter can be met without our having the capacity to act or refrain.

My response to this challenge is two-fold. First, even were we to concede the weaker principle, and adopt Yaffe's New Maxim over (2), it is still the case that we can get Weak PAP-Blame, as Yaffe is well aware. Although philosophers have disagreed about its significance (see Fischer and Yaffe), it is nevertheless true that a derivation of Weak PAP-Blame from an Ought-Implies-Can-inspired principle would be silent on a counterpart for praise. So some sort of asymmetrical view for praiseworthy and blameworthy actions would still be supported.

However, I want to resist Yaffe's argument, as well, because I believe that (2) is correct and a robust PAP-Blame follows. Yaffe is right that the second clause of OIC does not follow validly from the first, because they are about different classes of obligations. However, both represent aspects of the same idea regarding obligation in general. As mentioned earlier, the driving idea of the Ought-Implies-Can principle is that we have the control required to meet our obligations; we can effect that they are met. And this seems equally to apply to what we ought not to do. In both cases, the simple idea is that our obligations are in our power to fulfill. So if Yaffe's argument is correct, it seems to me to be a rejection of the principle itself, or to the guiding idea, not merely to a conception of it. Interestingly, Copp argues that the rationales discussed earlier speak in favor of understanding OIC in something like the way I have, rather than the way Yaffe has. (In fact, he elaborates further, indexing to times in the very content of obligations.) Although I reject those rationales, I do think that there is something to the idea of action-guidingness, or, rather, action-directedness. Rather than appeal to the *point* of ought-statements, I think it is preferable to appeal to the nature of obligation itself. Action-directedness is built into the very idea of obligation. This is why rocks don't have any. I am in general sympathy with Copp, then, even though I do not think one has to go beyond OIC itself to adopt this picture.

So is the sleeping person or the person struck by lightning a counterexample to (2)? Do the examples offer reason to reject this way of thinking about obligation? The examples are odd. It doesn't sound at all natural to say that we discharge our duties while struck by lightning. And I find it very easy to resist the idea that while I am asleep I am discharging my obligation. Is it always easy to resist that way of talking? No, but in those cases, I think we can explain the naturalness of talking in that way without undermining the force of the Ought-Implies-Can idea. For example, I might be discharging a duty to get rest so that I can take care of my children. But insofar as that is true, it is because I have done something to ensure that I get sufficient sleep. It is that action that fulfills my obligation directly. Only in a derivative sense are the consequences of that action implicated in my obligation.

Another Challenge: The Frankfurt-style Cases

There are at least two ways that the Frankfurt-style cases themselves have been used to cast doubt on OIC, and (2) in particular. The first is by accepting (1), denying PAP-Blame, and so concluding that (2) must be false.[18] One person's *modus ponens* is another person's *modus tollens*. The second is to take the cases to be direct counterexamples to OIC.

Because I have committed to premise (1), I think the replies to both arguments should be the same. And it seems that a defense of PAP-Blame in the face of Frankfurt-style examples is called for. There have been many replies to the Frankfurt-style examples designed to show that they fail to undermine PAP-Blame, when understood correctly. I will here adopt the notion of abilities introduced in chapter 3, as well as the accompanying strategy for resisting the Frankfurt-style counterexamples.

We saw earlier that one way of understanding the possession of an ability is that an agent has an ability to X if (i) the agent possesses the capacities, skills, talents, knowledge and so on that are necessary for X'ing, and (ii) nothing interferes with or prevents the exercise of the relevant capacities, skills, talents and so on.[19] Since in the Frankfurt-style examples, Joe satisfies these conditions, there is a sense in which he has the ability to do otherwise. Now of course, there is *a* sense of "ability to do otherwise" in which Joe lacks such an ability. Joe will push the child off the pier, even if he wavers. In this sense, having an ability to do X is precluded when it is inevitable that the agent will not do X (I called this the "inevitability-undermining" sense in chapter 3). But in another sense, both have their abilities to do something different from what they do intact. It is plausible that this same notion of ability plays a role both in OIC and in PAP-Blame.

---

[18] See Fischer (2003, p. 248).

[19] This is a notion of abilities that Wolf offers in a different context. Compare the recent attempts to offer compatibilist analyses of abilities such as the dispositional accounts of Smith, M. (2003), Vihvelin (2004), and Fara (2008). See Clarke (2009) for an insightful criticism of the approach.

5: Conclusion

So, to sum up, I have shown that (1) and (2) can withstand strong challenges, that (2) really does capture the spirit of the intuitively plausible Kantian Ought-Implies-Can principle, and that together (1) and (2) support an alternate possibilities condition for blameworthy action. At the same time, a parallel principle to the Ought-Implies-Can principle that would support an alternate possibilities condition for praiseworthy action is not plausible. Thus, we have at least one explanation for the asymmetrical rational abilities view of responsible action. As mentioned, even *if* all of this is correct, it does not directly entail that the view itself is correct. But the reasoning does offer an explanation of why alternatives are needed in the case of blameworthy actions, and, *in the absence of successful rationales for a general PAP*, why alternatives are not needed in the case of praiseworthy ones. Thus, this chapter, taken together with the arguments of chapter 2, constitutes a strong case for the asymmetrical character of the rational abilities view.

6

Deliberation and Alternatives

1: Self-Conception: Theories and Their Implications

As we have seen, there are powerful skeptical challenges to the idea that we are free and responsible agents. In earlier chapters, I have tried to show how these can be met, in part by developing a particular account of freedom and responsibility. In this chapter and the next, I turn to another kind of response to the skeptical challenges: the insistence that we cannot escape the *sense* that we are free in the way required for responsibility.

It is a striking fact that many, on all sides of the debate, agree to being unable to shake the sense of themselves as free. Kant famously wrote that we must "act under the Idea of Freedom", and Reid wrote of our "natural conviction of our acting freely".[1] More recently, Galen Strawson, a skeptic about true freedom, has written that "people cannot help believing that [they are free]", and van Inwagen writes sympathetically of the hypothesis that human beings who truly ceased to believe that they were free would enter a state of catatonia.[2] The seemingly unshakeable feeling or conviction that we are free presents a powerful challenge to the idea that we are not free.

Yet, at second glance, the fact that we can't help but feel free might seem to lose some force; it might seem to be the kind of response that could be made on behalf of any view one wants to defend—"but it *seems* true!". In this case, however, the response can be developed in a way that allows it to take a more powerful form, and also in an impressive variety of ways that allow it to have an impact not only on the debate about whether we are free and responsible, but also on the debate about what shape our freedom and responsibility takes.

---

[1] Kant (1785/1981, 448, 455, pp. 50, 56), and Reid (1788/1983, p. 336).
[2] Strawson (1986, p. viii), and van Inwagen (1983, p. 157).

Two features of the initial response set it apart from the general "it seems true" strategy. One is emphasized by Reid, who pointed out that the sense of freedom appears to be universal, at least among human beings. Importantly for Reid, our "natural conviction of our acting freely" is *natural*, existing even in those who deny that we are free. Even if we do not follow Reid himself who thought that this fact "ought to throw the whole burden of proof" on the skeptics, the fact that the conviction seems universal does make it something to be explained and reckoned with. Why, if it is not true, would we be stuck living under an illusion about something so central to our self-conception?

Of course, it is possible that all human beings are, by their nature, simply stuck with a false conviction. After all, human beings are susceptible to perceptual illusions under certain conditions. And we have an explanation for this sort of illusion that involves facts about human perceptual systems. Perhaps our sense of freedom is like such perceptual illusions, and, in both cases, we should consider ourselves fortunate to be able to discover that our natural convictions are false.

Yet, there is an important point of disanalogy between the perceptual illusion case and the sense of freedom case—a disanalogy that would seem to rob us of a ready explanation for our allegedly false sense of freedom. While it is in virtue of being human and so of having the physiology we have that we are subject to perceptual illusions, it is in virtue of being *rational deliberators* that we have a sense of freedom. In other words, we possess this sense because of our capacity to consider and evaluate reasons for acting with a view to making a decision and ultimately acting. This idea is suggested by Kant:

(K)   We must necessarily attribute to *every rational being who has a will* also the idea of freedom, under which only can such a being act.[3]

Kant went on to make the claim, stronger than Reid's "shift the burden" one, that if we accept this point then we must conclude that such beings are "for this very reason free from a practical point of view".[4] It is one

[3] Kant (1785/1981, 448, p. 50), emphasis mine. In Kant's terminology, "will" means "a kind of causality belonging to living beings in so far as they are rational" (p. 49). Without going into a detailed exegesis of Kant, I take it that such a being is similar to what we would call a "deliberative agent", i.e., a being with the capacity to act on considered reasons. In my terminology, being a rational deliberator is a necessary condition for being a deliberative agent, as a deliberative agent is one who deliberates and acts on those deliberations.

[4] Kant (1785/1981, 448, p. 50).

thing to suggest that it is a contingent fact about human beings that we have to think of ourselves as free, perhaps in the way that human beings are subject to perceptual illusions like seeing straight sticks in water as appearing bent. We can explain this human tendency in a way that shows why we are subject to the illusion. But if we have this conviction in virtue of being *rational* agents, a similar sort of explanation, say, in terms of specifically human optical systems, will not be forthcoming. Further, it might seem that if *rationality* itself is what endows us with such a conviction, it must be a true one.

As Kant wrote,

The ideas of pure reason can never be dialectical in themselves; rather it is merely their misuse which brings it about that a deceptive illusion arises out of them; for they are given as problems for us by the nature of our reason, and *this highest court of appeals for all rights and claims of our speculation cannot possibly contain original deceptions and semblances.*[5]

At this point, I want to draw a more modest, but still significant conclusion. The sense of freedom appears to be a powerful part of our self-conception, and one admitted by a variety of participants on all sides of the debate. At the very least, then, it would seem to serve as strong motivation for the anti-skeptical position, and a first step in shifting the burden of proof to the skeptic.

Now in addition to playing a role in answering the skeptic, the claim that we have an inescapable sense of freedom also plays an influential role in the debate about what freedom (in the sense required for responsibility) *is*. I believe this fact has not always been made as explicit as it deserves to be. This second role, at least until recently, is played largely by its having been given a certain kind of interpretation, one which has then been claimed to express the existence of a specifically *libertarian* self-conception. If indeed, we have an inescapable sense of ourselves as free, where the notion of freedom is itself libertarian, then we not only have motivation and, at the least, a first compelling argumentative move against the skeptic, we also have motivation and a first compelling argumentative move for a *libertarian* anti-skeptical position.

---

[5] Kant (1781/1997, A669/B697, p. 605, emphasis mine). Kant is not here writing of the Idea of freedom, but the passage reveals the general strategy that might be employed to defend the thesis that we are free, based on the commitment to freedom our rational agency entails.

Here is how I see this happening. First, one way of understanding Kant's claim (not that it is usually claimed to be a faithful interpretation of Kant's own views) is this:

(R) Rational deliberators, in virtue of their very nature as rational deliberators, must represent themselves as free.

Note here, that while Kant wrote of rational beings with wills, we have instead employed the idea of "rational deliberators". There is something compelling about this idea right away: deliberation seems to provide paradigm occasions when we can become consciously aware of a sense of freedom. Should I go straight to graduate school or serve in the Peace Corps first? Should I read a novel or go for a walk? Should I speak out against a prayer at a children's sporting event or let it go?

Cases like this have led some to an even more specific refinement of (R). A key feature of deliberation, it has been claimed, is that we think of ourselves as having choices among various alternatives. A popular way of cashing this out is as follows:

(DA) Rational deliberators must believe, in virtue of their nature as rational deliberators, that they have alternatives from which to choose.

I call this "DA" or the "Deliberative Alternatives Thesis". DA provides one understanding of the Kantian claim about freedom. As I will argue in chapter 7, it is not the only way to understand this Kantian claim.[6] But it is also a widely accepted and plausible claim in its own right. And even by itself it has been used to support the idea that we are natural indeterminists about our future actions, because it has frequently been understood as claiming that we see ourselves as having *multiple undetermined* alternatives.

The most widely held view, I believe, is that the alternatives one considers in deliberation are believed to be genuine alternatives in the sense that each is consistent with prior conditions together with the laws of nature. Having alternatives in this sense is incompatible with causal determinism. The reason is that causal determinism allows that there is only one possibility consistent with the past and laws of nature. But in deliberating,

---

[6] See also Nelkin (2004a).

on this view, we must assume that we have more than one such possibility from which to choose. More formally:

(I)   Rational deliberators who deliberate about an action A must believe, in virtue of their nature as rational deliberators, that there exist no conditions that render either A or not-A inevitable.[7]

(I call this "the Indeterministic Thesis".) There are many ways to put this point, and we find it in a variety of places.

Some have claimed to find something like it in the work of Aristotle, including passages such as the following:

About other [things] not only existence and non-existence is possible, but also human deliberation; these are things the doing and not doing of which is in our power.[8]

And much more recently, van Inwagen posed this challenge:

To deliberate is to try to decide between (or, it may be, among) various incompatible courses of action . . . when one deliberates, one's behaviour manifests a belief that what one is deliberating about is possible . . . It would seem to follow from that conclusion, a proposition as near to being uncontroversial as any philosophically interesting proposition could be, that either Holbach [a determinist] never deliberated or else he believed in the case of some pairs of incompatible courses of action that each was within his power.[9]

---

[7] This is taken from R. Taylor (1964, p. 76).

[8] Aristotle (1984b) [EE 1226a, pp. 26–7]. Although it first appears that Aristotle is claiming that we cannot deliberate unless each of two alternatives *is* within our power, Aristotle qualifies his claim elsewhere so that he makes the weaker claim that we cannot deliberate unless we *believe* each of our deliberative alternatives is within our power. See, for example, Aristotle (1984b, 1941 [EE 1225b, pp. 34–6] and 1942 [EE 1226a, pp. 25–6]). Interpreters divide as to whether Aristotle here claims that deliberators are committed to causal indeterminism. For an interpretation on which Aristotle does make this claim, see Sorabji (1980), and for an interpretation on which Aristotle does not, see Fine (1981). I discuss these passages briefly in Nelkin (2004a), notes 4 and 16.

[9] Van Inwagen (1983, pp. 154–6). For van Inwagen, having two alternatives each within one's power, together with plausible assumptions, entails the falsity of determinism. But one need not believe that determinism is false by believing that one has two alternatives each within one's power. Nevertheless, if the inference follows from a few self-evident steps, then there is at least rational pressure to adopt the conclusion of indeterminism when one recognizes one's commitment as a rational deliberator. This provides reason for saying that on this view, at least *reflective* deliberators are natural indeterminists. See Campbell (2007) for a subtle discussion of van Inwagen's claims.

John Searle assumes that a commitment to causal indeterminism is part of our very experience as deliberators:

The gap is that feature of our conscious decision-making and acting where we sense alternative future decisions and actions as causally open to us . . . (2001, p. 62)

The Indeterministic Thesis clearly has a natural appeal. Yet, as I argue in what follows, we have very good reason to reject it.

Before assessing the thesis, it is worth reflecting a bit more on its significance. An example will help. Timothy O'Connor begins his book, *Persons and Causes*, with a description of a piece of deliberation that is worth pondering:

Shall I join my children on the floor, and await instructions about my role in their pretend play? Shall I return to my work instead? . . . I would describe how making this decision seemed to me as follows: each of the options I considered (and perhaps some others) was open to me, such that I could have chosen it, just then. Put differently, it was entirely up to me to decide the matter, and I did so in a particular way, all the while being conscious that I might have chosen differently. (2000, p. 3)

This passage begins an argument that determinism is incompatible with our ordinary view of things, including our view of ourselves as free. Thus, implicit in O'Connor's view of his own deliberation is something like the Indeterministic Thesis and, in turn, the Kantian claim that as deliberators we must take ourselves to be free. And indeed this understanding of the Kantian claim lends itself to the view that we are natural incompatibilists about freedom and determinism. O'Connor is not alone in suggesting that the incompatibilist position is highly motivated by, if not strongly supported by, our experience, as rational deliberators, of what seems to be free choice.[10]

If these suggestions are correct, then we are natural libertarians, and we have not only a motivation for libertarianism, but also a challenge to both skeptics *and* compatibilist non-skeptics to explain this fact. And it is an explanation that would seem difficult at the least if we are stuck with our sense of freedom not because of anything special about us as humans, but because of our status as rational deliberators. In the next two chapters, I aim to do three main things: (1) argue that (R) is true, and that DA may be true, providing a challenge to the skeptic, but (2) reject the idea that DA

---

[10]   See, for example, Reid (1788/1983, p. 344), Chisholm (1964/2003, p. 31), Campbell (1957, pp. 158–79), and Taylor (1983, pp. 23–50).

is best read in a libertarian way, leading to my being able to (3) defend readings of both (R) and DA that dovetail in mutually illuminating ways with the account of freedom and responsibility developed in the first part of the book. In this chapter, I take on (2) and begin (3) by defending a compatibilist reading of DA.

In the next section, I begin exploring our commitments concerning our deliberative alternatives by setting out the case for the Indeterministic Thesis. Given the plausibility of DA in the first place, the strongest case against the Indeterministic Thesis includes as a part a defense of alternative interpretations of DA.[11] In sections 3 and 4, I evaluate two classic alternative interpretations that I call "epistemic versions" and "counterfactual versions". In section 5, I consider a combination strategy, suggested by Kapitan and recently developed by Pereboom, which combines virtues of both. In section 6, I introduce what I call "nexus versions" of DA, and show that the explanatory nexus view in particular has great explanatory power. Finally, while finding alternative belief constraints on deliberation is an important part of the case against the Indeterministic Thesis, and also important in its own right, there are also other reasons to question it, and I bring these out in sections 2 and 7.

2: The Indeterministic Thesis

Let us begin by looking at one kind of direct argument in favor of the Indeterministic Thesis: an argument by examples. Van Inwagen is one who takes this general sort of approach, and I suspect that reflection on examples in general is what accounts for much of the appeal of the Indeterministic Thesis. Consider the following case: while you were sleeping, you were injected with some sort of paralyzing drug, such as curare.[12] It seems that you can deliberate about whether to get out of bed, as long as you don't know what has happened. But once you discover the paralysis, and realize that it is impossible to move, getting up is no longer a live alternative about which to deliberate. It seems that a natural explanation of this deliberative failure is that once you learn of your paralysis, you no longer believe that getting up is causally open to you. And this suggests

---

[11] See, for some examples of this strategy, Bok (1998), Clarke (1992), Fischer (2006b), Kapitan (1986), and Pettit (1989).
[12] Thomas (unpublished).

that in order to deliberate about something, you must believe it is causally possible.

Turn next to van Inwagen's much-discussed "two-door" case: imagine that you are in a room with two doors and believe one of the doors to be unlocked and the other to be locked and impassable, though you have no idea which is which. Then see if you can imagine yourself deliberating about which door to leave by.[13] If you have trouble with this task, your difficulty will be natural, according to van Inwagen, for it looks as though what prevents you from deliberating is your belief that only one thing is causally open to you to do. This is a powerful thought-experiment. But the argument for the Indeterministic Thesis that appeals to it is successful only if there are no plausible alternative explanations for your difficulty in deliberating here. So a full assessment of this argument will require an examination of alternative accounts.

In the meantime, one might be tempted to reject the Indeterministic Thesis outright on the following grounds: "There have been plenty of determinists who deliberate, so surely one need not presuppose that one's actions are not determined in order to deliberate".[14] This sounds like a strong argument, but alas, there is a possible reply that promises to extend the debate. Van Inwagen avails himself of a variant of this reply, and it is implicit in the quoted passage above: "Of course, there are determinists who have deliberated. But they must thereby be holders of contradictory beliefs".[15]

---

[13] Van Inwagen (1983, p. 154). Note that van Inwagen does not here claim to argue that we are natural libertarians, committed explicitly to the truth of indeterminism. See Coffman and Warfield (2005) on this point.

[14] One might argue that the concept of "indeterminism" does not appear in the content of the Indeterministic Thesis, and so deliberators do not necessarily have an explicit commitment to indeterminism if the thesis is true. While this might very well be true, I take it that the thesis is usually understood in such a way that one's being able to do more than one mutually incompatible thing entails (with the help of a few easy inferences) indeterminism. Thus, at least determinists who have been made aware of the implications of the beliefs they have in virtue of being deliberators would be in danger of inconsistency. Further, insofar as they are *rational*, they would be under pressure to recognize the implications of their beliefs.

[15] Other sorts of purported counterexamples to the Indeterministic Thesis can be treated in the same way. For a survey and criticism of other attempts at providing counterexamples to the thesis, or rather to a related thesis that Coffman and Warfield call "BAT", see their paper (2005, p. 26). Also, see Levy (2006, pp. 456–9) for an interesting attempted counterexample that is meant to avoid Coffman and Warfield's criticisms.

At this point, the dialectic can take a number of turns, but a natural way to proceed is to suggest that *if* there is a way of accounting for deliberation and its failure without attributing contradictory beliefs to otherwise rational people, we should do so. The question that faces us, then, is again whether there is an alternative way of accounting for the data. As I will argue in chapter 7, attributing to all rational deliberators beliefs entailing indeterminism must rest on a mistaken view of the point of rational deliberation. If we focus on the idea that the aim of deliberation is to find and adopt good reasons for acting, and to decide and act on the basis of those reasons, then we will see that the aim of deliberation is *not* the aim of actualizing one of multiple indeterministic possibilities. In fact, when we focus on this reason-centered aim of deliberation, we can generate a plausible understanding of the Kantian claim that deliberators must take themselves to be free that makes no obvious use of alternatives at all.[16]

Yet, even if DA is not the best way of making sense of the Kantian claim concerning our sense of freedom, it would be good to have a plausible understanding of DA by itself that does not commit all rational deliberators to indeterminism. For even if we can offer a point to deliberation in the absence of indeterminism, it is fair for others to demand an account of what deliberative alternatives are; and, in particular, of how they are proscribed, if not by their being limited to those scenarios that we believe are causally open to us. It is also true that others have worked with a different conception of deliberation, one that might make the Indeterministic Thesis more appealing.[17] So it seems that we must explore alternative accounts of deliberative alternatives after all.

It is important to note at the outset that the Indeterministic Thesis itself has variants worthy of consideration. For example, according to a "negative" variant of the thesis, we need have no particular beliefs about our abilities to perform alternative actions; rather, for each alternative, we must *lack* the belief that we are unable to perform it.[18] In addition to its appealing simplicity, this negative variant has the advantage of requiring less of deliberators. But it cannot by itself account for the two-door case. For it seems that given the description of my situation facing the two

---

[16] See Nelkin (2004a).
[17] See Coffman and Warfield (2005, pp. 27–8) and Pereboom (forthcoming). I discuss their characterizations in section 5.
[18] See Pettit (1989), for example, for this suggestion.

doors, I do not believe of either action that I cannot perform it. And yet I cannot deliberate about which to open, despite fulfilling the negative condition. Thus, this negative variant of the Indeterministic Thesis does not have the explanatory power of the thesis itself.[19]

Let us turn, then, to a different family of alternative accounts: epistemic versions of DA.

3: Epistemic Versions

A natural suggestion as to how to understand deliberative alternatives is that they are epistemic possibilities. In particular, they are alternatives, or open possibilities, relative to what we know.[20] More precisely:

(K)   Rational deliberators must believe, in virtue of their nature as rational deliberators, that they have multiple alternatives from which to choose, where those alternatives are each consistent with what they know.

(K) (or the "Knowledge Thesis") seems plausible; when you think about deliberating about what to do with your life, for example, you don't know how it is all going to turn out. And this seems important. Could you deliberate about what to do with your life or even what to order for lunch if you already knew how you were going to decide and act?

Perhaps surprisingly, I think that reflection suggests that the answer is not obvious. Consider, for example, a situation in which you are engaged in a long-anticipated activity (for example, watching an overtime period of a championship basketball game, attending a concert, taking a once-in-a-lifetime trek). You receive a call from a friend who desperately needs to talk to someone about the sudden and unexpected death of a family member. In the past, you have always deliberated about what to do in situations of this

---

[19] Coffman and Warfield (2005, pp. 37–8) criticize this variant on other grounds, namely, that it is false.

[20] "He has not yet decided what to do" entails "He does not yet know what he will do" (Hampshire and Hart 1958, pp. 2–3); "The concept of a decision does not allow the possibility of a person's knowing what his decision will be before he makes it" (Ginet 1962, p. 52); "One cannot deliberate about what he is going to do, even though this may be something that is up to him, at the same time, knowing what he is going to do" (Taylor 1964, p. 75). See also Dennett (1984, p. 113), Pereboom (1995, pp. 32–3), and Fischer (2006b, p. 330), for example.

sort and have always resolved things in favor of talking to your friend; indeed, this is the kind of person you are. Based on these considerations, and perhaps others, you know you will decide the same way today. However, you haven't deliberated and decided to do so yet. But you can and do.

Or take an example of Clarke's:

> Imagine that Edna is trying to decide where to spend her vacation this year. She mentions this fact to her friend Ed, who, as it happens, is in possession of information that Edna does not yet have. Ed knows that Edna will soon learn that she can, with less expense than she had expected, visit her friend Eddy in Edinburgh. And given what Ed knows about Edna and her other options, he knows that after she learns of this opportunity, she will eventually decide to take it. However, Ed is a playful fellow, and he doesn't tell Edna all of this. He tells her only that he knows that she will eventually learn something that will persuade her to spend her vacation with Eddy in Edinburgh.
>
> ... [Edna] knows, let us suppose, that whenever Ed says anything of this sort, he is right. She believes then, with justification, that she will spend her vacation in Edinburgh.[21]

Can Edna deliberate about where to go on her vacation? It seems so.

I find it plausible that these cases are counterexamples to (K). But if you find these examples hard to evaluate, it might be because "knowledge" is a notoriously difficult concept. How much justification do we need for knowledge, for example?

One reaction to this worry is to avoid it, and so avoid apparent counterexamples, as well, by moving from "knowledge" to "certainty":

(C) Rational deliberators must believe, in virtue of their nature as rational deliberators, that they have multiple alternatives from which to choose, where those alternatives are each consistent with what they are certain of.

This seems to help when it comes to the examples. Perhaps you are not certain of what you are going to decide while you are on the phone with your friend; perhaps Edna is not certain of Ed's conclusion, even if both know what she will do.

There are several challenges facing (C), however. One is unique to it: it purchases immunity from counterexamples at the price of a loss of

---

[21] Clarke (1992, p. 108). For other counterexamples, see Canfield (1962) and Stocker (1968).

explanatory power. The reason is that we are certain of very little. As a result, as far as (C) allows, there is a very large number of things that can count as deliberative alternatives. And, yet, there are circumstances in which we seem *unable* to deliberate in certain situations, precisely because we lack deliberative alternatives. (C) does not have the resources to explain these, since it rules out so little in the way of deliberative alternatives. For example: we seem to be unable to deliberate about whether to jump out of a window from a high floor and float on the air currents, despite perhaps lacking certainty about whether this is possible (perhaps we do not rule out a "miracle" or even a perfect sequence of wind gusts). Thus, even if (C) provides a correct condition, it does not capture the whole story of what it is to be a deliberative alternative.

Responding to this sort of worry, Pereboom has proposed an epistemic condition that seems to avoid the problems of both the belief constraint that appeals to knowledge (K) and the belief constraint that appeals to certainty (C).[22] The basic idea is that we can deliberate when we have alternatives that are open relative to what we consider "settled", or relative to what we disregard doubts about. More precisely:

(S)   In order to rationally deliberate among alternative actions A1...An, for each Ai, S cannot be certain of the proposition that she will do Ai, nor of the proposition that she will not do Ai; and either (a) the proposition that she will do Ai must be consistent with every proposition that, in the present context, is settled for her, or (b) if it is inconsistent with some such proposition, she cannot believe that it is.

---

[22] Pereboom (2008a, p. 294). This is a revised version of the condition I discussed in my (2004b). For a different attempt to improve on (K), see Pereboom (2001) which appeals to a "doxastic" condition initially presented by Kapitan (1986); call it "B" for "Belief": (B) an agent presumes that his Φ'ing is an open alternative for him *only if* he presumes that if S is any set of his beliefs then his Φ'ing is contingent relative to S (p. 240). Kapitan adopts this condition after rejecting something like (K), on the basis of the following example. We can imagine that Kapitan's flying to Copenhagen tomorrow is actually contingent relative to what he knows, because some unforeseen emergency will call him to Copenhagen. Yet he cannot deliberate about doing so. Kapitan concludes that what is preventing the deliberation in this case is that he believes he will not fly to Copenhagen tomorrow. While I think that Kapitan is right to raise questions about (K), the Copenhagen example does not inevitably lead us to (B). Further, there is good reason to think (B) is false. For example, consider again the case in which your friend calls while you are engaged in a long anticipated activity. You might believe that you will talk to your friend in the end (and might even have excellent evidence for that conclusion), but it seems clear that you can deliberate about whether to do so.

Pereboom offers an elaboration on what it is to be settled:

(Settled) A proposition is settled for an agent just in case she believes it and disregards any doubts she has that it is true, e.g., for the purposes of deliberation.

The "Settledness Thesis" (or "S" for short) avoids any worries about the nature of knowledge that threaten to undermine (K), and, since we seem to regard more things as settled than we are actually certain of, it avoids the relative lack of explanatory power provided by (C). It is worth noting that this view also focuses on decisions, rather than actions, as occupying the central role of deliberative alternatives. The objects of deliberation are decisions about acting, then, not actions.

However, even this suggestion has limitations. For even if (S) avoids the original counterexamples to (K) and offers a correct and informative condition on deliberation, it does not follow that it captures all there is that makes something a deliberative alternative. That is, (S) may not provide a sufficient condition for being a deliberative alternative either. For there might be cases in which we are unable to deliberate, and this seems to have something to do with lacking deliberative alternatives, despite the fact that the condition in (S) appears to be met. (As we will see, some proponents of epistemic conditions, including Pereboom himself, do not intend for (S) to tell the whole story.)

Defenders of the Indeterministic Thesis can always agree that some epistemic conditions are correct, without their being sufficient. For, by themselves, they don't rule out a commitment to indeterminism as an additional condition. So consider the following case: Suppose that I am deliberating about whom to vote for in an upcoming presidential election—Obama or McCain, say. Suppose further that voting for each (and deciding to vote for each) is consistent with all that I regard as settled (suppose I've just emerged from the jungle if you like!). But now I learn that an evil neuroscientist is going to take things into his own hands, and make me decide to vote for the candidate he favors on election day. Can I deliberate about which decision to make? Presumably not. But why not? It seems important that in this case I see any potential deliberation of mine as cut off from my decision. If I don't think that my deliberation will be efficacious, then it seems that I can't deliberate—even if in some important epistemic sense it is open to me to decide to vote for any of the three candidates. To be genuinely open *for me*, it seems I must think that my deliberation will be connected to my decision in the right way. What I think is not captured here is the idea of efficacy between deliberation and decision. (I can, of course, decide who is the best candidate, who has the best ideas, and so on. But in doing this, I am not doing anything relevantly different from deciding what I should propose as my next executive order were I President of the United States, for example. Perhaps unfortunately, I cannot actually deliberate about what presidential order to issue or even which to decide to issue, despite the fact that I can think about which one would be best.)

Now it might seem that the Indeterministic Thesis is well poised to handle this sort of case all by itself. The reason I can't deliberate in the voting case, a defender of the Indeterministic Thesis might say, is that I don't think it is causally open to me to decide to vote for more than one candidate. But, as we will see, there are ways of capturing the idea of deliberative efficacy other than by the Indeterministic Thesis.[23]

Van Inwagen's two-door case reveals a different, albeit related, limitation of (S). While it seems that I can deliberate about which door to decide *to try* and even which door handle to decide to jiggle, if I know one of them to be locked and impassable, it also seems that I cannot deliberate about which door *to open*—or even which door to *decide* to open. Why is this? It looks like on the view under consideration, the answer must be that the scenarios of deciding to open door A and of deciding to open door B are inconsistent with propositions about which one disregards any

---

[23] One might try to build this idea of efficacy into an epistemic version as follows:

(S') In order to deliberate, the agent must believe that for some incompatible actions, A and B, deciding to A *on the basis of one's deliberation* and deciding to B *on the basis of one's deliberation* are both possible in the relevant epistemic sense (namely, where both alternatives are each consistent with what the agent regards as settled, that is, consistent with any proposition about which she has no doubts, and with any proposition about which she disregards any doubts she might have for the purposes of deliberation in the present context).

The basic idea is that the alternatives that must be epistemically open include my decision's being connected to my deliberation in the right way. Now this incorporates an idea of deliberative efficacy. But there is reason to think that (S') does not fully capture the notion of deliberative efficacy. Suppose that the case is the same as before, but although I believe that the neuroscientist is planning to intervene in my voting, I also know that there is a significant chance that he will be waylaid. Is having a doubt about whether I could decide on the basis of deliberation enough to allow for genuine deliberation about what to decide here? Must I have the further independent belief that my deliberation *will* be efficacious? Or at least lack the belief that it won't? If I can't deliberate about what to decide even in this revised voting case, despite meeting the condition, (S'), then it seems that an additional condition must be met in order to have genuine deliberative alternatives.

doubts for the purpose of deliberation. If so, what are the relevant propositions? I do not see any obvious answer here, since opening door A is consistent with what I don't entertain doubts about, and so is opening B.

Fortunately for those who wish to resist the Indeterministic Thesis, it is a more powerful tool than is actually needed here. The problem is not that we require both alternatives to be causally undetermined; the problem here is that we lack a commitment to our "decisional efficacy" (as contrasted with deliberative efficacy). Whereas earlier our concern was with the relation between deliberation and decision, here the concern is with the relation between decision and action. To put it crudely as a first pass: if I do not believe my decision will issue in action, I cannot deliberate.[24]

It is true that the Indeterministic Thesis appears to be in good position to capture the idea of both kinds of efficacy. Deliberative alternatives are viewed as not causally determined by the past; it seems up to you at the moment of decision to make one decision actual on the basis of your deliberation. Notice, though, that even the Indeterministic Thesis might need elaboration to bring out this point. It is not mere contingency of outcomes that is at stake; it seems that it must be possible in some sense for the agent to bring them about in the right way, whatever that may be.[25]

---

[24] We could try to add, as we did in note 23, a clause incorporating decisional efficacy:

(S") In order to deliberate, the agent must believe that for some incompatible actions A and B, deciding to A *and doing A* on the basis of one's deliberation and deciding to B *and doing B* on the basis of one's deliberation are both possible in the relevant epistemic sense (namely, where both alternatives are each consistent with what the agent regards as settled, that is, consistent with any proposition about which she has no doubts, and with any proposition about which she disregards any doubts she might have for the purposes of deliberation in the present context).

But the suggestion will not succeed in explaining our reaction to the two-door case. For it does not seem inconsistent with propositions about which I disregard doubts that I deliberate and decide to open door A on the basis of my deliberation. And the same goes for deliberating and deciding to open door B. Thus, if this epistemic version provided a sufficient condition for deliberation, deciding to open door A and deciding to open door B count as deliberative alternatives. But intuitively it seems that they do not, and precisely for that reason, I cannot deliberate in the case.

[25] Further questions might be raised here. For example, suppose that one believes that getting out of bed, say, is causally open—that is, it is not causally necessitated that one won't get out of bed, and yet one also believes that the odds of one's getting out of bed are .01. Do beliefs about one's chances make a difference to whether one can deliberate? If one is tempted by the indeterministic belief constraint, should one also be tempted by constraints concerning probabilities? Further, imagine a situation in which someone believes that, in a sense, everything is causally open, because God could reset the universe in any way at any time.

But we need not resort to the Indeterministic Thesis to capture the idea of efficacy. The remaining families of views attempt to capture the idea of both deliberative and decisional efficacy, while also avoiding the other worries with epistemic versions that we have seen.[26]

4: Conditional Versions

The so-called "conditional analysis" of freedom says that the ability to do otherwise that constitutes freedom is understood as follows: you can do otherwise if and only if you would do otherwise, if you so chose. This understanding of freedom has been widely dismissed on the grounds that these two phrases—the ability to do otherwise and the ability to do otherwise if you so chose—are not equivalent.[27] But we are not now focusing on what freedom is. We are exploring what it takes for something to be a genuine deliberative alternative for you; something you can deliberate about. So even if we reject the conditional analysis as an account of freedom, it is worth considering whether it has something to offer when it comes to deliberative alternatives.

Presumably, that would not make everything a deliberative alternative. So it would seem that even for one who is tempted by the indeterministic belief constraint, more would be needed to explain failures of deliberation.

[26] Coffman and Warfield (2005) offer a distinct objection to any epistemic belief constraint on deliberation, namely, that it requires too much in the way of cognitive sophistication. For example, they point out that it would seem to require that deliberators have the concept of consistency and also have concepts of their own epistemic states, while deliberation itself requires no such conceptual capacities. One line of response would point to the sophistication required to be a deliberator in the first place, and conclude that whatever level of sophistication is required for deliberation itself is more than adequate for the concepts of consistency and epistemic states. Coffman and Warfield would reject this, however, since they insist on a fairly "narrow" construal of deliberation as the trying to choose what to do among an incompatible set of actions, and doing so after reasons have been weighed and evaluated (p. 28). On the basis of the narrowness of their construal of deliberation, they argue that non-human animals and other hypothetical beings without such sophistication could in principle deliberate. While I believe that Coffman and Warfield are right to press discussants of these issues to be clear about the nature of deliberation, I also believe that whatever its nature, it must require a fair amount of sophistication and perhaps more than Coffman and Warfield would admit. One reason is that Coffman and Warfield, like many other parties to the debate, favor an alternative belief constraint that they believe captures our sense of freedom. On my understanding of the significance of the thesis that we have a sense of our own freedom, it is not a sense of ourselves that we share with (most) non-human animals. I discuss this point further in section 5.

[27] See, for example, Chisholm (1964/1982, pp. 26–7).

And a natural suggestion that captures the idea of deliberative efficacy is captured by "CT" for "Conditional Thesis":

(CT) In order to deliberate, an agent must believe that there are at least two distinct actions, A and B, such that the agent believes that were she to choose to A, she would A, and were she to choose to B, she would B.[28]

Now the Conditional Thesis nicely captures a causal relation between choosing to A and A'ing. This is one way of capturing the idea of decisional efficacy discussed above. CT helps explain why we can't deliberate in van Inwagen's two-door case, without recourse to the Indeterministic Thesis.[29] For in that case, we don't believe that were we to choose B, we would B, for example. In other words, we don't believe that in the two-door case, we have the right kind of decisional efficacy.

But, alas, there is a problem here that can be brought out by means of another example we considered earlier. Suppose that I believe that were I to choose to vote for Obama, I would, and were I to choose to vote for McCain, I would. Still, it seems that this is not sufficient for deliberating about whether to vote for Obama or McCain if I believe that someone else will cause me to vote in a certain way, despite my deliberation. For we seem to want not only decisional efficacy here, but also deliberative efficacy. Can we supplement the Conditional Thesis in order to capture this?

Clarke considers the proposal that we should invoke a series of conditionals: An agent must believe that if she so decides, she can A (B); if she finds better reason, she can decide to A (B); and if there is better reason to A (B), she can find it.[30]

---

[28] See, for example, Kapitan (1986, p. 234), Bok (1998, p. 114), and Fischer (2006b, pp. 330–1) for related suggestions. For a variant, see Clarke (1992, p. 104): In order to deliberate, one must believe that if one so decides, one *can* A (B). As we will see below, this is only one part of Clarke's suggestion, and his entire proposal is tentative in the sense that he thinks it is right, *if* there are any positive attitude constraints on deliberation that concern abilities at all.

Velleman (1989) suggests that our feeling of freedom and of the openness of the future is the belief that, within a certain range, whatever we decide to do, we will do. Since decisions are, in Velleman's view, self-fulfilling predictions, this means that within a range we (rightly) take it that whatever we predict will come true. While Velleman calls this experience of openness an experience of "epistemic freedom", I believe that it bears a closer resemblance to the belief captured in the conditional analyses views than to what I call the "epistemic" version of DA. One major difference between Velleman's view and the one discussed in the text is Velleman's claim that decisions are self-fulfilling predictions.

[29] As Kapitan (1986), Clarke (1992), and Bok (1998) have pointed out.

[30] Clarke (1992, p. 104).

Adding clauses to bring out explicitly the idea of deliberative efficacy, we get something like this:

(CT')   In order to deliberate, an agent must believe that there are at least two distinct actions, A and B, such that (i) were she to choose to A (B), she could A (B) on that basis, (ii) if she were to find better reason to do A (B), she could decide to A (B) and (iii) if there were better reason to A (B), she could find it.

Now I think that something like CT' might be on the right track as a necessary condition on deliberation, although there may be reasons for thinking it too strong.[31] But even if it, or some suitably modified version of it, captures a necessary condition on deliberation, it isn't clear that it captures all there is to the idea of deliberative alternatives. Could there be situations in which CT' is met, despite the fact that we seem to lack genuine deliberative alternatives? Could I believe, for example, that were there good reasons for me to fly out of the window, I could find them, and decide and act on those reasons, without my taking flying out of the window to be a genuine deliberative alternative? If so, then while CT' might give an informative necessary condition on being a deliberative alternative, it does not seem to tell the whole story. More seems needed.[32]

---

[31] One might try a more cautious "negative version of CT'", according to which what is necessary is not that one have the attitudes described in clauses (i)–(iii), but rather that one lack attitudes to the contrary. However, a negative version will not by itself explain our deliberative failure in the two-door case. We might also wonder whether a probabilistic version of CT' is more plausible, as is considered by Kapitan (1986, p. 234). Would it be sufficient to believe that were you to decide to perform action A you *probably* would A, and that were you to decide to perform action B you *probably* would B? In my view, it is far from obvious how a defender of a conditional analysis belief constraint should answer this question.

[32] See Coffman and Warfield (2005, pp. 40–1) for an objection to a conditional analysis belief constraint similar in its general strategy to the one they offer for epistemic belief constraints. They claim that deliberation itself does not require the cognitive sophistication that is required by the counterfactual belief constraints. Therefore, such constraints, which require facility with counterfactual reasoning, must not apply to deliberators. Here again, a possible reply would begin with the premise that deliberation itself is sufficiently cognitively sophisticated that at least a crude understanding of counterfactuals (of the form, "if I were to do x, then y") should be expected of deliberators.

5: A Combination Strategy

The natural move at this point is to combine the best of both of the previous approaches. Interestingly, Clarke, who offers what is perhaps the most subtle version of a conditional account, rejects various versions of the epistemic belief constraint. Bok, on the other hand, accepts an epistemic belief constraint in the form of (K), and seems to suggest at one point that it entails CT: "But if it is in principle impossible for an agent to know, before making a choice, what she will choose to do, then no conceivable correction of her beliefs could allow her to narrow the set of actions that she regards as alternatives beyond those that she would perform if she chose to perform them" (1992, p. 108). I do not believe this inference is justified. For even if I cannot know whether I will do A or B, I could consistently rule out C as an alternative, even where I believe that I would do C were I to choose to do C. Further, I have offered reasons for thinking that (K) is not correct as it stands. Setting these worries aside, though, the idea of recognizing more than one type of belief constraint on deliberation that can explain deliberative failures seems a promising step in the right direction. Kapitan (1986) takes this step quite explicitly. Fischer (2005) also accepts both an epistemic condition and a conditional one. I will here focus on Pereboom's recent development of these ideas.

Pereboom argues that two beliefs—one concerning a kind of epistemic openness and one concerning the efficacy of deliberation—better explain the phenomena that the belief in indeterminism was meant to explain, and provide a more plausible overall account. Pereboom's specific suggestion is as follows. First, Pereboom understands deliberation as follows:

(D)   S deliberates just in case S is engaged in an active mental process whose aim is to figure out what to do from among a number of distinct, i.e., mutually incompatible, alternatives, a process understood as one that can (but need not) include the weighing and evaluating of reasons for the options for what to do.[33]

Pereboom's characterization of deliberation is somewhat different from the way I characterized it earlier. In particular, Pereboom's (D) is *in one way* more minimal than the one I introduced earlier in which deliberation aims at finding and adopting good reasons for acting, as well as so acting.

---

[33] Pereboom (forthcoming), ms. p. 6.

My characterization included a kind of aim at acting on adopted reasons, while Pereboom's does not. At the same time, there is another way in which Pereboom's characterization includes something that mine does not. For Pereboom's characterization includes in deliberation the aim of "figuring out what to do" which in turn suggests an explicit aim at an epistemic achievement that mine does not. While I believe the first difference is not important for the purposes of evaluating Pereboom's proposal here (though it will be important for the concerns of chapter 7), the second difference, as we shall see, is important in the comparison of belief constraints presented here.

Now according to Pereboom, two belief conditions must be met in order to deliberate. The first is a belief in a kind of epistemic openness, one that we have already seen captured by

(S)   In order to rationally deliberate among alternative actions A1 . . . An, for each Ai, S cannot be certain of the proposition that she will do Ai, nor of the proposition that she will not do Ai; and either (a) the proposition that she will do Ai must be consistent with every proposition that, in the present context, is settled for her, or (b) if it is inconsistent with some such proposition, she cannot believe that it is.

together with

(Settled)   A proposition is settled for an agent just in case she believes it and disregards any doubts she has that it is true, e.g., for the purposes of deliberation.

The second is a belief in the efficacy of one's deliberation, captured by

(DE)   In order to rationally deliberate about whether to do A1 or A2, where A1 and A2 are distinct and incompatible actions, an agent must believe that if as a result of her deliberating about whether to do A1 or A2 she were to judge that it would be best to do A1, then, under normal conditions, she would also, on the basis of this deliberation, decide to do A1, and do A1; and similarly for A2. (Pereboom 2008, p. 209)

This proposal has the resources to answer the serious worries plaguing each of the previous views that take the following form: "Well, the condition in question might be necessary, but it does not explain all the phenomena;

it does not give a sufficient condition for deliberation in the way that the Indeterministic Thesis seems to do". It does so while also preserving the intuitively appealing ideas behind each of the previous views. DE also improves upon CT' in one important way, namely, by qualifying the claim that we must believe that were we to judge it best to do A, we would do it. DE leaves it open that one might believe a weaker claim— namely, that we would do what we judge best, *under normal conditions*.[34]

Nevertheless, I will raise two questions for the proposal. The first questions whether (S) is in fact a necessary condition on deliberation. The second raises the possibility of finding a single unifying belief that can do the work of both conditions, making it structurally more similar to the indeterministic belief proposed by those Pereboom calls "deliberation-incompatibilists".

First, consider (S), together with (Settled). As we saw, (S) and (Settled) are designed to avoid counterexamples like Clarke's Edna, who it seems can deliberate about where to go on her vacation despite the fact that she knows that she will go to Edinburgh. As long as Edna is not *certain* she will go, writes Pereboom, she can fulfill condition (S), and this explains why she is able to deliberate, while at the same time knowing what she will do. It is not clear to me that (S) avoids all of the counterexamples that target previous attempts to capture an epistemic openness condition. For example, suppose that you are engaged in an enjoyable activity (watching the seventh game of the world series, reading the seventh Harry Potter book, dining at your favorite restaurant), and you receive a call from your friend in need. It seems possible that you could know what you are going to do, and even be certain of what you will do (help your friend) and so, *a fortiori*, be settled with respect to this fact, without having made the decision or formed the intention to do it. I am not sure why this isn't coherent: one simply has no doubts about what one is going to choose, and still not yet have chosen from among one's alternatives. Pereboom writes that "If an agent is certain of what she will do, she cannot also still figure out what to do, and the intention to do it be produced as the result"

---

[34] One might still worry that this is not a sufficiently weakened constraint. Pereboom considers a suggestion of Kapitan's that it be altered to account for one's acknowledgment that one might be subject to akratic action—which presumably might constitute a normal condition for some. But I will set aside this worry here.

(forthcoming, p. 10). This suggests that we read "figuring out what to do" as an epistemic achievement. This is one place where Pereboom's characterization of deliberation seems to encourage the idea that there is no more work for deliberation to do once an agent has figured out what to do in the sense of figuring out what one will do. In contrast, characterizations which include the idea that an agent aims at adopting reasons, or even simply the idea that an agent aims at the best (or a good) action, make it more natural to think that there is still more work for deliberation to do. And if there is more—or other—work for deliberation to do, then it is much less plausible that one could not be settled—epistemically—while deliberating.

How should we decide between different conceptions of deliberation? It makes sense to consider every conception that we human beings instantiate for the purposes of identifying the nature and content of our sense of freedom. I see inherent value in this, and, at the same time, also believe that there are special reasons to focus on a notion of deliberation that appeals to our reason-evaluating capacities when it comes to answering the skeptic. Also, there are reasons for focusing on a conception of deliberation that requires some cognitive sophistication, insofar as we are engaged in capturing the idea that deliberation commits us to a sense of our own freedom.

Coffman and Warfield (2005) argue for an even broader characterization of deliberation than Pereboom, suggesting that "to deliberate is to try to choose what to do from among a number of incompatible courses of action under certain conditions", and that deliberation occurs "after reasons for various actions have been weighed and evaluated".[35] They contend that such an understanding of deliberation is true to that of van Inwagen and Searle, and so is the one most relevant to the debate to which they contributed so much. However, even if this is correct (and see Pereboom (2008a) for some reasons for doubt), employing such an understanding of deliberation is in some tension with the project of showing that deliberation generates our sense of freedom. Coffman and Warfield may be right that on their conception of deliberation, non-human animals and human infants deliberate, but insofar as van Inwagen and Searle are concerned to show that humans have a sense of freedom, it is natural

---

[35] Coffman and Warfield (2005, p. 28).

to suppose that they did not also intend to show that non-human animals do, as well. Thus, if we are interested in showing a commitment to human freedom, it is reasonable to adopt an understanding of human deliberation that presupposes some cognitive sophistication that is not necessarily possessed by non-human animals.

In the end, then, I do not dispute the interest in examining a number of different characterizations of deliberation, focusing on different features, and seeing what commitments they seem to entail on the part of deliberators. I do wish to emphasize, however, the special reason we have for focusing on ones that emphasize our reason-evaluating and reason-adoption capacities. This will become even more important in the next chapter.

Setting aside this question, however, I would like to raise one more question for Pereboom's proposal that does not hinge on a particular characterization of deliberation. It concerns the claim that there should be two separate conditions, one concerning openness and one concerning efficacy. Although Pereboom has nicely spelled out the virtues of having two separate conditions, there are also some attractive aspects to having a single one. One is that the defenders of the Indeterministic Thesis offer a single one, and so it would be nice if it were possible to find the same simplicity in a deliberation-compatibilist condition (that is, in Pereboom's terminology, one which takes S's deliberating and being rational to be compatible with S's believing that her actions are causally determined). A second is that the distinction might seem somewhat artificial when it comes to particular cases. For example, in van Inwagen's two-door case, it does not seem that it would be inappropriate to say that what is lacking is a belief in a kind of openness. The deliberation-incompatibilists combine the two kinds of considerations by saying, "in deliberating, I sense that more than one thing is open *to me*". Can the deliberation-compatibilist do the same thing? In the next section, I make an attempt to do just that.

6: Nexus Versions

So a real opportunity is an occasion where a self-controller "faces"—is informed about—a situation in which the outcome of its subsequent "deliberation" will be a decisive (as we say) factor. In such a situation more than one alternative is "possible" so far as the agent or self-controller is concerned; that is, the critical nexus passes through its deliberation. (Dennett 1984, p. 118)

The view contained in this passage is easy to overlook because it is often not clearly distinguished from one of the previous families of views. The basic idea is to make absolutely central the idea of deliberative efficacy, and suggest that alternative actions are genuine deliberative alternatives for an agent when she believes that only her own deliberation will determine which of the two (or more) alternatives is actualized. More formally:

(N)   Rational deliberators must believe, in virtue of their nature as rational deliberators, that they have multiple alternatives from which to choose, where their deliberation is the critical nexus (or decisive factor) among those alternatives.

There is something very attractive about this idea. For example, when we turn to the two-door case, we can understand the idea that the person in the room simply does not see her deliberation as determining which of the doors is opened. And this seems a natural explanation of why she cannot deliberate in this case. But, as always, we need to look at the details.

Let us begin by taking a closer look at Dennett's claim. He seems to equate the idea of "the critical nexus passing through deliberation" with the idea that more than one alternative is possible for the deliberator. But it isn't at all obvious how these two ideas are connected. Perhaps the idea of efficacy is one thing, and the idea of alternatives another thing altogether.

It seems natural to say that deliberation is the critical nexus between, say, my going to dinner or a movie. At the same time, in order for the idea of a critical nexus to explain deliberative failures, it must be the case that my deliberation is not seen as the nexus among *all* logically possible alternatives. For example, it cannot be that, as a deliberator, I see my deliberation as the nexus between my walking to dinner at a restaurant around the corner and my flying to the moon for dinner. But if determinism is true, and I can only do one thing (given the past and laws of nature), what is there to distinguish between the action I am determined not to take here on earth and my flying to the moon? Both are equally precluded by the actual past state of the world (and the laws of nature). Why does my deliberation get to be the critical nexus between my two earthly alternatives about which I deliberate, and not between an earthly alternative and going to the moon, about which I cannot deliberate?

Again, the Indeterministic Thesis has a natural way of distinguishing the cases: what matters is whether it is causally open to you to deliberate and decide and go to dinner or a movie. And if we do not assume the truth of determinism, it appears to be causally open to you to go to a movie, but not for you to go the moon. However, if we do assume causal determinism, then we cannot distinguish between alternatives that are genuine nodes on the nexus and those that are not. We cannot see deliberation as the decisive factor, or "critical nexus".

As appealing as it might be at first glance, this reasoning is too hasty. It is possible to provide an answer, and, not surprisingly, doing so requires some development of the idea of a critical nexus. The motivating idea encapsulated by the nexus view is that deliberation is the "difference-maker"; that is, your deliberation is what will explain why you do what you do, rather than something else. Crucially, this idea can be very naturally captured in ways that make no appeal to indeterminism.

To begin, we can learn a great deal from other contexts in which the notions of explanation and of difference-making arise. The first thing to note is that there are many such contexts, most notably in scientific explanation. It seems clear that many of our demands for explanation have the form: "why did X happen rather than Y?". Answers to these questions are commonly known as contrastive explanations, and these are pervasive in our everyday experiences.[36] We ask questions like, "why did Bush win the election rather than Dukakis?" and "why was the photon absorbed rather than transmitted?".[37] We suppose that there is an answer to each, an answer that explains why one thing happened rather than another. Interestingly, asking such questions does not presuppose the truth of indeterminism. If anything, asking such questions would appear to presuppose the truth of *determinism*; it is *more* controversial that contrastive explanation is possible if both alternatives are undetermined than if they are determined. For if things really could have gone either way given the past history, then nothing about the past history could seem to explain why things went the way they did.[38] The past history might easily explain why things going the

---

[36] See, for example, van Fraassen (1980).

[37] Barnes (1994, p. 36) and Hitchcock (1999, p. 586) respectively.

[38] See Lewis (1986/1993, pp. 197–8) for a defense of the claim that contrastive why-questions cannot be answered in the indeterministic case. See Hitchcock (1999) and Percival (2000) for responses. Nagel (1986, pp. 116–17) also suggests that contrastive why-questions cannot be answered in the indeterministic case and concludes that this is a special problem for those who hold libertarian views of free will. He suggests that in order to be free, our actions must be undetermined, but, at the same time, we must be able to give contrastive explanations of why we adopt certain reasons for doing what we actually do rather than reasons for doing otherwise. See Clarke (1996) for one response to Nagel.

way they actually did was probable; but that is not the same thing as explaining why what was probable (and *a fortiori* what was improbable) actually happened.

At the same time, it seems that certain demands for contrastive explanation are legitimate, while others are not. For example, it seems sensible to ask why Bush won the election rather than Dukakis, but not why Bush won the election rather than there never having been life on earth. In other words, some alternatives can participate together in genuine contrastive explanations, while some cannot. There is some controversy about how to distinguish the ones that can from the ones that cannot, and several criteria have been offered in the case of scientific explanation.[39] I discuss one in particular below, but it is important to note at the outset that, despite the controversy over the details, none of the main proposals on offer draws the distinction in terms of determined and undetermined alternatives.

My proposal is that when we deliberate, we take our deliberation to be the difference-maker (or explanatory nexus) among the alternatives we consider.[40] Thus, we should understand "critical nexus" as "*explanatory nexus*", that is, as what explains why we do one thing rather than another. Making this detail explicit, we get "the Explanatory Nexus Thesis":

(EN)   Rational deliberators must believe, in virtue of their nature as rational deliberators, that they have multiple alternatives from which to choose, where their deliberation is the *explanatory nexus* among those alternatives.

Fulfilling this condition does not mean that we rational deliberators have access to a clear criterion that distinguishes the scenarios for which our deliberation is the explanatory nexus and those for which it is not. Our notion of being a difference-maker is probably quite unspecific, in fact. What we learn from discussions of contrastive scientific explanation is simply that a commitment to our deliberation being a difference-maker

---

[39] See Lipton (1990/1993, especially pp. 217–18), for example. Also, see Barnes (1994) for a helpful survey of several suggested criteria, in addition to his own favored one, which I discuss below.

[40] This might be overstated. More cautious formulations include the following: As deliberators, we must take it that our deliberation *can* be the difference-maker, or as deliberators, we must take it that that our deliberation is the kind of thing that could be the difference-maker.

among a range of alternatives does not in turn require a commitment to indeterminism. And at the same time, we can see that there is room for the idea that our deliberation cannot be a difference-maker with respect to just any logically possible alternative, just as we find in the case of scientific explanation. This means that we have a model from scientific explanation that allows us to conceive of our deliberation as the difference-maker among the alternatives we consider in deliberation, and not among others. A commitment to this conception of our deliberation can then help us understand why, say, I can deliberate about whether to order an appetizer or a salad, while I cannot deliberate about whether or not to fly to the moon for dinner. The reason is that I conceive of my deliberation as capable of explaining why I order an appetizer instead of a salad, but not of why I go to a restaurant rather than the moon.

It will be useful to examine a particular suggestion about how to distinguish these sorts of cases in the context of scientific explanation. Eric Barnes suggests a criterion for evaluating "the sensibility of a why question".[41] To understand the criterion, we need just a bit of terminology. In a question of the form, "Why did P happen rather than Q?", the "fact" is what actually occurs, represented by P, whereas the "foil" is an alternative that does not occur, represented by Q. Barnes's proposal is that if the fact and foil can be viewed as culminating outcomes of some single type of natural causal process, then a question contrasting the fact and foil is sensible. If the fact and foil cannot be so viewed, then a question contrasting them is not sensible. In other words:

A class of propositions C is a contrast class just in case the propositions of C each describe culminating events of a single type of natural causal process.[42]

Thus, "why did Lewis go to Oxford rather than to Monash at time T?" is sensible, because both alternatives can be assumed to be possible outcomes of a single type of natural causal process (namely, deliberation), whereas, "why did Lewis go to Oxford rather than sneezing in a Monash museum shortly after T?" is not, because both alternatives are not assumed to be outcomes of a single type of natural causal process.

<hr />

[41] Barnes (1994, p. 50).   [42] Ibid.

The question naturally arises: "what counts as 'same type of natural causal process'?". To this, there are a variety of possible answers. Barnes considers two very general sorts: according to the first, there is some objective feature that distinguishes natural types from contrived ones, and, according to the second, there is not an objective feature of this kind, in which case the possibility of sensible contrastive explanations depends on our preferences "to think of the world in terms of certain causal processes rather than others".[43] Fortunately, I do not believe it is necessary to decide between these for our purpose here; it is sufficient to identify a coherent model of contrastive explanation that makes sense of our intuitions about cases without presupposing that difference-makers must actualize causally undetermined alternatives. No matter how we resolve the question of whether natural process types are "objective" in some sense, the model of contrastive explanation on offer treats the cases in an intuitive way—when it comes to deliberation as explanation and (other) scientific explanation. At the same time, it does so without any commitment, explicit or implicit, to indeterminism.[44]

An additional advantage for this suggestion is that it explains the appeal of other suggestions, such as the counterfactual belief constraints. Using counterfactuals is a well-known way of capturing explanatory claims, and it is easy to see how they might be used to try to cash out the idea of an explanatory nexus or difference-maker. However, seeing the Conditional Thesis as motivated by this independent idea of an explanatory nexus allows us to pursue the motivating idea while freeing us from the difficulties surrounding conditional claims.

Equally importantly, the Indeterministic Thesis could itself be confused with the idea that we must believe our deliberation is a difference-maker among our deliberative alternatives. It might be seen as one way, but as we have now seen, certainly not the only way of capturing that idea.

---

[43] Ibid.
[44] While the account in the text is of contrastive explanation, there have been several recent attempts to construe causation itself as a contrastive relation (see, for example, Maslen 2004, Northcott 2007, Schaffer 2005, and Woodward 2003). Parallel issues arise for this sort of account, including what constraints there are on legitimate contrasts. See, for example, Northcott (2007).

7: Where We Are

Each of the three families of suggested belief constraints on deliberation has something to offer.[45] The explanatory nexus view, while providing a strong motivating idea behind the Conditional Thesis, is also a view worthy of development in other directions. Here I have tried to show that there is a fruitful model for it in a kind of explanation that is both pervasive in our experience and central to our understanding of the world.

Notably, none of the belief constraints in the last three families considered requires a commitment, either implicit or explicit, to indeterminism, while each of them has the ability to account for at least some of the intuitions that the Indeterministic Thesis claims to explain. Further, even the Indeterministic Thesis may require supplementation in order to account for all deliberative failures.

There is also independent reason to resist the temptation to select a single simple rationalizing belief for deliberation. Given the complexity of the activity of deliberation, it should not be too surprising to find that a number of different commitments, perhaps operating in different situations, explain the possibility of deliberation. Take an activity that in some ways seems simpler—walking to the door. It might be that my walking to the door requires me to believe that the floor will not disappear under me (or at least that it requires my not believing that it will, or my not being certain that it will). But under other circumstances, perhaps I could consistently believe that the floor will disappear, as long as I also believe that gravity will temporarily be suspended at that moment. And we can imagine a variety of other combinations of belief that would make my walking to the door possible.[46]

The fact that it is not obvious just how "strong" or "weak" a belief constraint within a certain family should be is an interesting datum that also supports the idea that more than one belief (or lack thereof) can

---

[45] In Nelkin (2004b), I discuss another family of interpretations of DA: Abstraction versions.

[46] When it comes to purposeful, goal-directed activity, there may be commitments that must be present in every instance of that kind of activity, such as commitment to one's having a certain purpose or goal. Applied to rational deliberation, this means that one must have a commitment to one's goal in deliberating. Just what that is, in the case of rational deliberation, is a question I discuss in some detail in Nelkin (2004a).

explain deliberative failure in different situations.[47] Perhaps, as in other cases in which we are trying to do something, how much we value the outcome can affect whether we are able even to try.[48] In sum, there is independent reason to think that a variety of beliefs could explain deliberative failures and successes in different circumstances. At the same time, there being a variety of beliefs that operate under different conditions is consistent with there being minimal belief constraints that obtain in all cases of deliberation.

Where does this leave us? It is true that providing alternative explanations for the data does not refute the Indeterministic Thesis. At the same time, since there is independent reason to reject the thesis (in the form of apparently rational and thoughtful deliberating determinists among others), the alternatives contribute to the case against it. To the extent that they are plausible in themselves, are rationalized by the nature of deliberation (at least in certain circumstances), and can account for the appeal of the Indeterministic Thesis, they constitute a very strong case. I believe that each of the three families of views discussed offers belief constraints that are as plausible as the Indeterministic Thesis, and that the explanatory nexus constraint in particular, as well as all collectively, have the resources to explain at least much of the appeal of the Indeterministic Thesis. Finally, when we focus on deliberation itself, there appears to be no clearer rationale for the Indeterministic Thesis than for any of the others. Even if *freedom* were to require indeterminism, deliberation could have a point without it. It could be the difference-maker among a variety of salient alternatives, it could resolve our commitments in our own minds, and it could successfully result in our adoption of a decision on the basis of good reasons, and our acting on that basis. Thus, there is very good reason to reject the Indeterministic Thesis, and to continue to pursue fruitful alternative ways of understanding our deliberative alternatives. The more of a positive picture of our deliberative alternatives we can construct in this way, the less hold the Indeterministic Thesis can have on us, and, in turn, the less motivation there is for libertarianism about freedom.

---

[47] Recall that there are variations of each. How strong should the epistemic component be in the epistemic versions? Should the counterfactual belief constraints be understood probabilistically?

[48] See, for example, Ludwig (1992, pp. 267–8). In his view, we can try to do something we believe impossible, as long we see our action as designed to meet our end and we attach some value to that end.

7

The Sense of Freedom, or Acting under the Idea of Freedom

In the previous chapter, I argued for the plausibility of the claim that as rational deliberators we take our deliberation to be the difference-maker among multiple deliberative alternatives. Importantly, this understanding of how we conceive of our alternatives in deliberation is a competitor to the traditional understanding of deliberative alternatives as options we take to be causally open relative to the past, or causally undetermined. Adjudicating between these different ways of understanding our attitudes toward alternatives in deliberation is crucial to evaluating a major motivation of libertarianism, because if we were "natural libertarians", that is, agents who necessarily see themselves as choosing among undetermined alternatives, then at the very least there would seem to be a burden of proof on others to show that libertarianism is incorrect. Thus, I hope to have gone some way toward pushing that burden back.[1]

At the same time, those arguing for a libertarian understanding of our attitudes toward deliberative alternatives have more than just one opponent in mind; not only do they attempt to shift the burden of proof to compatibilists who reject libertarianism, they also hope to shift the burden of proof to *skeptics* who reject the idea that we are free, period. And one might wonder, now that I have adopted a non-libertarian understanding

[1] In Nelkin (2007b), I take up some of the mixed empirical evidence concerning actual human commitments. For consistent with the arguments given so far is the possibility that as *humans* we cannot shake a sense of ourselves as libertarian agents.

of our attitudes toward our deliberative alternatives, whether I have, in the process, dashed the hope of shifting any burden of proof onto the skeptic.

To put the question in a different way, we can ask whether, having offered a non-libertarian reading of DA, we now have no way to capture the idea that as deliberators we have an inescapable sense of freedom. The short answer is "no", and in this chapter I explain why. On the one hand, I concede that DA by itself, even if true on my proposal, does not entirely capture our sense of freedom. On the other hand, that is consistent with there *being* a sense of freedom that we have in virtue of our nature as rational deliberators. And it is this latter claim that I wish to defend here. In other words:

> (R)   Rational deliberators, in virtue of their very nature as rational deliberators, must represent themselves as free

is true. In this chapter, I will argue that by paying special attention to the nature of rational deliberation, we can see that engaging in it does commit us to our own freedom.

In section 2, I begin by further elaborating the way I understand rational deliberation, and in section 3, I set out and explain the nature of our commitment to our own freedom. In section 4, I spell out the argument for our having the particular commitment we do, and in section 5, I consider objections and replies, allowing for an elaboration of the argument.

1: Rational Deliberation

As we saw earlier, I understand rational deliberation to be a goal-directed activity, one aimed by the agent at the evaluation of reasons with a view to deciding and acting. The culmination of rational deliberation is the adoption, on the basis of one's evaluation, of certain reasons *as* one's reasons for performing an action, and the consequent decision so to act.

As we have begun to see, this understanding of deliberation differs from other conceptions along a number of dimensions. Hobbes, for one, seems to understand deliberation as something that happens to the agent. As he puts it:

When in the mind of man appetites and aversions, hopes and fears, concerning one and the same thing arise alternately, and diverse good and evil consequences of the doing or omitting the thing propounded come successively into our thoughts, so that sometimes we have an appetite to it, sometimes an aversion from it ... ; the whole sum of desires, aversions, hopes and fears, continued till the thing be either done or thought impossible, is that we call DELIBERATION.[2]

In contrast, I take deliberation to be an activity, directed by the agent toward a goal. More recently, Galen Strawson has described a case of deliberation that has some things in common (although not all) with Hobbes' view. Describing the rational deliberation of an imaginary being, the Spectator, he writes that she is "experientially detached from her desires—from her motivations generally—in some curious way" (1986, p. 234). For her rational deliberation is a series of "practical-rational calculations going on in" a person in such a way that the person need have no sense that *she* is the decider and rational planner of action (p. 235). Although for Strawson this is an anomalous case of rational deliberation, it seems to reveal a divergence between his conception and my own. For it seems possible to be passive insofar as deliberation is a set of calculations "going on" rather than being an activity directed by the agent. Strawson suggests at an earlier point that "practical reasoning is itself plausibly seen as an *activity*, in certain cases at least ... " (p. 130) but does not commit himself to this position, writing that, given that it is being allowed that "dogs can act" it might "become questionable to what extent mental practical reasoning is an activity, in the sense of something intentionally directed, given the notion of practical rationality that would emerge (p. 131). Now Strawson accepts that *qua* human beings, we are committed to the (false) proposition that we are free; but not that all rational deliberators are. My argument to the contrary that follows depends explicitly on a conception of rational deliberation that is active.

Yet other conceptions of deliberation de-emphasize the adoption of reasons for action. As we saw in chapter 6, Coffman and Warfield, for example, take deliberation to be "the attempt to choose what to do from among a number of incompatible courses of action ... " and explicitly leave out of deliberation the weighing of reasons. In allowing for more creatures to qualify as deliberators, their view has something in common

---

[2] (1668/1994, p. 33). For a detailed explication of Hobbes' view (among other seventeenth century thinkers on the will and motivation), see Rickless (forthcoming).

with Strawson's; but in taking deliberation to be active and in leaving out reasons, their view diverges from his.

In the end, there might very well be a variety of cognitive processes that can go by the name "rational deliberation". I am interested in showing that engaging in one specific kind of these commits us to our own freedom. Whether or not we share these sophisticated cognitive abilities to weigh and adopt reasons with other beings, it is an important question whether being rational deliberators of this kind brings with it a certain self-conception as free and responsible agents.

2: The Sense of Freedom Explained

The Sense of "Freedom"

To explain the sense of "freedom" in the type of reading of (R) I favor, it will be useful to return to some terminology from John Rawls, and distinguish between the *concept* of freedom and particular *conceptions* of freedom.[3] First, there is a concept of freedom that all (or at least many) people grasp, even if, as we've seen, they disagree as to the necessary and sufficient conditions for its instantiation. There must be such a concept if compatibilists, incompatibilists, and those who believe freedom impossible are rightly said to disagree. Of course, it is possible to argue that the whole problem with the free will debate is that the participants are indeed speaking different languages, and that agreement could be reached immediately if this fact were only acknowledged. I do not believe the debate is so easily dissolved, however. Rather there is a single concept about which there is disagreement.

Second, as we have also seen, there are different analyses of freedom offered (such as the ability to choose from among various undetermined actions or the ability to act in accordance with good reasons). These are *conceptions* of freedom, attempts to spell out in detail the conditions under which actions are free.

It is easy to describe various conceptions of freedom, then. But what is the concept of freedom? In my view, the concept of free agency is the notion of one's actions being up to one in such a way that one is, in a basic sense, responsible or accountable for them.

---

[3] Rawls (1971, p. 5).

This account must be clarified in various ways. First, let me emphasize that in identifying the concept of freedom in this way, I mean to suggest that the mutual implication between "free" and "being up to one in such a way that one is accountable" should be recognized by anyone in possession of the concept of freedom. Second, as we have seen, it is also very important that "responsible" and "accountable" not be read as "*morally* responsible" and "*morally* accountable", despite the fact that the former locutions are often used as shorthand for the latter. I think that we have a more basic notion of responsibility (or accountability) that underlies various *kinds* of responsibility: responsibility for one's productivity and creativity, moral responsibility, and so on. Responsibility in this basic sense is a necessary, but not sufficient, condition for moral responsibility. The reason is that moral responsibility requires certain sorts of understanding and knowledge, both general and particular. But this does not mean that the concept of freedom I have characterized is a weak notion. It captures what is traditionally known as the "freedom" condition for moral responsibility, while leaving open the question of how to characterize the "knowledge" condition.

I believe that this concept remains neutral as among various particular conceptions of freedom. To see this, consider that libertarian agent causationists argue that if one's actions are to be up to one in this way, they must be indeterministically agent-caused.[4] Alternatively, some argue that if one's actions are to be up to one in this way, they must be determined by one's valuational judgments.[5] The first of these views requires the truth of indeterminism, while the second does not.

Now some might argue that the true concept of freedom is *not* in fact neutral, and that the concept of freedom just is the notion that "one could have done otherwise" or that "one is the undetermined source of one's actions". Yet, there have been a large number of attempts to provide such conditions that do not allude to having the ability to do otherwise, or being undetermined. If the concept of freedom were the notion that one can do otherwise, then it would seem that agreement as to the entailment between freedom and the ability to do otherwise, or indeterminism, would be readily forthcoming. The fact that many who have attempted to provide necessary and sufficient conditions for freedom have not

---

[4] See, for example, Chisholm (1964), and O'Connor (2000).
[5] See Watson (1975/2004).

granted the point suggests that the concept of freedom is not simply the notion that one can do otherwise or that indeterminism is true. Further, even if we were to accept the point of the objection for the sake of argument, we can still accept that the notion I have described is an important condition for moral and other sorts of responsibility.[6] Thus, if it can be shown that we must represent ourselves as free in the sense that I have described, that would be a significant result.

Finally, the concept I have described satisfies widely accepted constraints on the notion of freedom that is at the heart of the free will debate. For example, philosophers often claim that the notion of freedom in which they are interested is a notion that applies to persons, but not to many non-human animals who are thought not to be persons.[7] That is, there is a sense in which the actions of humans can be up to them, or be their own, in a way that the actions of a spider cannot. Since the notion of accountability might be thought to be limited in its applicability in such a way as to exclude many non-human animals, the concept that I have described matches this widely accepted feature of freedom. The readings I will consider in what follows take "free" in (R) to pick out the concept of freedom. Hence, they are "conception-neutral".[8]

The Sense of "Sense"

There are a number of different ways one might understand "sense" in the "sense of freedom", including "feeling", "appearance", "belief", and

---

[6] In this connection, see Jackson (1998): "I find compelling Peter van Inwagen's argument that [...] determinism is inconsistent with free will. What compatibilist arguments show, or so it seems to me, is [...] that free action on a conception near enough to the folk's [i.e., common-sense] to be regarded as a natural extension of it, and which does the theoretical job we folk give the concept of free action in adjudicating questions of moral responsibility and punishment, and in governing our attitudes to the actions of those around us, is compatible with determinism" (pp. 44–5). Although the concept that I offer is neutral as between compatibilism and incompatibilism, the spirit of Jackson's point applies to it, as well. Even if one doubts that the concept I offer is *the* concept of freedom, one can still accept that it can do the theoretical work we want it to do, including supporting our attributions of moral responsibility.

[7] See, for example, Frankfurt (1971).

[8] Bok (1998) has defended what might naturally be thought of as an explicitly compatibilist reading of (R). In particular, she argues that being practical reasoners gives us reason to regard ourselves as free in a compatibilist sense. We are free in the relevant sense when we can determine our conduct through practical reasoning, and we have genuine alternatives among which we can choose, where genuine alternatives are those actions we would perform *if we chose to perform them*. See especially pp. 118–19.

"rational commitment". I begin by arguing that the sense of freedom in (R) is an epistemic commitment, or belief, that one is free. It does not follow from this reading that all rational deliberators can articulate their commitment without considerable probing and reflection; but it does follow that they actually represent themselves as free. In this respect, it is like the Indeterministic Thesis reading of (R). In what follows, I call the conception-neutral reading that understands "sense" in this way the "Belief-Concept" reading. I also consider a weaker reading of (R) according to which the sense of freedom is a rational commitment that one is free. Roughly, one is rationally committed to a proposition when reflection and recognition of features of one's own mental states and reasoning is sufficient for one's believing that proposition. But one need not actually believe that one is free in order to be rationally committed to the proposition. I call the reading of (R) that incorporates both the conception-neutral reading of "free" and the rational commitment reading of "sense", the "Commitment-Concept" reading. Although I believe that there is good reason to accept the Belief-Concept reading, it is true that even weaker premises are needed to support the Commitment-Concept reading, and thus, that the latter requires less in the way of defense. At the same time, as I will explain, both readings can do powerful explanatory and justificatory work.

3: An Argument for the Belief-Concept Reading

Now that this reason has causality, or that we can at least represent something of the sort in it, it is clear from the **imperatives** that we propose as rules to our powers of execution in everything practical. The **ought** expresses a species of necessity and a connection with grounds which does not occur anywhere else in the whole of nature.[9]

We can begin by focusing once again on the nature of rational deliberation. Given the nature of rational deliberation described earlier, deliberators are the sorts of beings who have a guiding conception of their purpose when they perform intentional, goal-directed actions. Further, it is important to note that they have a sense of their purpose whether or not they explicitly deliberate about what to do. For example, if a rational

---

[9] Kant (1781/1997, A547/B575, p. 540).

deliberator is engaged in seeking the latest international news, then she has a conception of the goal that defines her activity. If she does not conceive herself to be seeking the latest news, then whatever activity in which she is engaged, she is not seeking the news. This point applies to rational deliberation itself. Here, too, one need not be able to articulate one's purpose in deliberating without considerable reflection, but one must have a conception of one's purpose when one deliberates, namely, that of finding, adopting and acting on good reasons.

Accepting this point depends crucially on an understanding of the nature of rational deliberation as an activity directed by the agent toward a particular goal. The fact that a set of mental states constitutes a genuine piece of rational deliberation is determined not merely by the content of those states (for example, "R is a reason to do action A"), and not merely by the fact that they tend to issue in action. It is also essential that the deliberator be *thereby* attempting to accomplish something, namely, the adoption of good reasons as her own. This requires that the deliberator have a guiding sense that her activity is aimed at this goal.[10]

Now if rational deliberators have a conception of themselves as seeking to adopt and act on good reasons, then they must take themselves to be capable, in general, of finding such reasons. This claim is independently plausible, but I believe it derives additional support from its being explained. Implicit in the sense of purpose that guides their intentional, goal-directed actions is a commitment to a plan (however incomplete) to achieve it. Yet if one does not view one's purpose as attainable, then one cannot envision a plan for its implementation. In other words, in order to have a guiding conception about *how* one can achieve one's purpose, one must believe *that* one can.[11] It is not necessary for deliberators to believe that they must succeed on each occasion of deliberation; but they must believe that they have the ability to succeed in at least some typical situations. In other words, they must believe that they are the sort of

---

[10] Strawson's rejection of (R) may ultimately rest on an understanding of rational deliberation that differs from mine on just this point.

[11] Adams (1995, p. 552) develops a similar idea. Adams there argues that all intentional action requires an attempt, and that trying to perform an action requires the lack of a belief that success is impossible. Thus, it would seem to follow that intentional action requires the lack of a belief that success is impossible. Sometimes Adams also seems to endorse the stronger claim that intentional action requires the belief in the possibility of success (see pp. 553–4, for example). And the stronger claim fits well with his reasoning that intentional action requires that one have beliefs about how to achieve one's end.

being who, by engaging in the activity of rational deliberation, can succeed in finding and adopting good reasons for acting. Otherwise, it would not be possible to conceive of their activity as constituting a way of achieving their purpose. Thus, rational deliberators must take themselves to be the sorts of beings who can and do sometimes find, adopt, and act on good reasons.

If this is the case, then rational deliberators must believe that there are good reasons to be found, adopted, and acted upon. In other words, they must believe that there are reasons they ought to act upon. But if one is the sort of being to whom such "ought-statements" apply and one takes as one's aim their fulfillment, then one's actions can be rationally justified or unjustified. And that one's actions are potential objects of this sort of justification is the way in which one can be accountable for one's actions.

At this point, the question arises whether rational deliberators must believe that they are accountable simply because they believe that there are reasons upon which they ought to act. Of course, it is not true in general that an agent must believe the consequent of a true entailment when she believes the antecedent. But this is a special case. There is a tight conceptual connection between the idea of there being reasons one ought to adopt and act on, and the idea of one's being accountable; it seems that in order to see oneself as the sort of being to whom such reasons apply, one must see oneself as the sort of being who is accountable for his or her actions.[12]

Further, as we saw in chapter 6, one must see one's own deliberative activity itself, one's adoption of reasons and action on their basis *as* the difference-maker among one's alternatives. We can see, then, how one must believe that one's actions are up to one in such a way that one is accountable for them: one believes that one's actions can be performed as a result of one's own adopted reasons and, further, that they are potential objects of rational justification. Thus, by identifying essential features of

---

[12] As Burge (1979) has pointed out, one might have "incomplete mastery" of a concept, have false beliefs about even some of the essential properties of its instances, and yet have genuine beliefs employing the concept, nevertheless. For example, one might believe that one suffers from arthritis, even if one believes it is not a disease of the joints. However, it may be that there are certain true beliefs that one cannot lack, and still be said to have the concept. The case at hand appears to be of this kind: it is constitutive of having the concept of having reasons that one believe one ought to act in certain ways if one has reasons to act.

rational deliberation, we can see why deliberators must have a sense of themselves as free (in the conception-neutral sense).

4: Objections, Replies, and Elaboration

At this point, a number of questions might be raised about this line of reasoning and addressing them will allow for elaboration of the view.

Rational Deliberation's Purpose

One natural question is whether rational deliberators can take their activity to have a different purpose from the one I identify. In particular, can rational deliberators who come to believe that they are not free continue to deliberate while taking themselves to have a different purpose in doing so? For example, they might take the purpose of their deliberation to be to achieve the maximal satisfaction of their desires, or to increase the beauty in the world by being a passive receptor of reasons.

Although this objection has some force, I believe that its force can be defused by focusing once again on the nature of deliberation. It is compatible with the reasoning above that rational deliberators take their activity to have more than one point or purpose. The claim that those engaged in rational deliberation take their activity to have as its purpose their acting for good reasons is perfectly consistent with the claim that they also take that activity to have an additional, or further, point. For example, a rational deliberator might be asked to deliberate and decide on a course of action as part of her participation in a researcher's psychological experiment. In deliberating, she might have as her purpose to please the researcher, but if she follows the researcher's instructions to the letter, she must also take as her purpose to act for good reasons. In order to do so, she must take it that her deliberation can be efficacious and that there are reasons on the basis of which she *should* act. Hence, as I argued earlier, she must have a sense that she is free. The fact that one can imagine a rational deliberator taking her activity to have any of a number of different points does not show that rational deliberators can avoid taking their activity to have the point of acting on the basis of good reasons.[13]

---

[13] Along lines similar to objections in the text, it might be argued that in rationally deliberating, one is sometimes guided only by the purpose of finding the best thing to do. Yet, as I argued earlier, if one's activity toward the goal of finding the best thing to do is to

Further, in addition to consulting our intuitions about the nature of rational deliberation in the abstract (as I have so far been urging us to do), it is useful to consider in more concrete terms the question of whether rational deliberators must take deliberation to have a particular purpose. To this end, consider our own behavior when we believe that there are no good reasons for acting in a certain way. For example, suppose you are at an ice cream shop, having decided to buy an ice cream cone. You believe that all the flavors are equally good. You don't generally deliberate in such circumstances, but simply pick a flavor at random. On my view, the reason for your lack of deliberation in such a case is that you see no point to deliberating. We see no point in engaging in the evaluation of reasons for acting when we think that there is no reason that we should act in a particular way. We are not in a position in which we could act for good reasons in choosing a flavor of ice cream, hence we see no point to deliberating, and so do not engage in it.

This thought experiment—together with the investigation into the nature of goal-directed intentional activity I sketched earlier—strongly suggests that the very activity of rational deliberation manifests the sense that there is a point or purpose to the activity. Further, these considerations suggest that rational deliberation manifests the sense that the point of one's activity is to decide and ultimately to act on the basis of good reasons.

Purpose and Possibility

At this point, a second objection might naturally arise: even if one has a conception of the purpose of one's activity, one need not believe that one's purpose can be achieved in order to be rational in engaging in it. In what follows, I defend the idea that one must believe that one has the general ability to succeed in order to have a conception of one's purpose in performing goal-directed intentional actions. There is a long history of controversy on this and related questions, and I cannot do full justice to it here.[14] But I will suggest one approach to it in the context of defending

---

constitute genuine rational deliberation (as opposed to other activities that might aim at that goal, such as making a sacrifice to the gods), one must also be guided by the purpose of finding good reasons for acting.

[14] For a small sampling of the literature on the connections among intentional action, intention, and belief, see Davidson (1985), who argues that intentional action requires the belief that one can succeed; Grice (1971), Harman (1976), and Velleman (1985), who argue that having an intention requires the stronger belief (or acceptance, in the case of Grice) that

a key premise in the reasoning for the Belief-Concept reading. Let me begin by emphasizing that I am not relying on the claim that one must believe one can succeed on every occasion. Rather the claim is that one must believe one can succeed in typical circumstances when one attempts the relevant type of action. This point might be sufficient to defuse the present worry about the Belief-Concept reading. For as I hope to show, those on both sides of the debate over the connection between intentional action and belief might be able to find agreement once this point is noted.

In thinking about the relation between intentional action and belief, intuitions about examples play an important role. Here is an example that provides support for the idea that one must believe one can achieve one's purpose, when one has a conception of it in acting intentionally: I cannot intentionally engage in any activity that might be described as either flying or trying to fly, no matter how much I desire to and how much I flap my arms. The natural explanation seems to be that I do not believe it possible for me to fly. In fact, I believe that I lack the general ability to fly. I can imagine circumstances in which someone else tries to fly. But these circumstances include delusions on the part of the person making the attempt. If someone were to believe that his physical abilities were very different from what they are, or that the laws of aerodynamics or gravity were different from what they are, then he could try to fly. (Of course, this would require a great number of changes in one's belief system and probably a great deal of irrationality.) Here, it seems that what explains the difference between this person and me is the difference between our beliefs about what our flapping our arms could possibly accomplish.

Those who argue against a necessary connection between belief and intentional action offer examples on the other side. Kirk Ludwig offers the following, among others:[15] Playing basketball, a friend insists that I can make a basket from half-court. I believe it impossible for me to make a basket from that distance, and set out to show him that even if I try as hard

---

one *will* succeed; and Bratman (1986), who argues that (normally) having an intention and being rational requires that one not believe that one will not succeed. Many have argued against one or more of these claims. For example, McCann (1986) argues against them all. Ludwig (1992) and (1995) also argues against all of these claims, and goes one step further. He defends the claim that one can be rational in both intending and acting intentionally even though one believes that one *cannot* succeed. I am grateful to Kirk Ludwig for an e-mail correspondence about his view. For a survey of some recent literature, see section 5 of Setiya (Spring 2010).

[15] See Ludwig (1992, p. 263).

as I can, I still can't do it. I try, and, amazingly, make the basket. This appears to be a case in which I intentionally succeed without believing that it is possible. According to Ludwig, my intentionally making the basket in this case shows that I also intended and tried to make it before surprising myself with my success. Since I have argued that rational deliberators engaged in intentional goal-directed activity have a sense of their purpose, the case seems to be one in which the sense of purpose is not accompanied by a belief that it can be achieved.

Reasons might be offered to resist this example and others like it, but what is more important for our purposes here is the kind of example it is (and is not). For even those who argue that intentional action does not require the belief that success is possible agree that there are some things one cannot intentionally do (or even try to do), like flying or making a basket from ten miles away. Some explanation for this fact is required.

Ludwig, for example, acknowledges that you could not try to hit a home-run by holding the bat in a "bunt" position.[16] Why not? The reason, according to Ludwig, is that this stance and the limited motion it permits are not *designed* to bring about the end of hitting home-runs. In cases like this in which one intentionally performs an action without believing that one can succeed, one might recognize that circumstances are special in such a way that one's activity cannot succeed. This is a cashing out of the idea that in order to act intentionally, one must conceive one's actions as of a type designed to bring about a certain end.

If this is right, then we have a way to distinguish between the cases of making a basket from half-court and swinging "all-out" for a home-run on the one hand, and making a basket from Mars and a home-run from a "bunt" position on the other. The view also suggests that we assume that when we act intentionally our actions are of a type that, under at least some typical circumstances, can succeed. Further, there is a rationale for this: if one views a certain kind of activity as one some of whose typical instances are successful in achieving their purposes, then one can have a conception of *how* they are successful. This makes it possible for us to envision our own activity of this type as a way of implementing a plan to achieve its purpose.[17]

---

[16] See Ludwig (1995, pp. 566–8).

[17] Albritton (1985) argues that one can try to do what one believes is impossible, but, like Ludwig, also recognizes the need to account for cases like the flying case. For example, he

Admittedly, it is difficult to give criteria for "type" of action here. But I think it is possible to rely on an intuitive idea. I can't try to fly, or make a home-run from the bunt position, because these are not the kinds of actions at which I could succeed under anything like normal circumstances. I must believe that I have the general ability to succeed, if I have a sense of my purpose in acting.[18]

This conclusion is all that is needed in order to defend the Belief-Concept reading of (R) from the present objection. For even if one need not believe that one can succeed on a particular occasion of deliberation, one must believe that one has the general ability to succeed, and one must take it that one's activity will be successful under at least some typical circumstances. Otherwise, one won't be able to view one's engagement in the activity as counting as a way of achieving the purpose of adopting good reasons for acting. Thus, one must believe that one is free in the conception-neutral sense.

Is Rational Deliberation Too Hard?

It might be argued that, according to this reasoning, rational deliberation requires too much in the way of conceptual development and self-reflection. We saw earlier that others have offered weaker accounts of

---

agrees that there are certain things he cannot try to do, including trying to jump over a building and even trying to do fifty push-ups. His explanation for this fact is that "in his present cognitive position and state of mind that description of him [as trying] would be inept whatever he did", and "It's that nothing I can think of to do this evening would be rightly *described* as trying to jump over this building, in a straightforward sense, unless, for example, my beliefs were to alter or go very dim" (p. 245). It seems to me that something important must be contained in the phrases, "present cognitive position" and "my beliefs". It is tempting to take them to include the lack of belief that success is possible or the lack of belief that one has the general ability to perform these kinds of actions.

[18] One consequence of this reasoning is that there is a certain kind of irrationality in simultaneously being a rational deliberator and a "practical reasons-nihilist" or even a skeptic about practical reasons. Against this, it might be argued that a skeptic about reasons could rationally deliberate (and be perfectly rational) simply by seeking reasons *if* they happen to exist. In reply, as argued earlier, one could not deliberate if one lacked the belief that one can succeed in at least *some* typical situations; otherwise, one would lack a conception of what one was doing in deliberating. Since deliberation requires such a conception, one must believe that one can sometimes succeed in finding reasons for acting. Importantly, this leaves open the possibility of a rational skepticism about the possibility of finding reasons on a particular occasion. See also Burge (1998) for a different argument that finds a similar, albeit more general, target in a broad reasons-skepticism. Burge argues persuasively that in order for one to fully understand reasons, "one must be susceptible to reasons", and "one must recognize" the effect of reasons on one's judgments and inferences (p. 250).

deliberation that did not require these sorts of cognitive tools, for example.[19] Young children and non-human animals would appear to be counterexamples to the reasoning for the Belief-Concept reading of (R), on such conceptions of rational deliberation, since they include rational deliberators who lack mental state and related concepts (for example, "action", "reasons", and "responsibility") and those who have not reflected on the purpose of their activity. In a different way, psychopaths pose a problem on this reading of (R), because insofar as they seem to lack relevant concepts, as well, they would also then be precluded from being rational deliberators. But that is highly implausible. Let us briefly consider the first sort of apparent counterexample—children and non-human animals—first.

I believe that the initial appeal of these cases fades when we are clear on the nature of rational deliberation. As elaborated earlier, deliberation is itself a very sophisticated cognitive activity: the consideration and evaluation of reasons with a view to deciding to act, where one's decision is based on one's evaluation and adoption of reasons as one's reasons for performing an action. Once this is understood, it becomes difficult to maintain that young children and non-human animals provide counterexamples to the claim that all rational deliberators must have the concept of reasons, for example. For the cognitive sophistication required to engage in rational deliberation itself would seem to rule out at least some members of these groups, and, in particular, the very same members who are excluded from possession of sophisticated concepts such as reasons.

Turn now to psychopaths. It seems clear that they are rational deliberators, but because they lack reactive attitudes, one might wonder whether they have a robust sense of freedom associated with moral responsibility. In fact, it is plausible that they do. To see why, recall that the sense of freedom is not the same thing as a sense of moral responsibility. It is true that the notion of freedom is meant to capture the freedom condition for moral responsibility. But it is not a moral notion in itself. This, I believe, is a virtue of the account here. For it is plausible that psychopaths do have a sense of their own freedom, even if they do not, and cannot, have a sense of themselves as morally responsible agents. For they lack moral understanding. It seems that they do not, therefore, take

---

[19] See Coffman and Warfield (2005) and Strawson (1986), for examples.

themselves to be accountable based on *moral* standards, and cannot understand moral reasoning. Nevertheless, it takes a great deal of cognitive sophistication to be able to recognize and adopt reasons, and to evaluate them with an aim to so act. But this is a set of skills that, perhaps for the worse, psychopaths possess.

Is Belief Too Strong?

Finally, there are many different accounts of what it is to believe something. There are disputes, for example, about whether having a belief requires actual representation and manipulation in one's mind.[20] And one might argue, on the basis of a demanding standard for belief, that it would be too much to demand representation of the proposition that we are free in the conception-neutral sense in order to deliberate. Without entering the debate over the nature of belief, I will instead show that even if lingering doubts remain about the strength of the Belief-Concept reading of (R), it is possible to adopt a weaker conception-neutral reading without giving up much of the explanatory and justificatory role of (R).

According to the Commitment-Concept reading, rational deliberators are rationally committed, in virtue of being rational deliberators, to their being free. They need not actually believe that they are free, but they are in a state such that mere reflection and recognition of features of their own mental states and activity would suffice for the beliefs in question. To reach this weaker conclusion, each premise of the reasoning for the Belief-Concept reading of (R) might be weakened in such a way as to incorporate rational commitment in place of belief, and thus, to require less in the way of self-reflection than the reasoning for the Belief-Concept reading. Equally importantly, the Commitment-Concept reading of (R) can do much of the work that the Belief-Concept reading can do. For it can explain the centrality of the belief that one is free for those (like us) who have reflected on the matter. And it can also play a powerful role in arguments like Reid's and Kant's that we are in fact free. To take the simplest example, Reid's burden-of-proof argument set out earlier does not seem to lose much of its force when we substitute "rational commitment" for "conviction". Thus, even if we adopt the

---

[20] See, for example, Schwitzgebel (2008).

Commitment-Concept reading of (R) over the Belief-Concept reading, (R) remains an important thesis.

Practical Deliberation and Theoretical Deliberation

Before concluding, it remains to consider one final objection that will allow us to follow out some important implications for the relationship between two different kinds of deliberation. Unlike the others, this one does not question the reasoning for the Belief-Concept reading of (R), but instead questions the meaning and significance of the conclusion. The objection is that once we see that freedom in the conception-neutral sense is closely tied to the ability to act for good reasons, it is not clear that the notion of freedom in the conception-neutral readings of (R) is really the concept of freedom after all. The quality of "being chosen, or up to us" seems to fade into the background, while the notion of rational capacity can be seen to undergird the conception-neutral notion of freedom described.

The objection can be pressed in the following way: consider theoretical deliberation, or the deliberation about what to believe. ("Practical deliberation" is then understood in contrast to theoretical deliberation; practical deliberation is what I have been calling "rational deliberation", which is deliberation about what to do.) When engaged in theoretical deliberation, it is reasonable to suppose that we are committed to our being able to believe (or judge) for good reasons. But there is nothing like a true sense of freedom associated with theoretical deliberation; to the contrary, we do not choose our judgments as we do many of our actions. So perhaps the sense of freedom as I have characterized it is not really the sense of freedom that seems intuitively associated with deliberation about what to do.

This objection relies on two key claims. On the one hand, it relies on the claim that

(1) Exactly the same reasoning that we used to derive the commitment claimed to be a genuine sense of freedom from certain features of deliberation about what to do can be used to derive the same commitment from the same features of deliberation about what to judge or believe.

At the same time, the challenge continues, surely

(2) Theoretical deliberation about what to do does not entail a genuine sense of freedom, and, in particular, not the commitment that many try to capture when deriving it from practical deliberation about what to do.

Therefore, the challenge concludes, whatever it is I derived earlier from practical deliberation about what to do cannot be the genuine sense of freedom I was aiming at. In the end, I will reject (1) on the grounds that there is no perfect parallel to the reasoning in the practical deliberation case that can be applied in the case of theoretical deliberation. At the same time, there is truth to be found in the vicinity, for there is an *imperfect* parallel. Theoretical deliberation, no less than practical deliberation, yields important commitments, some of which overlap with those delivered by practical deliberation.

Before we can go further, we need to become clearer about what theoretical deliberation is. Since the objection assumes that there is such a thing, and that it parallels practical deliberation about what to do, a natural first suggestion is this: just as rational deliberation about what to do is activity aimed at adoption of reasons and decision to act on their basis, theoretical deliberation is activity aimed at adoption of reasons and decision to believe on their basis. But, as Williams famously claimed, and Shah and Velleman have recently reminded us, "deciding what to believe is notoriously impossible" (2005, p. 502). Still, as they point out, even if it is impossible to *decide* what to believe, the activity can aim at judgment itself, even if not at deciding as an intermediate step. Thus, deliberation about what to believe is reasoning designed to issue in belief on a subject based on good reasons.[21] Let us take this as a working understanding of deliberation about what to believe.

Now we can look more closely at the challenge at hand, and at (1) and (2) in particular.

Some epistemologists have made claims that support the denial of (2), insofar as they explicitly associate freedom with deliberation about what to believe.[22] On this view, it is easy to conclude that we are committed to

---

[21] This understanding is similar to that of Shah and Velleman who write that "deliberating whether to believe constitutes deliberation . . . simply because it is reasoning aimed at issuing or not issuing in a belief in accordance with the norm for believing" (2005, p. 506). Of course, not everyone takes it to be obvious that one cannot decide to believe.

[22] See Ryan (2003), Steup (2001), and Chisholm (1968/1977).

our freedom in both theoretical and practical deliberation. The substantial literature (both contemporary and historical) on deontology in epistemology is also especially interesting in this regard. Epistemological deontologists take justification of belief to be a matter of believing what one ought. On many variants of this general view, denying (2) becomes a live option since associated notions of freedom, control, praise, and blame are taken to be essentially connected with justified (or unjustified) belief. If, indeed, as seems plausible, we ought to believe certain things and not others, we must be free to do so, goes one line of reasoning.

John McDowell, in an influential passage, writes that

Judging, making up our minds what to think, is something for which we are, in principle, responsible—something we freely do, as opposed to something that merely happens in our lives. Of course, a belief is not always, or even typically, a result of our exercising this freedom to decide what to think. But even when a belief is not freely adopted, it is an actualization of capacities of a kind, the conceptual, whose paradigmatic mode of actualization is in the exercise of freedom that judging is. This freedom, exemplified in responsible acts of judging, is essentially a matter of being answerable to criticism in the light of rationally relevant considerations. So the realm of freedom, at least the realm of the freedom of judging, can be identified with the space of reasons.[23]

William Alston, who in the end rejects the deontological conception of justification of belief, finds the picture "natural" and understands it in terms of "obligation, permission, requirement, blame, and the like" (1988, p. 258).

Further, as epistemic deontologists point out, there are other apparent parallels between belief and action. We demand that people answer for their beliefs, just as much as for their actions, and we find it intelligible and appropriate to say that "I should not have come to that conclusion" or that "I should have realized that . . . ".[24] We blame people for their beliefs as much as for their actions. Consider someone who holds racist beliefs, in the face of good evidence against their truth, for example.[25]

---

[23] McDowell (1998, p. 434).

[24] See Watson (2003/2004, p. 150).

[25] See Adams (1985) for an argument that we can indeed be blameworthy for such attitudes (while at the same time, in his view, they are involuntary). See also Montmarquet (1993) for an argument that blameworthiness for action derives ultimately (most of the time?) from blameworthiness for beliefs.

Of course, not everyone is a deontologist about justification, and some, including Alston, reject the deontological position precisely because they believe that it would require our having freedom with respect to our beliefs (which they in turn deny is possible).[26] And even among those who do count themselves as deontologists, there are an interesting variety of views on what being a deontologist about the justification of belief requires. There are some who believe that all of freedom, control, voluntariness, up-to-oneness, praise, and blame, are also appropriately attributed to believers.[27] Others make do with less, accepting that epistemic justification entails epistemic responsibility, but denying, say, that this in turn requires freedom or even voluntariness.[28]

Yet others reject the idea that freedom comes with belief. A common line of reasoning for this view appeals to the idea that we lack control over our beliefs. After all, as Plantinga writes:

Driving down the road I am confronted with what appears to be an approaching automobile; it is ordinarily not, in such a case, up to me whether I believe that there is an automobile approaching… (1993, p. 24)

As Owens puts it, "In the end, it is the world that determines what I believe, not me", and once we decide to attend to the evidence, "the evidence takes over and I lose control" (2000, p. 12). Thus, in opposition to those who infer freedom from the obligation to believe, this kind of reasoning infers a lack of freedom from a fundamental passivity or lack of control when it comes to believing.

Claims like Plantinga's and Owens' are certainly initially plausible, but I think the conclusion that there is no control when it comes to belief is too hastily arrived at. Even in the realm of action, having control is not understood as being in contrast to receptivity to reasons; it is precisely in

---

[26] See Plantinga (1993) and Alston (1988), cited in Feldman (2001). See also Ryan (2003) for a helpful survey of such views, including a critical evaluation of them.

[27] See Steup (2001); McDowell (1998); Montmarquet (1993).

[28] Feldman (2001), for example, offers an interesting variant of the deontological position, according to which epistemic "oughts" are best understood as role "oughts" (similar to the oughts that apply to parents qua parents, or gardeners qua gardeners). He rejects the idea that belief is voluntary in the way that action is. Owens (2000) offers a book length defense of the view that justification requires responsibility, but that responsibility does not in turn require control. See also Adams (1985), Hieronymi (2008), and Smith, A. (2005) who are not immediately concerned with justification, but are concerned to show that we can be responsible for a variety of attitudes without their being voluntary.

virtue of being sensitive to reasons that we take ourselves to have control. Taking control is a matter of bringing one's own faculties to bear on the reasons there are. It is true that sometimes reasons seem utterly decisive (as in Plantinga's driving case, for example). But this is sometimes the case when it comes to action, too. Watson vividly illustrates the latter when he points out that he takes himself to be powerless to form the intention to lop off his leg, given his other commitments, albeit without any loss of either control or agency.[29] Doxastic control, according to Watson, just is "being determined, in accordance with some 'belief-relevant norms', by the 'world'" (2003/2004, p. 144).

So far, then, we have seen a line of reasoning that moves from similarities in belief and action, particularly with respect to the obligations we have in both spheres, to the idea that we have freedom in both spheres, as well. We have also seen a line of reasoning that moves from a seeming passivity and lack of control with respect to belief, to the idea that freedom is lacking in that sphere. At the same time, despite the appeal of examples like Plantinga's driving one, it is not obvious that control is really lacking. This does not settle the question of whether the same freedom is associated with belief and action, but it does provide reasons to keep the question open.

Before continuing to evaluate this debate, it is worth stepping back for a moment and seeing how it is related to our question about whether we are committed to freedom in theoretical deliberation. For, so far, we have entered the debate about belief and freedom quite generally; we have not attended specifically to *our beliefs about* our freedom to believe, let alone our beliefs formed as the result of deliberation in particular. In other words, we have not yet focused on the beliefs or commitments we form as the result of being theoretical deliberators. It is worth noting two points in this connection. First, the best case for a lack of control over beliefs would seem to be the more spontaneous cases like Plantinga's driving case. So if even in these cases it turns out to be harder to

---

[29] See also Ryan (2003) who compares some belief acquisition to this choice: "I am given a choice of a cup of fresh and delicious pumpkin soup or a cup of one-month-old lima bean and raw calf's liver stew for dinner . . . " (p. 73). She takes herself to have only one option she can take seriously, and writes that "my selection of the soup was causally determined by a lot of things including my intention to pick the pumpkin soup, my severe aversion to liver and lima beans, my commitment to vegetarianism, my fear of illness, the laws of nature, and a lot of other things . . . ". See also Ginet (2001).

say that we have control, it seems at least an open question whether we have control over beliefs formed as the outcome of deliberation. Second, so far, while we have been discussing the connection between justified belief and freedom, we have not directly examined the relationship between theoretical deliberation and the *commitment* to freedom. These two questions are connected, however. For if the aim of theoretical deliberation is itself justified belief and theoretical deliberation is itself an intentional, goal-directed activity, then, by similar reasoning to that which we saw before, theoretical deliberators are committed to the possibility of the constitutive conditions for meeting their goal, and these now arguably include agents' control over their beliefs.

Now let us return to our guiding question. Is the sense of control agents have in theoretical deliberation the same as the sense of control that they have when it comes to practical deliberation? My own view is that there very well might be *a* notion of freedom and control that is appropriate even in the case of justified belief arrived at as a result of deliberation. And this might be the kind of freedom of which we are sometimes aware when we are deliberating with an aim to achieving justified belief. But it is not exactly the same as that associated with practical deliberation. So I accept (2) in its current form, and instead reject (1) in the objector's challenge. That is, I deny that there is an exact parallel of the reasoning I offered for practical deliberation available in the case of theoretical deliberation. At the same time, I am impressed by arguments just described that reveal a great overlap between the two sorts of deliberation.

Still, there is this difference. Deliberation about what to do aims at action via decision, whereas theoretical deliberation about what to believe aims directly at judgment or belief. In turn, this points to another difference: decision, which has no obvious counterpart in theoretical deliberation, is an act of the will, and essentially voluntary. As McCann writes, "'Volition' can be voluntary in the way water can be wet—that is, essentially, in a way that does not require some means as explanation".[30] The sense of freedom accompanying deliberation about what to do embodies the commitment to one's own deliberation making the difference in one's own voluntary activity, in such a way that one can be called upon to give reasons in defense of one's voluntary activity. The

---

[30] McCann (1974, p. 472).

commitment manifested by theoretical deliberation on this view is a different one: it is at most a commitment to the idea that one is answerable for one's (in the relevant sense, involuntary) judgments.[31] Thus, the objects of one's commitments when it comes to the two kinds of deliberation are different, and this can give rise to a substantial difference in the nature of those commitments. And these differences provide an answer to the objection at hand. Recall that the objection at hand is that we have lost the sense of "up-to-usness" in defending the Belief-Concept reading in part by appealing to rationality. But the difference between practical and theoretical deliberation that we have identified suggests why this worry is out of place. The sheer voluntariness of decision involved in rational deliberation distinguishes this kind of deliberation from theoretical deliberation—at least as we have understood it here.

5: Conclusion

In this chapter, I have argued that being rational deliberators commits us to our own freedom, to the idea that our actions are up to us in such a way that we are responsible for them. In the previous chapter, we saw that insofar as we have beliefs about our alternatives in deliberation, we take our deliberation to be able to explain why we choose and act as we do, rather than in other ways. Although these commitments have often been mistakenly assumed to entail indeterminism, they are nevertheless central and important aspects of our self-conception. Thus, while, on the one hand, they allow us to show that a major source of motivation for incompatibilism is undermined, they also present an explanatory challenge for the skeptic who claims that we are not free and responsible agents. For we have a powerful and unshakeable commitment to our being free and responsible in a way that is dependent on our nature as beings obligated by reasons.

---

[31] Watson (2001/2004) argues that there is no "doxastic will". But see Nickel (2010) for an interesting response.

Concluding Thoughts

1: Putting It All Together

In the last two chapters, we explored the nature of our commitments as rational deliberators. Such commitments have been assumed as a central motivation, if not the ground, of libertarianism. Here I have argued that libertarians who appeal to such commitments are right about one thing and wrong about another. They are right that we are committed to our freedom, and so the skeptic faces a challenge. But they are wrong that the freedom to which we are committed is essentially indeterministic. For these reasons, our exploration of our commitments as rational deliberators offers mutual support to the anti-skeptical and compatibilist account of responsibility developed in the first part of the book. But the support goes even deeper, as we can see when we focus on the particular nature of our commitments and their grounds.

Rational deliberation is itself an activity directed toward finding the best (or at least good) reasons for acting, adopting them as one's own, and acting upon them. This rational activity itself gives rise to a commitment to our being rationally evaluable in such a way that we can be answerable for our actions. Such a commitment dovetails perfectly with our account of responsibility as accountability, and, in particular, as one that requires that we act with the ability to act for good reasons.

This is the simple account with which we began, an account of responsibility as a kind of accountability, one connected to obligation and answerability. When we searched for a rationale—and one that could explain the asymmetry of the account—we found one that fits neatly with our commitments as rational deliberators. For its focus on obligation connects it directly with our commitment to our answerability in virtue of our ability to do what we ought. The very features that make the rational abilities account appropriate for responsibility as accountability are also what make it cohere with the nature of rational deliberation, from which our sense of freedom has long been thought to arise.

With these points in hand, it is possible to return to the challenge raised earlier in chapter 3, according to which the rational abilities view has the unacceptable consequence that only praiseworthy actions and not blame-worthy actions are consistent with determinism. I pointed out that this objection can go through only if determinism entails that there is inter-vention in one's capacities that prevents one from exercising any other than the ones one actually exercises. Thus, much hangs on whether determinism has this consequence, and on the relevant senses of "inter-vention" and "ability to do otherwise". In chapter 3, I argued that whether one has the relevant ability (to act well) is not undermined to any greater extent by determinism than by indeterminism—at least when it comes to worlds in which causes are merely events and not agents. Then, in chapter 4, I argued that, while an agent-causal picture is attractive in many ways, it is no more attractive in an indeterministic form than in a deter-ministic form, nor does it better capture a notion of control that might be thought essential to having the relevant abilities. Now we are in a position to add to the argument that the relevant abilities are not undermined by determinism by appealing to our conception of ourselves and our abilities. One powerful reason for resisting a compatibilist notion of abilities to act differently than one does is that having a libertarian view of our own abilities is built into our very nature as rational agents. But we have seen good reasons to reject this claim; our fundamental commitments to our abilities as rational deliberators and to having deliberative alternatives are of central importance, but they are not essentially commitments to indeter-minism.

It is still possible to embrace part of this account—namely, that libertar-ians are in no better position than compatibilists—without embracing the positive rational abilities account itself. That is, one might respond by rejecting the idea that it is possible to give a coherent account of responsi-bility that captures all that is needed for deserved praise and blame. Yet, here, holistic considerations come into play, and the account's ability to withstand a variety of challenges, to explain a variety of phenomena, and to cohere with the commitments we have in virtue of being rational deliberators all speak against taking this skeptical option.

2: Leeway in the Account

It is important to highlight some of the ways in which the account is flexible, and in which it can be combined with one of a number of competing theses. While the account comes down very firmly on some questions, on others it retains some leeway, so to speak. When it comes to the metaphysics of causation, emotional capacities required for responsible agency, and the reactive attitudes that are appropriate responses to responsible action, different options are available. I will here consider these points in turn.

As we saw in chapter 4, it is possible to adopt a coherent compatibilist picture of responsible agents as the (agent) causes of their actions. Agents cause what they do in virtue of their nature and causal powers. On the compatibilist picture, their nature and causal powers might, in conjunction with the natures of all else in the world, determine what they will do. Nevertheless, it is agents themselves who are, quite literally, the causes of their actions, and in virtue of their own natures that they are so. The rational abilities view is consistent with this picture, and one attraction of it is that it addresses directly worries that compatibilist views have a "disappearing agents" problem. On this picture, agents are front and center in the causal story, despite the fact that their natures might be such as to ensure certain actions rather than others. A somewhat less metaphysically robust view can still address the disappearing agents problem, and that is to hold that "agent-talk" and "event-talk" are interchangeable. There is a glass-half-empty way of looking at this and a glass-half-full way. Some agent-causal libertarians take the former view, and this makes sense when set against the assumption that agents are supposed to be special in being alone as substance-causes. For if agent-talk were equivalent to event-talk, then agents would simply become just like the rest of the world in this way. But since I have advocated a return to the idea that while agents are special in their particular causal powers, there is no reason to think that they are alone in being substance-causes if they are, this is not a problem. Thus, the "half-full" view is that, while translation is possible for both human agents and all other substances so that humans aren't in *this* way special, it is also the case that agents don't disappear in the way they would if it were a mistake to speak as though they were causes. Both of these agent-causal views are consistent with the rational abilities account, as is a traditional event-causal view.

I have not argued in detail for any one of these views over the others. However, it is an advantage for the rational abilities view, I believe, that it is consistent with each. If the reasons for adopting the strongest agent-causal account turn out to be overriding, then the rational abilities view can accommodate them.

A second area in which the rational abilities view is flexible concerns the role of emotional capacities in responsible agency. The view is consistent with a variety of roles for emotional capacities, along at least two dimensions. The account is consistent with certain emotional capacities being required for responsibility, via their being required for relevant rational capacities; it is consistent with the idea that certain emotional capacities are necessary for humans to be responsible agents, because we can only recognize and be motivated by relevant reasons through certain emotions. And, finally, it is consistent with there being no requirement—either for agents generally or for human beings—for the possession of emotional capacities. Along a second dimension, the view is also consistent with differing accounts of the particular emotional capacities that might be required for responsible agency. For example, on many views, the ability to have reactive or even retributive emotions is essential. But an alternative view, equally consistent with the rational abilities account, has it that other sorts of emotional capacities are required, including those that underlie or constitute empathy, for example. The rational abilities account does come down firmly on one point that can begin to help us decide which way to answer these questions, and that is in its requirement that responsible agents be able to grasp and act on specifically moral reasons. Current research into psychopathology suggests that this last requirement may indeed be satisfied—at least by humans—only if they possess certain emotional and social capacities, such as empathy.[1] This is one key reason for my having used "rational abilities" (plural) to describe the view; there might not be a single so-called "cold" rational faculty that suffices for responsible agency. It may be that emotional capacities are required, either necessarily or as contingent, but crucial, epistemic guides or motivational foundations.

---

[1] See, for example, Fine and Kennett (2004). Even if humans did require such specific emotional capacities, it remains a question whether they require them as developmental predecessors to achieving the ability to, say, grasp a moral reason, or whether they constitute present capacities to detect such reasons.

A third way in which the rational abilities account is flexible concerns the reactive attitudes and their relationship to responsibility. We began by identifying a notion of responsibility as entailing deserved praise and blame, but we left as an open question what is essential to praise and blame. Does blame, for example, require retribution or retributive sentiments? Is it essentially punitive? In chapter 2, we saw some reasons to think that it need not be. That is, there is a central notion of blame, connected to obligation and accountability, that need not entail either the intrinsic goodness of, or the (unqualified) right to inflict, harm on those who violate their obligations. However, this is also consistent with there being obligations to compensate on the part of those who are to blame, as well as the appropriateness of certain reactive attitudes. It is even consistent with a kind of "side-constrained consequentialism" about punishment, according to which punishment can be justified by its benefits, but only insofar as those punished are responsible and only insofar as it is proportional,[2] as well as related accounts of punishment that require that one be blameworthy in order to be punished or to have harm inflicted.[3]

The question naturally arises whether, depending on which option is taken on punishment, the notion of responsibility captured by the account is the central one we were supposing initially. For some may assume that the concept of responsibility is picked out by its license of, or even

---

[2] See Duff (2008).

[3] See Scanlon (2008) for a recent defense of the idea that blame is something that can be deserved, together with a rejection of the idea that it is "morally better that [the one blamed] should suffer some loss in consequence" (p. 188). On Scanlon's view, one is blameworthy when an action shows something about the agent's attitudes toward others that impairs the relations that others can have with him or her. And "to *blame* a person is to judge him blameworthy and to take your relationship with him or her to be modified in a way that this judgment of impaired relations holds to be appropriate" (p. 128). I do not believe that this view fully accounts for the notion of blameworthiness with which we have been concerned here. There are apparent counterexamples that would in some way have to be dealt with (for example, that people who are dead can be blameworthy, without their actions impairing their relationships). And this view also seems to have lost its tight connection with obligation and accountability. Scanlon takes this to be a positive feature of his view: "It explains why . . . not every blameworthy action need be impermissible" (p. 152). See chapter 5 for arguments against this claim. Despite my differences with Scanlon's particular account, however, I do agree that there is room to accept that blame and praise are deserved and appropriate without accepting certain theses standardly associated with unqualified retributivism, such as that it would be good for those who are blameworthy to suffer. See McKenna (forthcoming) and Vargas (in preparation) for illuminating discussions of various theses about desert. The correct view of punishment requires much more discussion than I have offered in the text, and I hope to contribute further to the conversation elsewhere.

obligation to inflict, retributive punishment (where this can take various forms, including being the target of retributive attitudes). I have given some reason to think our concept of responsibility as accountability that invokes notions of obligation and reasons-responsiveness, and is central to our self-conception, is separable from such accounts of punishment. At the same time, if such an argument does not ultimately succeed, considerations of fairness can both support a combination of the rational abilities view with this kind of retributive theory of punishment, as well as the asymmetry of the rational abilities view itself. Despite its neatness (as we saw in chapter 2), however, I have resisted this combination of views thus far.

Another possible response to this challenge that rests on tying responsibility as accountability more closely to a standard retributive theory of punishment is to embrace a limited degree of revisionism. As I have argued, the concepts of obligation and accountability come apart from the idea that we are licensed, or even obligated, to inflict harm on those who are responsible and act badly. But it could still be that our concept of responsibility combines both of these aspects. If so, and the rational abilities view is not combined with this sort of view about harm, then it would count as "moderately revisionary" in Manuel Vargas' sense.[4] It would not require us merely to get clearer about our concept, nor would it require elimination of the concept, but it would require some change to it. This is not necessarily an ultimately unwelcome result. As Vargas points out, it is not exactly clear why revisionism is often taken to be a last resort, and one which people avoid acknowledging. I believe that there are good reasons for beginning one's inquiries with an assumption that one will not revise. This is to give our important commitments an initial presumption of correctness, and to see whether we can identify justification for them. But if reflection reveals mistaken assumptions, then we must follow out the implications of our theories. Of course, how much we give up as a result in terms of our practices and judgments depends greatly on the particular assumptions in question. In this case, one might argue that revision follows from our recognition that we had made a mistake in assuming that obligation and sanction were connected in a very particular way. How problematic is that? It could be thought to be problematic if we were committed to keeping every one of our past assumptions and

---

[4] See Vargas (2005a) and (2007).

practices, but, faced with good reason to reject some of them, doing so should not be avoided.

A related reason for resisting revisionism would arise if one takes our choice of account to have an "all or nothing" quality. That is, one might think that revising our view about the relationship between blameworthiness and the goodness of harm, for example, would undermine the justification and appropriateness of making demands on ourselves and others, all of the reactive attitudes and, in turn, what makes human relationships meaningful. Susan Wolf, for example, describes a world without the reactive attitudes as one in which

> an act of heroism or saintly virtue would not inspire us to aim for higher and nobler ideals, nor would it evoke in us a reverence or even admiration for its agent . . . We would not recoil from acts of injustice or cruelty as insults to human dignity, nor be moved by such acts to reflect with sorrow or puzzlement on the tide of events that can bring persons to stoop so low . . .[5]

And she goes on to describe the most "gruesome" difference between such a world and our own as concerning our closest personal relationships. "Love" and "friendship" would take on a "hollow ring", and a world of this kind would be "so cold and dreary that any but the most cynical must shudder at the idea of it".

This is indeed a depressing picture. But on the account I have offered, even a revisionist version need not entail it. There is no reason why rejecting the idea that it is good that harm comes to those who are blameworthy, or that we have the unqualified right to inflict such harm, means that we inhabit such a world. On the account offered, we still retain obligations (including those that require that we compensate when we fail to meet others), appropriate demands, and many reactive and other attitudes. Even on a skeptical view, it is possible to resist the *bleakness* of the picture in various ways.[6] It is somewhat easier to do so if we retain the

---

[5] Wolf (1981, p. 391).

[6] See Pereboom (2001) and Sommers (2007). One way to do this is to propose "analogs" of reactive attitudes in place of our current ones. Notably, Pereboom considers the possibility of retaining moral obligation without responsibility and deserved praise and blame, expressing sympathy with arguments by Honderich (1988) and Smilansky (1994) in favor of doing so. However, in the end, after considering an objection articulated by Haji, he writes that he is not sure that moral ought-judgments can be retained (p. 147). At the same time, as we saw in chapter 5, Pereboom questions whether the truth of "ought" judgments is necessary for the truth of judgments of wrong-doing. Thus, on his view, even if obligation is not possible,

notion that we are responsible agents, accountable for our actions, and jettison only the claim that blame encompasses the commitment to harm being an intrinsic good or to our unqualified right to inflict it. In chapter 2, we saw in some detail that an important notion of one paradigmatic reactive attitude, forgiveness,[7] wholly survives the rejection of the idea that it is intrinsically good that the blameworthy suffer, for example.

Thus, the rational abilities view is consistent with at least three theses regarding punishment. The first is to adopt a very traditional and unqualified retributivist thesis, thereby allowing for yet an additional argument for the asymmetry of the view, namely, the sort of fairness argument considered, but not ultimately adopted, in chapter 2. A second is to reject the thesis, while denying that doing so requires revision of a concept. Rather, on this view, what is required is simply the rejection of a common misconception about the relationship of responsibility and punishment. A third is to accept genuine revision of the concept of responsibility. Because the second and third options do not differ significantly in their upshots for our practices, and because there is great controversy over the correct theory of punishment, even independently of the considerations raised here regarding responsibility, flexibility on this choice at this point is not unwelcome.

3: Conclusion

While there is a great deal of flexibility in the account, as just noted, there are also a number of firm and substantive commitments. It is a compatibilist view with asymmetric commitments about the ability to do otherwise; it maintains a strong connection via its rationale to the notions of obligation and reasons for acting; and it makes sense of our self-conception as free and accountable beings.

---

other aspects of morality survive. Although both a revisionary version of the rational abilities view and a skeptical view are in a position to resist the charge of bleakness, the rational abilities view, in part by bringing with it a conceptual commitment to obligation, takes a different approach.

[7] In introducing the reactive attitudes, Strawson (1963/2005) writes: "I want to speak, at least at first, of something else: of the non-detached attitudes and reactions of people directly involved in transactions with each other; of the attitudes and reactions of offended parties and beneficiaries; of such things as gratitude, resentment, *forgiveness*, love, and hurt feelings" (p. 75, emphasis mine).

Because of these features of the view, it is a clear competitor to both traditional compatibilist accounts and incompatibilist ones. It is true that because the account shares aspects of each kind, parts of the reasoning for it can be embraced by each. But at least some of the strength of the account lies in its ability to capture insights of each traditional competitor that build on one another, making the whole greater than the sum of its parts. It is in this way, and because it recognizes and indeed incorporates at least some skeptical challenges to each kind of traditional view, that it is possible to offer a stronger answer to the skeptic in the end.

Bibliography

Adams, F. (1995) "Trying: You've Got to Believe", *Journal of Philosophical Research* 20, 549–61.

Adams, R. (1985) "Involuntary Sins", *Philosophical Review* 94, 3–31.

Albritton, R. (1985) "Freedom of the Will and Freedom of Action", Presidential Address, *Proceedings of the American Philosophical Association* 59, 239–51.

Alston, W. (1988) "The Deontological Conception of Epistemic Justification", *Philosophical Perspectives* 2, 257–99.

Aristotle (1984a) *The Complete Works of Aristotle*. J. Barnes (ed.). Princeton: Princeton University Press.

—— (1984b) *Eudemian Ethics*. J. Solomon (tr.). In Aristotle (1984a), 1922–1981.

—— (1984c) *Nicomachean Ethics*. W. D. Ross (tr.), revised by J. O. Urmson. In Aristotle (1984a), 1729–1867.

—— (1984d) *De Interpretatione*. J.L. Ackrill (tr.) In Aristotle (1984a), 25–38.

Austin, J.L. (1956) "Ifs and Cans", in his *Philosophical Papers*, 3rd edn, pp. 205–32, Oxford: Clarendon Press (1979). Originally published in *Proceedings of the British Academy* 42.

Baker, L. (2006) "Moral Responsibility without Libertarianism", *Noûs* 40, 307–30.

Barnes, E. (1994) "Why P Rather Than Q? The Curiosities of Fact and Foil", *Philosophical Studies* 73, 35–53.

Benn, P. (1996) "Forgiveness and Loyalty", *Philosophy* 71, 369–83.

Bennett, C. (2003) "Personal and Redemptive Forgiveness", *European Journal of Philosophy* 11, 127–44.

Blumenthal, R. (2005) "Sentencing Hearing Starts for G.I. Featured in Abu Ghraib Pictures", *The New York Times* (May 4).

Bok, H. (1998) *Freedom and Responsibility*. Princeton: Princeton University Press.

Bowers, F. (2005) "Abu Ghraib's Message for the Rank and File; Six Lower-level Enlistees have been Punished, though Lynndie England's Fate is Unsettled", *The Christian Science Monitor* (May 6).

Bratman, M. (2000) "Fischer and Ravizza on Moral Responsibility and History", *Philosophy and Phenomenological Research* 61, 452–58.

—— (1986) *Intention, Plans, and Practical Reason*. Cambridge: Harvard University Press.

Brink, D. (2004) "Immaturity, Normative Competence, and Juvenile Transfer: How (Not) to Punish Minors for Major Crimes", *Texas Law Review* 82, 1555–85.

Brink, D. (1994) "Moral Conflict and Its Structure", *Philosophical Review* 103, 215–47.

Broad, C. D. (1952) "Determinism, Indeterminism, and Libertarianism", in *Ethics and the History of Philosophy: Selected Essays*, pp. 195–217. New York: Humanities Press.

Burge, T. (1998) "Reason and the First Person", in C. Wright, B. Smith, and C. MacDonald (eds), *Knowing Our Own Minds*, pp. 243–70. Oxford: Clarendon Press.

—— (1979) "Individualism and the Mental", *Midwest Studies in Philosophy* 4, 73–121.

Butler, J. (1726/1896) *Fifteen Sermons Preached at the Rolls Chapel* in J. H. Bernard (ed.), *The Works of Bishop Butler*. London: Macmillan.

Byerly, H. (1979) "Substantial Causes and Nomic Determination", *Philosophy of Science* 46, 57–81.

Campbell, C. A. (1957) *On Selfhood and Godhood*. London: Allen and Unwin.

Campbell, J. K. (2007) "Pereboom on Deliberation", 2nd Online Philosophy Conference (OPC2). http://experimentalphilosophy.typepad.com/2nd_ann ual_online_philoso/files/cambells_commentary_on_pereboom.pdf. Accessed January 12, 2011.

—— (2005) "Compatibilist Alternatives", *Canadian Journal of Philosophy* 35, 387–406.

—— (1997) "A Compatibilist Theory of Alternative Possibilities", *Philosophical Studies* 88, 319–30.

Canfield, J. (1962) "Knowing About Future Decisions", *Analysis* 22, 127–9.

Chalmers, D. (2002). "Does Conceivability Entail Possibility?", in Tamar Szabó Gendler and John Hawthorne (eds), *Conceivability and Possibility*, pp. 145–200. Oxford: Oxford University Press.

Chisholm, R. (1968) "Lewis' Ethics of Belief", in P. A. Schilpp (ed.), *The Philosophy of C.I. Lewis*, pp. 223–42. Lasalle, IL: Open Court.

—— (1964) "Human Freedom and the Self", *The Lindley Lecture*. Reprinted in Watson (2003), pp. 26–37.

Clarke, R. (2009) "Dispositions, Abilities to Act, and Free Will: The New Dispositionalism", *Mind* 118, 323–51.

Clarke, R. (2005) "Agent Causation and the Problem of Luck", *Philosophical Quarterly* 86, 408–21.

—— (2003) *Libertarian Accounts of Free Will*. Oxford: Oxford University Press.

—— (1996) "Contrastive Rational Explanation of Free Choice", *Philosophical Quarterly* 46, 185–201.

—— (1992) "Deliberation and Beliefs About One's Abilities", *Pacific Philosophical Quarterly* 73, 101–13.

Coffman, E. J. and Warfield, T. (2005) "Deliberation and Metaphysical Freedom", *Midwest Studies in Philosophy* 29, 25–44.

Copp, D. (2008) "'Ought' Implies 'Can' and the Derivation of the Principle of Alternate Possibilities", *Analysis* 68, 67–75.

Copp, D. (2003) "Ought Implies Can, Blameworthiness, and the Principle of Alternate Possibilities", in D. Widerker, and M. McKenna (eds) (2003) pp. 265–99.

—— (1997) "Defending the Principle of Alternate Possibilities: Blameworthiness and Moral Responsibility", Noûs 31, 441–56.

Damasio, A. (1995) Descartes' Error: Emotion, Reason, and the Human Brain. Pbk edn, New York: Harper Perennial.

Damm, L. (2010) "Emotions and Moral Agency", Philosophical Explorations 13, 275–92.

Darwall, S. (2006) The Second-Person Standpoint: Morality, Respect and Accountability. Cambridge: Harvard University Press.

Davidson, D. (1985) "Reply to Pears", in B. Vermazen and M. Hintikka (eds), Essays on Davidson: Actions and Events, pp. 211–15. Oxford: Clarendon Press.

—— (1980) Essays on Actions and Events. New York: Oxford University Press.

—— (1969) "The Individuation of Events", in N. Rescher (ed.), Essays in Honor of Carl G. Hempel. Dordrecht: Reidel. Reprinted in Davidson (1980), pp. 163–80.

—— (1963) "Actions, Reasons, and Causes", Journal of Philosophy 60. Reprinted in Davidson (1980), pp. 3–20.

Dennett, D. (1984) Elbow Room. Cambridge: MIT Press.

Doris, J. and Knobe, J. (forthcoming) "Strawsonian Variations: Folk Morality and the Search for a Unified Theory", in The Handbook of Moral Psychology. Oxford: Oxford University Press.

Doris, J. and Murphy, D. (2007) "From My Lai to Abu Ghraib: The Moral Psychology of Atrocity", Midwest Studies in Philosophy: Philosophy and the Empirical 31, 25–55.

Duff, A. (2008) "Legal Punishment", in Edward N. Zalta (ed.), The Stanford Encyclopedia of Philosophy (Fall 2008 Edition), <http://plato.stanford.edu/archives/fall2008/entries/legal-punishment/>.

Easterbrook, G. (2004) The New Republic. http://webcache.googleusercontent.com/search?q=cache:pJmJT5pA7PEJ:www.belgraviadispatch.com/archives/003924. Accessed January 13, 2011.

Fara, M. (2008) "Masked Abilities and Compatibilism", Mind 117, 843–65.

Feldman, R. (2001) "Voluntary Belief and Epistemic Evaluation," in Steup (2001), pp. 77–92.

Finch, A. and Warfield, T. (1998) "The Mind Argument and Libertarianism", Mind 107, 515–28.

Fine, G. (1981) "Aristotle on Determinism: A Review of Richard Sorabji's 'Necessity, Cause, and Blame'", Philosophical Review 90, 561–80.

Fine, C. and Kennett, J. (2004) "Mental Impairment, Moral Understanding and Criminal Responsibility: Psychopathology and the Purposes of Punishment", International Journal of Law and Psychiatry 27, 425–43.

Fischer, J. M. (2008) "Freedom, Foreknowledge, and Frankfurt: A Reply to Vihvelin", Canadian Journal of Philosophy 38, 337–42.

Fischer, J. M. (2006a) *My Way: Essays on Moral Responsibility*. Oxford: Oxford University Press.

—— (2006b) "Free Will and Moral Responsibility", in D. Copp (ed.), *The Oxford Handbook of Ethical Theory*. Oxford: Oxford University Press.

—— (2004) "Responsibility and Manipulation", *Journal of Ethics* 8, 145–77.

—— (2003) "'Ought-Implies-Can,' Causal Determinism and Moral Responsibility", *Analysis* 63, 244–50.

—— (1994) *The Metaphysics of Free Will: An Essay on Control*. Cambridge: Blackwell.

—— (1982) "Responsibility and Control", *Journal of Philosophy* 79, 24–40.

—— and Ravizza, M. (1998) *Responsibility and Control, A Theory of Moral Responsibility*. Cambridge: Cambridge University Press.

—— and —— (1992) "Responsibility, Freedom, and Reason". Critical Review of *Freedom Within Reason* by Susan Wolf. *Ethics* 102, 368–89.

Fischette, C. (2004) "Psychopathy and Responsibility", *Virginia Law Review* 90, 1423–85.

Frankfurt, H. (1988) *The Importance of What We Care About*. Cambridge: Cambridge University Press.

—— (1983) "What We Are Morally Responsible For", reprinted in Frankfurt (1988), pp. 95–103.

—— (1971) "Freedom of the Will and the Concept of a Person", *Journal of Philosophy* 68, 5–20.

—— (1969) "Alternate Possibilities and Moral Responsibility", *Journal of Philosophy* 66, 829–39.

Gandhi, M. and Desai, M. (1957/1993) *Gandhi, an Autobiography: the Story of my Experiments with Truth*. Boston: Beacon Press.

Garrard, E. and McNaughton, D. (2003) "In Defense of Unconditional Forgiveness", *Proceedings of the Aristotelian Society* 103, 39–60.

Garvey, S. (1998) "Aggravation and Mitigation in Capital Cases: What Do Jurors Think?", *Columbia Law Review* 98, 1538–76.

Ginet, C. (2001) "Deciding To Believe," in Steup (2001), pp. 63–76.

—— (1962) "Can the Will Be Caused?", *Philosophical Review* 71, 49–55.

Graham, P. (forthcoming) "'Ought' and Ability", *Philosophical Review*.

Grice, P. (1971) "Intention and Uncertainty", *in Proceedings of the British Academy* 57, pp. 263–79. London: Oxford University Press.

Haji, I. (2003) "The Emotional Depravity of Psychopaths and Culpability", *Legal Theory* 9, 63–82.

—— (2002) *Deontic Morality and Control*. Cambridge: Cambridge University Press.

Hampshire, S. and Hart, H. L. A. (1958) "Decision, Intention, and Certainty", *Mind* 67, 1–12.

Hanser, M. (2005) "Permissibility and Practical Inference", *Ethics* 115, 443–70.

Harman, G. (1976) "Practical Reasoning", *Review of Metaphysics* 29, 431–63.

Harré R. and Madden, E. H. (1975) *Causal Powers: A Theory of Natural Necessity* Oxford: Blackwell.

Hart, H. L. A. (1961) *The Concept of Law*. Oxford: Clarendon Press.

Hieronymi, P. (2008) "Responsibility for Believing", *Synthese* 161, 357–73.

—— (2004) "The Force and Fairness of Blame," *Philosophical Perspectives* 18, 115–48.

Hitchcock, C. (1999) "Contrastive Explanation and the Demons of Determinism", *British Journal for the Philosophy of Science* 50, 585–612.

Hobbes, T. (1668/1994) *Leviathan*. E. Curley (ed.). Indianapolis: Hackett.

Hoffman, M. L. (2000) *Empathy and Moral Development: Implications for Caring and Justice*. Oxford: Oxford University Press.

Honderich, T. (1988) *A Theory of Determinism*. Oxford: Oxford University Press.

Howard-Snyder, F. (2006) "'Cannot' Implies 'Ought Not'", *Philosophical Studies* 130, 233–46.

Jackson, F. (1998) *From Metaphysics to Ethics*. Oxford: Oxford University Press.

Kane, R. (1996) *The Significance of Free Will*. Oxford: Oxford University Press.

Kant, I. (1785/1981) *Grounding for the Metaphysics of Morals*. J. Ellington (tr.). Indianapolis: Hackett.

—— (1781/1997) *The Critique of Pure Reason*. P. Guyer and A. W. Wood (trs). Cambridge: Cambridge University Press.

Kapitan, T. (1986) "Deliberation and the Presumption of Open Alternatives", *Philosophical Quarterly* 36, 230–51.

Kotlowitz, A. (2003) "In the Face of Death", *New York Times Magazine* (July 6).

Levy, N. (2006) "Determinist Deliberations", *Dialectica* 60, 453–59.

Lewis, D. (1986/1993) "Causal Explanation", *Philosophical Papers II*, 214–40. Oxford: Oxford University Press. Reprinted in Ruben (1993), pp. 182–206.

Lewis, M. (1993) "The Emergence of Human Emotions", in M. Lewis and J. Haviland (eds), *Handbook of Emotions*, pp. 265–80. New York: Guilford Press.

Lipton, P. (1990/1993) "Contrastive Explanation", in D. Knowles (ed.), *Explanation and Its Limits*, pp. 247–66. Cambridge: Cambridge University Press. Reprinted in Ruben (1993), pp. 207–27.

Lowe, E. J. (2001) "Event Causation and Agent Causation", *Grazer Philosophische Studien* 61, 1–20.

Ludwig, K. (1995). "Trying the Impossible: A Reply to Adams", *Journal of Philosophical Research* 20, 563–70.

—— (1992) "Impossible Doings", *Philosophical Studies* 65, 257–81.

McCann, H. (1986) "Rationality and the Range of Intentions", *Midwest Studies in Philosophy* 10, 191–211.

—— (1974) "Volition and Basic Action", *Philosophical Review* 83, 451–73.

McDowell, J. (1998) "Having the World in View: Lecture One", *Journal of Philosophy* 95, 431–50.

McKenna, M. (forthcoming) *Agent Meaning and Conversation: A Theory of Moral Responsibility*. Oxford: Oxford University Press.

—— (2008) "A Hard-line Reply to Pereboom's Four-Case Manipulation Argument", *Philosophy and Phenomenological Research* 77, 142–59.

—— (2005) "Reasons Reactivity and Incompatibilist Intuitions", *Philosophical Explorations* 8, 131–43.

—— (2003) "Robustness, Control, and the Demand for Morally Significant Alternatives: Frankfurt Examples with Oodles and Oodles of Alternatives", in Widerker and McKenna (2003), pp. 201–18.

—— (2000) "Assessing Reasons-responsive Compatibilism: J. M. Fischer and M. Ravizza's Responsibility and Control," *International Journal of Philosophical Studies* 8, 89–114.

—— (1998) "Does Strong Compatibilism Survive Frankfurt Counter-Examples?", *Philosophical Studies* 91, 259–64.

—— and Russell, P. (2008) "Introduction", in McKenna and Russell (eds), *Free Will and Reactive Attitudes: Perspectives on P. F. Strawson's "Freedom and Resentment"*. Burlington, Vermont: Ashgate.

McKinley, J. and C. Pogash (2009). "Kidnapping Victim Was Not Always Locked Away", *New York Times*, 29 August 2009. Available at http://www.nytimes. com/2009/08/29/US/29abduct.html?_r=1&pagewanted=2

Malle, B., Moses, L., and Baldwin, D. (eds) (2001) *Intentions and Intentionality*. Cambridge: MIT Press.

Markosian, N. (1999) "A Compatibilist Version of the Theory of Agent Causation", *Pacific Philosophical Quarterly* 80, 257–77.

Maslen, C. (2004) "Causes, Contrasts, and the Nontransitivity of Causation", in J. Collins, N. Hall, and L. A. Paul (eds), *Causation and Counterfactuals*, pp. 341–57. Cambridge, MA: MIT Press.

Mele, A. (2006) *Free Will and Luck*. New York: Oxford University Press.

—— (2005) "A Critique of Pereboom's 'Four-case' Argument for Incompatibilism", *Analysis* 65, 75–80.

—— (2001) "Acting Intentionally: Probing Folk Notions", in Malle et al. (2001), pp. 27–43.

—— (1995) *Autonomous Agents: From Self Control to Autonomy*. New York: Oxford University Press.

—— and Robb, D. (2003) "Bbs, Magnets, and Seesaws: The Metaphysics of Frankfurt-style Cases", in D. Widerker and M. McKenna (eds) (2003), pp. 127–38.

—— and —— (1998) "Rescuing Frankfurt-Style Cases", *Philosophical Review* 107, 97–112.

Milgram, S. (1969) *Obedience to Authority*. New York: Harper and Row Publishers.

Montmarquet, J. (1993) *Epistemic Virtue and Doxastic Responsibility*. Lanham: Roman and Littlefield.

Morse, S. (2002) "Uncontrollable Urges and Irrational People", *Virginia Law Review* 88, 1025–78.

Moya, C. (2006) *Moral Responsibility: The Ways of Scepticism* (London: Routledge).

Murphy, J. (2003) *Getting Even: Forgiveness and Its Limits*. New York: Oxford University Press.

—— (1982) "Forgiveness and Resentment", *Midwest Studies in Philosophy* 7, 503–16.

Nagel, T. (1986) *The View from Nowhere*. Oxford: Oxford University Press.

Nahmias, E., Morris, S., Nadelhoffer, T., and Turner, J. (2006) "Is Incompatibilism Intuitive?", *Philosophy and Phenomenological Research* 73, 28–53.

——, ——, —— and —— (2005) "Surveying Freedom: Folk Intuitions about Free Will and Moral Responsibility", *Philosophical Psychology* 18, 561–84.

Naylor, M. (1984) "Frankfurt on the Principle of Alternate Possibilities," *Philosophical Studies* 46, 249–58.

Nelkin, D. (2009) "Responsibility, Rational Abilities, and Two Kinds of Fairness Arguments", *Philosophical Explorations* 12, 151–65.

—— (2007a) "Good Luck to Libertarians: Reflections on Al Mele's Free Will and Luck", *Philosophical Explorations* 10, 173–84.

—— (2007b) "Do We Have a Coherent Set of Intuitions about Moral Responsibility?", *Midwest Studies in Philosophy: Philosophy and the Empirical* 31, 243–59.

—— (2005) "Freedom, Responsibility, and the Challenge of Situationism", *Midwest Studies in Philosophy: Free Will and Moral Responsibility,* 29, 181–206 Cambridge: Blackwell.

—— (2004a) "The Sense of Freedom", in J. Campbell, M. O'Rourke, and D. Shier (eds), *Freedom and Determinism*, pp. 105–34. Cambridge, MA: MIT Press.

—— (2004b) "Deliberative Alternatives", *Philosophical Topics* 32, 215–240.

—— (2001) "The Consequence Argument and the *Mind* Argument", *Analysis* 61, 107–15.

Newberry, P. (2001) "Joseph Butler on Forgiveness: A Presupposed Theory of Emotion", *Journal of the History of Ideas* 62, 223–44.

Nichols, S. and Knobe, J. (2007) "Moral Responsibility and Determinism: The Cognitive Science of Folk Intuitions", *Noûs* 41, 663–85.

Nickel, P. (2010) "Voluntary Belief on a Reasonable Basis", *Philosophy and Phenomenological Research* 81, 312–34.

Northcott, R. (2007) "Causation and Contrast Classes", *Philosophical Studies* 139, 111–23.

O'Connor, T. (2009) "Agent-Causal Power", in T. Handfield (ed.), *Dispositions and Causes*, pp. 189–214. Oxford: Oxford University Press.

—— (2000) *Persons and Causes: The Metaphysics of Free Will*. Cambridge: Cambridge University Press.

Otsuka, M. (1998) "Incompatibilism and the Avoidability of Blame", *Ethics* 108, 685–701.

Owens, D. (2000) *Reason Without Freedom: The Problem of Epistemic Normativity*. London: Routledge.

Percival, P. (2000) "Lewis's Dilemma of Explanation Under Indeterminism Exposed and Resolved", *Mind* 109, 39–66.

Pereboom, D. (in preparation), "Living Without Free Will" (revised version).

Pereboom, D. (forthcoming), "Optimistic Skepticism About Free Will", (presented at SUNY, Brockport, November 2009).

—— (2008a) "A Compatibilist Account of the Epistemic Conditions on Rational Deliberation", *Journal of Ethics* 12, 287–306.

—— (2008b) "A Hard-line Reply to the Multiple-Case Manipulation Argument", *Philosophy and Phenomenological Research* 77, 160–70.

—— (2006) "Reasons-Responsiveness, Alternate Possibilities, and Manipulation Arguments Against Compatibilism: Reflections on John Martin Fischer's *My Way*", *Philosophical Books* 47, 198–212.

—— (2003) "Source Incompatibilism and Alternative Possibilities", in D. Widerker and M. McKenna (eds) (2003), pp. 185–199.

—— (2001) *Living Without Free Will*. Cambridge: Cambridge University Press.

—— "Determinism Al Dente", *Noûs* 29, 21–45.

Pettit, P. (1989) "Determinism with Deliberation", *Analysis* 49, 42–4.

Plantinga, A. (1993) *Warrant: The Current Debate*. Oxford: Oxford University Press.

Ramirez, E. (in preparation) *A Sensible Sentimentalism: The Role of the Emotions in Evaluative Concepts and Reactive Attitudes*. UCSD Dissertation.

Rawls, J. (1971) *A Theory of Justice*. Cambridge: Harvard University Press.

Reid, T. (1788/1983) *Essays on the Active Powers of Man*, in R.E. Beanblossom and K. Lehrer (eds), *Inquiry and Essays*. Indianapolis: Hackett.

Reider, L. (1998) "Toward a New Test for the Insanity Defense: Incorporating the Discoveries of Neuroscience into Moral and Legal Theories", *UCLA Law Review* 46, 289–342.

Rickless, S. (forthcoming). "Will and Motivation", in P. Anstey (ed.), *The Oxford Handbook of British Philosophy in the Seventeenth Century*. Oxford: Oxford University Press.

Ruben, D.H. (ed.) (1993) *Explanation*. Oxford: Oxford University Press.

Russell, P. (2004) "Responsibility and the Condition of Moral Sense", *Philosophical Topics* 32, 287–305. [Special Issue on Agency, ed. J.M. Fischer]

Ryan, S. (2003) "Doxastic Compatibilism and the Ethics of Belief," *Philosophical Studies* 114, 47–79.

Scanlon, T. (2008) *Moral Dimensions: Permissibility, Meaning, and Blame*. Cambridge: Harvard University Press.

—— (1998) *What We Owe To Each Other*. Cambridge: Harvard University Press.

Schaffer, J. (2005) "Contrastive Causation", *Philosophical Review* 114, 327–58.

Schwitzgebel, E. (2008) "Belief", in Edward N. Zalta (ed.), *The Stanford Encyclopedia of Philosophy (Fall 2008 Edition)*, URL = <http://plato.stanford.edu/archives/fall2008/entries/belief/>.

Searle, J. (2001) *Rationality In Action*. Cambridge: MIT Press.

Setiya, K. (2010) "Intention", in Edward N. Zalta (ed.), *The Stanford Encyclopedia of Philosophy (Spring 2010 Edition)*, URL = <http://plato.stanford.edu/archives/spr2010/entries/intention/>.

Shah, N. and Velleman, J. D. (2005) "Doxastic Deliberation", *Philosophical Review* 114, 497–534.

Sher, G. (2006) *In Praise of Blame*. New York: Oxford University Press.

—— (2005) "Kantian Fairness", *Philosophical Issues* 15, 179–92.

Shirer, W. (1979) *Gandhi, A Memoir*. New York: Simon and Schuster.

Shoemaker, D. (2007) "Moral Address, Moral Responsibility, and the Boundaries of the Moral Community", *Ethics* 118, 70–108.

Smilansky, S. (1994) "The Ethical Advantages of Hard Determinism", *Philosophy and Phenomenological Research* 54, 355–63.

Smith, A. (2005) "Responsibility for Attitudes: Activity and Passivity in Mental Life", *Ethics* 115, 236–71.

Smith, M. (2003) "Rational Capacities, or: How to Distinguish Recklessness, Weakness, and Compulsion", in S. Stroud and C. Tappolet (eds), *Weakness of Will and Practical Irrationality*, pp. 17–38. Oxford: Oxford University Press.

Sommers, T. (2007) "The Objective Attitude", *Philosophical Quarterly* 57, 321–41.

Sorabji, R. (1980) *Necessity, Cause, and Blame*. Ithaca: Cornell University Press.

Steup, M. (ed.) (2001) *Knowledge, Truth, and Duty: Essays on Epistemic Justification, Responsibility, and Virtue*. Oxford: Oxford University Press.

Stocker, M. (1968) "Knowledge, Causation, and Decision", *Noûs* 2, 65–73.

Strawson, G. (1986) *Freedom and Belief*. Oxford: Oxford University Press.

Strawson, P. (1962/2003) "Freedom and Resentment", *Proceedings of the British Academy* 48, 1–25; reprinted in Watson (2003).

Suarez, F. (1597/1994) *On Efficient Causality: Metaphysical Disputations 17, 18 and 19*. A.J. Freddoso (tr.). New Haven: Yale University Press.

Sundby, S. (2007) *A Life and Death Decision: A Jury Weighs the Death Penalty*. New York: Palgrave Macmillan.

Swinburne, R. (2000) "The Irreducibility of Causation", *Dialectica* 51, 79–92.

Talbert, M. (2008) "Blame and Responsiveness to Moral Reasons: Are Psychopaths Blameworthy?". *Pacific Philosophical Quarterly* 89, 516–35.

Taylor, R. (1983) *Metaphysics*. New Jersey: Prentice-Hall.

—— (1964) "Deliberation and Foreknowledge", *American Philosophical Quarterly* 1, 73–80.

Thomas, G. (unpublished manuscript), "Deliberation and Determinism".

Tiboris, M. (in preparation) *Youth and Diminished Responsibility*. University of California, San Diego dissertation.

van Fraassen, B. (1980) *The Scientific Image*. Oxford: Clarendon Press.

van Inwagen, P. (1983) *An Essay on Free Will*. Oxford: Oxford University Press.

Vargas, M. (in preparation) "Desert, Retribution, and Moral Responsibility".

—— (2007) "Revisionism", in J.M. Fischer, R. Kane, D. Pereboom, and M. Vargas, *Four Views on Free Will*. Oxford: Blackwell Publishing.

—— (2005a) "The Revisionist's Guide to Responsibility," *Philosophical Studies* 125, 399–425.

Vargas, M. (2005b) "The Trouble With Tracing", *Midwest Studies in Philosophy: Free Will and Moral Responsibility* 29, 269–91.

—— (2004) "Responsibility and the Aims of Theory: Strawson and Revisionism", *Pacific Philosophical Quarterly* 85, 218–41.

Velleman, J.D. (1989) "Epistemic Freedom", *Pacific Philosophical Quarterly* 70, 73–97.

—— (1985) "Practical Reflection", *Philosophical Review* 94, 33–61.

Vihvelin, K. (2004) "Free Will Demystified: A Dispositional Account", *Philosophical Topics* 32, 427–50.

Vranas, P. (2007) "I Ought, Therefore I Can", *Philosophical Studies* 136, 167–216.

Wallace, R. J. (1994) *Responsibility and the Moral Sentiments*. Cambridge: Harvard University Press.

Watkins, E.T. (2010) "Kant", in T. O'Connor and C. Sandis (eds), *Blackwell's Companion to the Philosophy of Action*, pp. 521–27. Oxford: Wiley-Blackwell.

—— (2005) *Kant and the Metaphysics of Causality*. New York: Cambridge University Press.

Watson, G. (forthcoming) "The Trouble With Psychopaths", in R.J. Wallace, R. Kumar, and S. Freeman, *Reasons and Recognitions: Essays on the Philosophy of T.M. Scanlon*. Oxford: Oxford University Press.

—— (2004) *Agency and Answerability: Selected Essays*. Oxford: Oxford University.

Watson, G. (2003/2004) "The Work of the Will", in S. Stroud, and C. Tappolet (eds), *Weakness of Will and Practical Irrationality*, pp. 123–157. Oxford: Oxford University Press; reprinted in Watson (2004).

—— (ed.) (2003) *Free Will* (2nd edn). Oxford: Oxford University Press.

—— (2001/2004) "Reasons and Responsibility", *Ethics* 111, 374–94; reprinted in Watson (2004).

—— (1996/2004) "Two Faces of Responsibility", *Philosophical Topics* 24, 227–48; reprinted in Watson (2004).

—— (1987/2004) "Responsibility and the Limits of Evil: Variations on a Strawsonian Theme", in F. Schoeman (ed.) *Responsibility, Character, and the Emotions: New Essays in Moral Psychology*, pp. 256–86, Cambridge: Cambridge University Press; reprinted in Watson (2004).

—— (1975/2004) "Free Agency", *Journal of Philosophy* 72, 205–20; reprinted in Watson (2004).

Widerker, D. (1995) "Libertarianism and Frankfurt's Attack on the Principle of Alternate Possibilities", *Philosophical Review* 104, 247–61.

—— (1991) "Frankfurt on 'Ought' Implies 'Can' and Alternate Possibilities", *Analysis* 51, 222–24.

—— and McKenna, M. (eds) (2003) *Moral Responsibility and Alternative Possibilities*. Burlington, Vermont: Ashgate.

Wolf, S. (1990) *Freedom Within Reason*. Oxford: Oxford University Press.

—— (1981) "The Importance of Free Will", *Mind* 90, 386–405.

—— (1980) "Asymmetrical Freedom", *Journal of Philosophy* 77, 151–66.

Woodward, J. (2003) *Making Things Happen: A Theory of Causal Explanation*. Oxford: Oxford University Press.

Yaffe, G. (2005) "More On 'Ought Implies Can' and the Principle of Alternate Possibilities", *Midwest Studies in Philosophy: Free Will and Moral Responsibility* 29, 307–12.

—— (1999) "'Ought' Implies 'Can' and the Principle of Alternate Possibilities", *Analysis* 59, 218–22.

Zimbardo, P. (2004) "Power Turns Good Soldiers Into 'Bad Apples'", *Boston Globe* (May 9).

Zimmerman, M. (in preparation) "Responsibility, Reaction, and Value".

—— (2008) *Living With Uncertainty*. Cambridge: Cambridge University Press.

—— (1997) "A Plea for Accuses", *American Philosophical Quarterly* 29, 229–43.

—— (1984) *An Essay on Human Action*. New York: Peter Lang.

Index

Lightning Source UK Ltd.
Milton Keynes UK
UKOW031602160713

213843UK00002B/2/P